FOO FIGHTERS

Also by Mick Wall

*Getcha Rocks Off: Sex & Excess. Bust-Ups & Binges. Life &
    Death on the Rock 'N' Roll Road*
Love Becomes a Funeral Pyre: A Biography of The Doors
Lou Reed: The Life
Black Sabbath: Symptom of the Universe
AC/DC: Hell Ain't a Bad Place to Be
Enter Night: Metallica – The Biography
Appetite for Destruction
When Giants Walked the Earth: A Biography of Led Zeppelin
W.A.R.: The Unauthorised Biography of W. Axl Rose
Bono: In The Name of Love
John Peel: A Tribute to the Much-Loved DJ and Broadcaster
XS All Areas: The Autobiography of Status Quo
Mr Big: Ozzy, Sharon and My Life as the Godfather of Rock
    (with Don Arden)
Paranoid: Black Days with Sabbath & Other Horror Stories
Run to the Hills: The Authorised Biography of Iron Maiden
Pearl Jam
Guns N' Roses: The Most Dangerous Band in the World
Diary of a Madman: The Official Biography of Ozzy Ozbourne

FOO FIGHTERS

LEARNING TO FLY

MICK WALL

St. Martin's Press
New York

www.stmartins.com

Library of Congress Cataloging-in-Publication Data

Names: Wall, Mick author.
Title: Foo Fighters : learning to fly / Mick Wall.
Description: First U.S. edition. | New York : St. Martin's Press, 2017. | Includes index.
Identifiers: LCCN 2017011001 | ISBN 9781250122339 (hardcover) | ISBN 9781250122346 (ebook)
Subjects: LCSH: Grohl, David. | Rock musicians—United States—Biography. | Foo Fighters (Musical group) | Nirvana (Musical group)
Classification: LCC ML420.G864 W35 2017 | DDC 782.42166092 [B]—dc23
LC record available at https://lccn.loc.gov/2017011001

Our books may be purchased in bulk for promotional, educational, or business use. Please contact your local bookseller or the Macmillan Corporate and Premium Sales Department at 1-800-221-7945, extension 5442, or by email at MacmillanSpecialMarkets@macmillan.com.

First published in Great Britain by Orion, an imprint of the Orion Publishing Group Ltd, an Hachette UK company

First U.S. Edition: August 2017

10 9 8 7 6 5 4 3 2 1

For Anna Valentine,
whose idea this book was

Contents

Acknowledgements

Without whom none of this would have been possible: Robert Kirby, Malcolm Edwards, Linda Wall, Maureen Rice, Vanessa Lampert, Harry Paterson, Emma Smith, Amy Elliot, Mark Foster, Mark Handsley, Susan Howe, Margot Weale, Jessica Purdue, Rebecca Gray, Richard King, Krystyna Kujawinska, Isadora Attab, Marianne Ihlen, Anna Hayward; Sarah and Martin Sando, Sandie Alcock, and not forgetting Ian Clark, Steve Morant, and all at the SNC. Extra special thanks: Dave Everley and Joe Daly the X Team.

1. Learning to Fly

Reading Festival, 26 August 2012. Sunday night. The one they've all been waiting for. Nearly 90,000 people, all ready to let themselves go, all ready to explode with pride on behalf of the most prideful band in rock, all ready already.

Knowing this, feeling the occasion more keenly than the most fish-eyed fan, Dave Grohl makes his move. His timing has always been excellent. This time, though, he knows he has excelled himself, for this is a special night: 20 years exactly since he first headlined Reading with Nirvana, before the shit hit the fan and the world went all wrong.

But now it is all right again. Now everything is just cool, brother. It's 20 years later, a new generation, another century, and Dave is feeling so good he decides to stop the show and tell the crowd, his people, all nearly 90,000 of them, a little story. It goes like this . . .

Strumming his guitar, stroking it like the hair on a baby's head, gently, playfully, sensually, absent-mindedly, the rest of the band shutdown, hidden in the shadows, listening as intently as the crowd, Dave just wants to share, to connect, to be like Bruce Springsteen but without the self-righteous bullshit, guitar twinkling.

'. . . so I grew up in Virginia, right outside of Washington, DC. I played in a punk rock band. We played in little clubs and squats and we toured and we fuckin' starved and it was really, really fun. One day this friend of mine says, "Hey, you ever heard of that band Nirvana?" . . .'

The crowd, Dave's crowd, some of whom have never owned a Nirvana record, but are smart enough to play along, give this an enormous roar of approval. Nirvana, golden name, golden band, golden age, now gone, lost in the single blast of a 20-gauge shotgun and the simple delirium of an OD-strength hit from a syringe, Kurt's loaded body shaking interminably then stopping. Abruptly. Bloodily. Stupidly.

'. . . I'm like, "Yeah, I've heard of Nirvana." He said, "Well, they're looking for a drummer and they think you're pretty good." I said, "Really?" "Yeah." So I flew up to Seattle . . .'

His guitar twinkling, drifting, like orphan stars high above. Black tee. Black jeans. Black-and-white sneakers. Black beard and white, spotlit face.

'. . . and they already had a drummer. This guy named Danny. He was a fucking great drummer. Danny was in a band called Mudhoney . . .'

Some modest yells of recognition. No one out there can actually name two good Mudhoney songs, let alone who the drummer was on the first Nirvana album, but here's a clue: it was neither Danny nor Dave. Yeah, and so?

'. . . and they'd been over here and toured and played a bunch. So the first day I ever hung out with Krist and Kurt and all those guys, we were having a little barbecue and I said to Danny, I said, "What's the biggest audience you've ever played to?" And he said, "Uh . . . 35,000 people." I said, "Where the fuck did Mudhoney play to 35,000 people?" He said, "Oh, this place called the Reading Festival" . . .'

Now comes the real sweet spot as the nearly 90,000 people at this Reading have a rippling, whole-body crowdgasm.

'About a year later, we had recorded the record *Nevermind*

and we had come over here to play some festivals . . .' The last of these words are drowned out as the crowd erupts into another fetishistic thunderclap. They can't believe what they're hearing, what they're witnessing. Dave Grohl never mentions *Nevermind*. Never talks about Nirvana. Not at a Foo Fighters show! Except, he is! He just fucking is!

Dave continues to spin his yarn, about the first time he and Nirvana played Reading, even further back, how he had 'never been so fucking scared in my entire life' at the prospect of playing to so many people. How it was 'beyond my wildest fucking dreams', and the 2012 Reading crowd continues to lap it up, baying and hooting and hanging on every gooey, sentimental syllable.

Then a little misstep: 'Over the years I've seen the stage get taller and taller and I've seen the barrier get farther and farther away.' It's leading up to something but the crowd doesn't give him time to finish. They start to booooooo.

But Dave Grohl didn't get where he is today without knowing how to recover from mistakes, to find the instant rejoinder that gets the conversation back on track, the evasive action that guarantees to right the ship, that gets the show back on the road.

Without even flinching, he just rolls it out, like a punch line, like he always knew what he was doing all along. 'But, from right here, it looks the same as it has for twenty-two years.'

The booing stops and the crowd melts as one. They knew they could rely on Dave. That he would never let them down, never stop making sense or call on them to get their eyes blackened.

But still it's not enough. He goes on, talking about his mother, who is there at the side of the stage, as she often is these days, as she sometimes was even in Nirvana days, and whose birthday it is in a few days' time, getting the crowd to sing her 'Happy Birthday', which of course they are more than happy to do, the giant video screens flashing on her at the side of the stage smiling, enchanted, bursting with pride for her most prideful son.

It's like one of those scenes from a Disney movie, where the handsome young hero, having fought his way up from nothing, against all odds, despite the haters, the bullies and the badmouthing, finally triumphs and gets to make his valedictory speech in front of an adoring crowd of whooping, cheering Hollywood extras.

It's exactly like that, except . . . well . . . this is *real*. Right?

'This festival' – he chokes out the words, his guitar becoming insistent – 'is not just a festival to me.' Pause, drama, pause, dingle-dangle-doo on the guitar, piercing stare into the crowd. 'Tonight . . . is like the most important gig of my life.' The tide of approval rolls in across the festival grounds, the mental visuals all in sweeping long shot, the dream panorama almost complete now . . .

'So this one' – small breath – 'is for all of you!' No blam into the song though, no band follow-up. 'It's called "Times Like These" . . .'

Dave, the master of delayed gratification, merely upping the stakes by singing the song alone, just him and the crowd and his almost 90,000 very best friends, on the occasion of the most important gig of his life.

'It's times like these you learn to live again,' he croons, sounding a little like Tom Petty, whom he nearly joined after Kurt died, but was too smart to. 'It's times like these you learn to give and give again . . .'

And there you have it: the reason why it isn't just the people at the Reading Festival that love Dave Grohl and his Foo Fighters;

it's the millions around the world who have bought his CDs and DVDs, his concert and festival tickets; the generations that bought into his story, his dream, his self-fulfilling prophecies. Dave's a giver. He may not have the savant glamour of Kurt Cobain, but Kurt was a taker. Kurt dwelled in darkness, on the wrong side of the moon. Dave is a sun worshipper, a lover not a loner, a bringer of light.

Above all, Dave is a fast learner: in everything he has, all that he does, picked up along the way, from the street, from the breast of his mother, from his kids, his fans, and the band mates he tolerates and conveys fame and wealth to. Everything Nirvana did wrong, the Foo Fighters do right. Everything Kurt could not stomach, that he choked on, Dave has chewed up and spat out and allowed to make him stronger. Where Kurt was the perpetual victim, inviting the stalkers to rape him, Dave is the ultimate survivor, daring the world to try and tell him different. Vanquishing foes with that big goofy smile and warm embrace; unafraid in private to draw the knife and strike whenever he really has to.

'It's times like these you learn to love again,' he sings that night at Reading. 'It's times like these, time and time again . . .'

And that's when the band does finally come in, the timing perfect, the drama heightened, cathartic, real, the stage now fully lit as Dave shows again just how well he has learned the game, become a master at it, and how we all can't help but love the nicest man in rock, while knowing no one gets this far down the road by simply being nice. That to be a real foo fighter you have to fly so fast across what passes for most normal people's radar that they really can't identify what or who you are, just follow the streak as it wends its way, zigzagging back and forth across the sky, night or day, in pretty colours, both alien and human, in revolving order.

That to be a real foo fighter you have to know how to pilot a ball of fire. Learning to fly so fast the only real trail left behind – the only truth left to be told – is all yours.

2. Foo are You?

They wanted this book to be about the Foo Fighters. But the Foo Fighters as a *band* is only a notional idea. Something that only exists in your head. There is only one real Foo Fighter and his name is Dave Grohl. The rest – the floating cast of members that surround him – play no part in the decision-making process. They are mere appendages. Staff members. Hired and fired by Dave. Musical actors. Who play their parts well but that doesn't make them intrinsic to the Foo Fighters' story any more than the Munchkins are in *The Wizard of Oz*. They are the dwarves in this story, dancing jauntily around the central figure of Grohl, who appears as both Dorothy and the Wizard, depending on his mood. And they are lucky to be there.

Even Nirvana – who could sustain the loss of five drummers and a second guitarist before Dave Grohl was hired, but not a single moment without Kurt Cobain – was more of a real band than the Foo Fighters have ever been. Kurt had Krist Novoselic to anchor Nirvana's band identity, even as he later pushed him into signing a contract that took away most of his ownership in the group's songs retrospectively. Dave has only the fantasy of a real friend in his band. Oh, much is made of his longstanding relationship with guitarist Pat Smear. But Pat bailed on Dave after just one album and didn't appear fully on another Foo Fighters album for 14 years, by which time Dave didn't need him any more, his empire already built. Good old Pat's back now but only by Dave's good graces.

Then there's the drummer Taylor Hawkins, the 'little brother' whom Dave sat beside in hospital in London in 2001 after he overdosed on heroin and alcohol and nearly died. Taylor was 29 and, by Christ, should have known better, and Dave was 32 and had already seen this movie with Kurt, thanks. Yet Dave stayed beside Taylor. Cancelled a European tour and allowed him to recover back home in Los Angeles, on the promise he clean up his act. Two months later Dave was playing drums with Queens of the Stone Age, leaving his own band stewing and Taylor, in particular, standing tiptoe on an emotional ledge, threatening to throw himself off. Dave never blinked and after three days Taylor was much better off. Or else.

How about the other 'original' Foo Fighter, the bassist Nate Mendel? Nate came in, like everybody else, after Dave had already formed the 'band', at a time when it consisted of just one member, Dave, who had written, recorded, produced, sung and played every instrument on the first Foo Fighters album. Nate came in because the guy who had been the drummer in Nirvana, the biggest band in the world, the best band in the world, the most influential and important band in the world since the Beatles, asked him to. Nate, whose own band, Sunny Day Real Estate, no one outside their own dreams had ever heard of, or could name a single song by, had folded through total lack of interest. Nate, in his earnest beard and awful dad-shorts, studiously gnawing away at his bass, who would never in a million years have had Pat Smear in the band, nor Taylor Hawkins, who called Dave one night in 1999 to tell him he was leaving the Foo Fighters, too, only to call him back at six the next morning to beg for his job back, realising what a dumb thing he had just done. Nate was lucky to still be on the scene and nobody knows it better than Nate. Except Dave, of course, who knows things none of the others could ever imagine.

As for Chris Shiflett, bless his heart; does anyone know how to pronounce his name properly, let alone what he's supposed to do as 'lead guitarist' in the Foo Fighters? Chris, the real nice guy in the Foo Fighters, who plays nice guitar but had never been credited with writing a song in his life before receiving co-credits on the fourth Foos album, *One by One*, in 2002 – an album he later admitted he kept turning up to work on, only to be left to sit around 'drinking coffee' and eating lunch until he was told to go home again. Until Dave scrapped it and began again, this time with Chris in the same room, at least. Chris the nice guy whose job was threatened every step of the way by the ever-present ghost of Pat Smear, whom Dave was talking to privately on the phone about coming back to the band for years until it was eventually made official in 2006. Chris was furious. 'I was just like, "You've got to be fucking kidding me."' But Chris didn't have any say in the decision. Nobody did. Just Dave. Well, duh.

So this is not going to be a book about the Foo Fighters the *band*. Because that would make this is a fairy tale for idiots. This is instead a book about the Foo Fighters the *man*. Cos that's what it is, millions of Foos fans. Don't pretend you would want it any other way, either.

The real story of the Foo Fighters goes back to Springfield, Virginia, in the late Seventies, where the nine-year-old David Eric Grohl, son of an Irish-American single mother, Virginia Jean, is practising guitar, trying to play along to his Led Zeppelin records. 'I don't think Dave was ever that much of an angry punk rock kid,' says Paul Brannigan, who would become Dave's first biographer. 'There was an element of that in his upbringing but people who talk about him from then always talk of him more as being goofy and a bit of a clown – the life and soul of the party rather than the intense young man sitting at the back of the classroom. Kurt Cobain was that archetypal rebel kid. But Dave wasn't really that. He liked the music but it wasn't like he was some sort of twisted ball of neurosis.'

Dave was always the comedian, always the attention-seeker. A Capricorn born in the Age of Aquarius, 14 January 1969, back when peace and love and long hair still meant something, man. According to Kurt Cobain, who also came from a broken home but came out of it with a completely different outlook, Dave Grohl was 'the most well-adjusted boy I know'.

Ironically, what helped Dave achieve this apparent state of grace was the fact that his father, James Harper Grohl, a hard-working news reporter of Slovak–German lineage, divorced Dave's mother, Virginia, an English teacher, in 1976, leaving his seven-year-old son to grow up with just his mother and older sister, Lisa. Consequently, 'there was no male balance,' Grohl reflected in 1996. 'There was no father who wanted you to be like Dad, so you were left to be an individual because of course your mother didn't want you to grow up to be like your mother, and your sister didn't want you to grow up to be like your sister.' Growing up without that strong 'male balance', he insisted, 'had a strong influence on me. When I was twelve, I was in theatre groups and they were predominantly gay – growing up in rural Virginia, where everyone's either a farmer or works in the Penta-gon, to be so accepting of gay people was a real bonus.'

The only words of fatherly advice he could recall, he later claimed, were: 'Never get into a pissing match with someone who buys their ink by the barrel.' Prophetic words of wisdom for a boy destined to spend most of his adult life being profiled and fingerprinted, defined then redefined by an over-eager media ready to laud or disdain him on the strength or weakness of his every utterance, his every gesture. His just being there, after the fall of Nirvana, the sole survivor who refused the guilt trip the world wished to foist on him. To make them feel better. Dave wasn't having any of that. Fuck you, man.

Instead, the boy Grohl grew up uninhibited by notions of Midwestern American manhood, neither enamoured of nor rebellious towards the idea of family, of home, and his cherished place in it. With only one parent's income to rely on, there was little money for treats or vacations. 'There were tough times when we'd eat peanut butter and pickle sandwiches for dinner,' he told Nirvana's biographer Michael Azerrad. But the family unit was tight, supportive, unwavering. As a result, Dave once explained, 'I've always craved stability. I've never gotten off on chaos. Throughout the whole Nirvana experience I retreated to Virginia whenever I felt sucked into the tornado of insanity. Same thing with the Foo Fighters – I wouldn't be able to do this if I didn't have my feet planted firmly on the ground.'

Yet not so firmly planted that he didn't let his mind roam free. He loved comic books and aliens and space travel. 'I used to sit on my porch and stare at the skies and fucking pray I would see a UFO,' he said. 'Even as a child, I just couldn't understand why anyone would be so close-minded as to think there was no life anywhere else but our tiny, ignorant planet.' Dreams of UFOs full of friendly ET-like beings coming in to land, offering him the chance to just fly away, were also to do with notions of escape, of course, of fleeing a normal rural life, whatever normal really means. Dave didn't even pretend to know the answer to that. Not as a kid with his eyes fixed on the sky. It was like he said: 'Every kid wanted their own spaceship. You wished you could get in it and fly above your school and look down at your friends. I used to sit on my lawn and wish I could see a UFO and that it would land, and that little aliens would come out.' He paused, reflected. 'When you're being pushed down by everything around you, you can fantasise about a UFO coming from somewhere you have never been and from somewhere you have never seen or heard of . . . or never knew there was.'

It was this same sense of wanting to leap beyond the bounds of reality that found him joining his sister, Lisa, at the dressing-up box. 'When I was young, I would put on a show for the family,' he remembered. 'I was always the comedian.' Except for when he cried. He'd dress up in 'clothing we had in the attic, something as outlandish and ridiculous as possible,' then prance around the living room in front of his mother and her friends, acting the clown, just as he would years later in Foo Fighters videos, like the one for 'Learn to Fly', where he dresses in drag as a goofy flight attendant.

Later he would suggest his behaviour was down to being 'hyperactive – extremely'. His teachers at school did not disagree. His old school report cards are remarkable for the number of requests for meetings with his mother to discuss her son's seeming inability to simply sit down and shut up. 'They always said the same thing: "David could be a great student if he could just stay in his fucking seat."'

Music – fast-as-fuck rock'n'roll music, fucker! – was more than an emotional salve, it was the older brother Dave never knew he had. 'Drums, to me, always seemed like the greatest toy,' he said in an early interview. 'You didn't have the nicest bike in the neighbourhood, you didn't have a tennis racket, you had a drum set. Drums are strange. Drums are for idiots. I am the idiot, and I'm comfortable with that. Drums are great, because nobody expects anything from you.'

Before drums, he'd played guitar – after a fashion. His father had left behind an old nylon-string Spanish guitar that Dave drove his mother so crazy with, she eventually begged him to get lessons. He did – for a while and with zero enthusiasm, but he couldn't handle the terrible tedium of one-string-at-a-time learning, so shut himself up in his room, kerranging along to anything he could get onto his record player that was loud, thumping and hot. His father had once played flute, his mother had briefly sung in acapella groups. Maybe it meant something. The first instrument he'd actually tried to play had been the trombone – like a flute, maybe, but with a much deeper, gravelly voice. But he just felt ridiculous. You couldn't join a high school rock band playing the fucking trombone, man. So Dave went for guitar, even though he couldn't name you a single chord, and by the time he was 12 he was thrumming along like he knew what he was doing, disguising his lack of ability with sheer exuberance.

The closest he came to an actual band was when he and his best pal Larry hooked up to record some songs they'd made up together about school friends and Dave's dog. Dave would plonk away on one string of the guitar while Larry used knives and forks to play 'drums' on his mother's kitchen pots and pans. They even had a name for their group: the HG Hancock Band. It was a laugh while it lasted, but it didn't last long and that was all.

He was a freshman at Thomas Jefferson High, in nearby Alexandria, a smart-ass in a bunch of genuinely smart kids. 'I was able to get along with anybody. I got along with the stoners, I got along with the geeks, I got along with pretty much everyone.' Music was the common denominator. And with the music came weed and with that came rock wisdom, mid-twentieth-century style. It all went together, dude: Zep and Sabbath and weed and feeling fine; tripping on The Who and Judas Priest and bong water and foot-long doobics.

None of this was remotely punk. This was teenage heartland America in the early Eighties, where rock with a capital 'R' ruled, alongside The Eagles and Fleetwood Mac and REO Speed-wagon on date-nights – if you could ever *find* a date. Which you could not, be real, dude. Looking back on those days, in 1997, Dave recalled getting 'pretty good grades until I got into high school. Then I started smoking pot and I couldn't give a shit about anything.'

It was Dave and his best pal Jimmy Swanson – 'we were like brothers'. Jimmy was a born metal freak. Didn't matter if it was Venom or Def Leppard, as long as they had guitars and kick-ass drums and they fuckin' rocked like a bitch – and sounded even better when you smoked pot. 'I was such a burnout,' Dave would say, shaking his head, years later. 'I was smoking all day long. My best friend was the bong. My friend Jimmy here – we both dropped out of high school and sat around and smoked pot and listened to King Diamond all day!' Then there was Sab-bath, Jimmy prompted him, then '. . . Venom, Overkill . . .' Dave shook with mirth. 'Jimmy and I actually went to see [Venom's singer] Cronos, his solo project.'

The real turning point came, though, when Dave was 13 and he and Lisa spent a summer vacation with their cousin Tracy. Tracy's family lived in Evanston, Illinois, within spitting distance of Chicago – the big city. The Grohl family would drive up every July. But then, in 1982, 'we showed up and Tracy was not the old Tracy we knew. She was now punk rock Tracy. And it was fucking wild, man,' said Dave. 'I'd only seen punks on TV, never in real life. She was part of this unbelievable underground net-work that I totally fell in love with.'

The first gig Tracy and her bondage pants took Dave to was Naked Raygun at the Cubby Bear, a local sports bar in Chicago, across from Wrigley Field, home of the Cubs baseball team. Originally known as Negro Commander, and fronted by Jeff Pezzati, who went on to become the bass player in Big Black (the Chicago-based band belonging to the future Nirvana and Foo Fighters producer Steve Albini – keep up, dude!), Naked Raygun played true-blood, all-American white punk stuff. Dave was so entranced that when he came home from the gig with punk Tracy he decided to become punk Dave. 'She took me to see a punk rock show and from then on that was it,' Dave would later testify. From then on we were totally punk. We went home and bought [the punk fanzine] *Maximumrocknroll*, and tried to figure it all out.'

Before the trip with Tracy to the Cubby Bear, Dave's mom hadn't even let him go to a Kiss concert (he had a giant poster of them on his bedroom wall). After being shown the light by Tracy, though, nothing could stop him. He still kept up his love of rock and metal, becoming an early adopter of Metallica and Slayer, and the whole thrash metal scene. ('I bought the first Metallica album [*Kill 'Em All*] on cassette from a mail-order catalogue in 1983,' Dave recalled. 'It blew my fucking mind. It was like someone had sent me the Holy Grail.')

Now, though, thanks to punk rock Tracy, at the same time as Dave was getting John Bonham's entwined triangle of circles logo tattooed onto his wrist, his horizons expanded to include original Brit-punks like The Damned and The Clash (the Damned's drummer, Rat Scabies, 'was one of the first people to do that crash cymbal/hi-hat thing. That's who I learned that from') and the latest hardcore American punk bands like Bad Religion, who mixed their street poetics with time-changes, guitar solos and – gulp! – occasional three-part vocal harmonies; The Germs, fronted by the already dead Darby Crash and a strikingly effeminate guitarist, now turned Hollywood bit-parter, named Pat Smear; Circle Jerks, a weak LA version of The Clash featuring a classically trained guitarist and a jazz-literate drummer who nonetheless achieved domestic punk godhead with their debut album, *Group Sex*, which featured 14 tracks with a combined running time of just 15 minutes; and DRI – short for Dirty Rotten Imbeciles – from Houston, Texas. Their first release, in 1982, was the *Dirty Rotten EP*, which featured 22 tracks, totalling 18 minutes, spread across two sides of a seven-inch vinyl EP. Only 1000 copies of the EP were ever pressed, making it now a highly sought-after collector's item. Dave and Jimmy owned one of them, which they shared. Most of all, Dave loved local punk heroes Bad Brains, a punk fusion – rock and reggae – outfit that had grown like a musical tumour from the jazz-funk origins of a mid-Seventies Washington, DC outfit called Mind Power.

'I started listening to Killing Joke or Hüsker Dü or Bad Brains and all these bands where the music was just a distorted melodic mess with these sweet harmonies over the top,' Dave later recalled. 'It's still the kind of music that I enjoy the most.'

He took to playing snatches of Circle Jerks and Bad Brains over the school Tannoy system every morning. But Jimmy wasn't feeling it and the two friends began to go their different ways. 'I discovered the B-52s and Devo,' Dave told *Rolling Stone*, 'he was going off to Loverboy and Def Leppard.' When Dave drew a comic strip in class featuring a character named Devo aiming his space gun at a character called Loverboy, Dave was pulled out of class and sent to see the school shrink, who asked him, 'What are you going to do with your life?' Dave replied that he'd like to find some sort of a career in the music business. 'And her first reaction was, "You only want to do that because you know where the drugs are."'

It couldn't last and it didn't. Dave's mother, appalled at her stoner son's unrepentant lust for marijuana, pulled him out of Thomas Jefferson and got him transferred to Bishop Ireton High, an all-male Catholic school known for its strict discipline, its tough love. Dave was there for two years before Virginia

took pity on him and allowed him to transfer to the more lib-
eral Annandale High School, known for its emphasis on racial
and cultural diversity and the quality of its student newspaper.
And for its freethinking, kickass, motherfucking students. Yeah,
buddy!

The first band Dave played in was at Annandale and it
was called Freak Baby. He was 15 and had recently become a
regular face at the 9.30 Club, the local stopping off point for
alternative and punk rock scenesters in the mid-Eighties: a
black-walled, weirdly shaped sweatbox on the ground floor of
the nineteenth-century Atlantic Building in sleazy downtown
Washington. 'I went to the 9:30 Club hundreds of times,' he
would boast. 'I was always so excited to get there, and I was
always bummed when it closed. I spent my teenage years at the
club and saw some shows that changed my life.'

One of the guys his age Dave used to bump heads with
there was named Brian Samuels, then playing bass in Freak
Baby. When the band decided to add a second guitarist, Dave
faked his way through an audition, playing random chords as
loudly and as fast as possible. Giving it loads with the goofy
smile and the bug eyes. The band only lasted six months but it
was during rehearsals one night that Dave decided to have a go
on the drummer David Smith's kit. He got so carried away he
didn't hear Samuels telling him to quit it until the irate bassist
dragged him by his nose off the drum stool and onto the floor.
Not digging this at all, the others told Samuels to get the fuck
out. No problem, he railed, and stormed out never to return.
The only other Freak Baby member that could do a reasonable
impersonation of a bass player was Smith – which left the band
looking for a drummer. Enter: our hero in battered 501s with a
sore nose.

The change in line-up demanded a change in name and Freak

Baby became Mission Impossible. True to their punk spirit, when Mission Impossible went in to make their first – and only – demo, at the Laundry Room Studio, in 1985, the seven tracks they recorded – half old Freak Baby material, half new stuff – were all barely a minute long but filled to bursting with frizzy guitars, choked vocals and – lo and behold – some surprisingly busy and accomplished-sounding drums. The demo did the trick and Mission Impossible began to get gigs. They even got a track onto a split single with another local DC punk act, Lunch Meat, released on the indie Dischord label. Things were moving fast, the music was moving faster. So they changed their name to Fast. Then stood around smoking cigarettes and bitching as everything slowed to a grinding halt.

When the bandleaders, the singer Chris Page and guitarist Bryant Mason, graduated from high school and headed off to college, the two Davids – Grohl and Smith – vowed to keep the faith and soldier on, which they did for more than a year with another local 'visionary' named Reuben Radding improvising vocals and guitar over the top of whatever fists of fury the two Davids could summon between them. They called the new trio Dain Bramage – geddit? Ha, yeah. Amped up on coffee and weed they jammed for all of one night in the living room of Dave's mother's house. As dawn came creeping like a sick friend through the windows, they found they had half a dozen not-at-all-bad punk songs that would later become the basis of a ten-track album titled *I Scream Not Coming Down* – released on Fartblossom Records, the deal struck just moments after Dain Bramage had completed their first ever gig at the 9.30 Club. 'It was already the greatest night of my life,' Dave remembered with that special glow. 'As a kid growing up in the DC punk rock scene, your first show at the 9:30 Club might as well have been Royal Albert Hall or Madison Square Garden.'

Only snag: Dain Bramage may have been several steps further up the musical ladder than anything he'd been involved in before – definite echoes of art-punk pioneers like Television and The Voidoids – but the regular 9.30 crowd was left cold. 'Everybody just hated us.' And the euphoria of getting a record deal lasted only for as long as it took Dave to find himself a bigger, better gig to play. The way he saw it, he had no choice. It was sink-or-swim time and, as he would demonstrate again and again throughout his minefield career, Dave was not a sinker.

He'd finally dropped out of high school at 16, worked briefly at a succession of hard, dull jobs (furniture warehouseman, manual labourer, general dickweed) and had secretly considered becoming a professional session drummer, learning to read music and earning enough money to put himself back through school. By now he was regarded, in Springfield, at least, as a proper kickass drummer. He'd actually found something he could excel at and he knew it, felt it every time he got behind the kit and taught it to fly. At the same time, he had smoked enough weed and played in enough whoop-de-doo punk rock outfits by the mid-Eighties to have developed a highly fatalistic attitude to his future. 'When I was twelve,' he once confessed, 'I thought for sure that I would die before I was sixteen, because sixteen is when you get your driver's license. When I was sixteen I thought I'd be dead before I was twenty-one, because when you're twenty-one you're old enough to drink.' He couldn't 'imagine myself being fifty years old'. He just couldn't 'see that far into the future'. Who the hell could? No one Dave knew, or wanted to know.

He couldn't even see himself ever leaving Springfield, Virginia, not unless he joined the army, as so many unskilled local guys did. And then it happened, his big break, the offer to join the best-known, most influential punk band on the Washington scene

– Scream. Three albums, all on Dischord, all highly regarded, all highly cool, and a national touring schedule that would, they told him, take them to Europe, fabled land across the shining, shit-filled sea, and home to the kind of punk that rocked as only gobbing, pogoing, tattooed skinhead second-wave punk music can. Especially in the UK, which Scream weren't yet going to but never mind that, you coming or what the fuck, man?

It was March 1987 and the 17-year-old Dave Grohl didn't need to be asked twice. He quit Dain Bramage on the spot. Reuben and the other David decided to try and continue on without their brilliant but recalcitrant drummer. But fuck, man, it just wasn't happening. As Reuben ruefully noted, years later, 'After you've spent a couple years with Dave Grohl as your drummer it's easy to feel like no other drummer exists.'

3. A Loud, Sharp, Piercing Cry

Scream was a crazy dream, shared by two brothers: Peter and Franz Stahl. Peter was the good-looking singer who wrote lyrics. Franz was the enigmatic guitarist who wrote music. There were two others, the drummer Kent Stax and bassist Skeeter Thompson. But Scream was all about the brothers. Kent was good, solid and reliable, and knew how to fuck-up his drums. Skeeter was a river-deep bass note bouncing off the walls. The brothers had been born at the crossroad – Bailey's Crossroads, in Fairfax County, Virginia – but behind the scenes it was Skeeter who did most of the devil's work; beginning with weed and wine before escalating to crack cocaine. But as Franz says now, speaking from his home in Los Angeles, 'Everybody has their moments.'

Scream were hardcore American punk at a time when the genre looked like it was screamed out; the last street serenaders of an age when playing loud and fast on instruments you had barely mastered was considered as far out as you could ever need to be. Peter and Franz fancied themselves a kind of Midwestern American collision between The Clash and The Damned, without the visual theatrics, but with the same almost clownish musical aplomb.

'We got to do two nights with The Dammed at the 9.30 Club,' says Franz, 'which was like playing in the World Series, for me.' He recalls with delight Kent leaning over to Rat Scabies and asking, 'Could I bum a cigarette off of you?' And Rat turning around and telling him to fuck off. 'I ran into Rat years later at the Viper Room and told him that story and he was all apologetic and I was like, "No, no, no! That's what punk was about to me!"'

Scream had the moves, the ideas, and even the momentum, each of their first three albums building on the last. And if they'd come along five years earlier – or five years later – they might have become the band they always felt they should have, could have, would have been. Instead, in 1987 bands like Scream were being supplanted in cutting-edge American youth culture by the new generation of thrash metal bands, led by Metallica, whose recent album, *Master of Puppets*, had actually made the US Top 30, something Scream would never come close to achieving – though not for the want of trying.

As far as the teenaged Dave Grohl was concerned though, Scream ruled. 'They were from Virginia,' he shrugged. 'I had roots in Virginia.' And though he had seen them play at the 9.30 Club many times, and knew they were local dudes like him, he knew absolutely nothing else. Scream were an enigma wrapped in a punk poster, awash in a punk wet dream. 'I loved the fact I could be walking past them every day without knowing it.'

No FB or Twitter to check them out on in those days, not even a blip on the regular music-magazine radar; all Dave had to go on was the music: hardcore, Brit-influenced punk – gritty, determinedly blokey and dry as Grandmothers' dead bones. Typically, it was the third Scream album, *Banging the Drum*, released on Dischord in 1986, that Dave liked best. The speed-kills riffs of their first two albums were still here and there but they had brought in a second guitarist to flesh out their sound and the tracks now lasted longer than a minute or two. They had also let their hair grow out and were coming up with more obvious rock anthems such as 'ICYUOD' (short for: 'I See Why

You Over Dose') and the sub-Who-style 'Feel Like That'. There were even power ballads like 'People, People', and when Dave later talked about the album sounding more like early Aerosmith than, say, The Damned, it said everything you needed to know. Dave thought of it as 'the album where Scream went from being a hardcore band into being a rock band'.

When Kent Stax was forced to quit Scream in 1987 – 'Kent had been married and he'd recently had a child,' Franz explains, 'and he just couldn't go on tour any more, because back then we were not making any money and he had to provide for his child' – the band placed a handmade flyer in the window of a local record store saying they were looking for a drummer and giving a phone number: Franz's. When Dave saw the handwritten poster up on the wall the next day, he knew he had to at least call the number. 'I thought I'd try out just to tell my friends I'd jammed with Scream.'

The first time Dave rang it though, the elder brother, Pete, blew him off, said he was too young. The Stahl brothers were already in their mid-twenties; Dave was barely 18. For anyone else, that would have finished things off right there. Not Dave. He left it a while then called Pete back: lied about his age, told them he was 20. They said awright, come on over. He did and the first thing Franz Stahl asked him was which numbers he wanted to play, maybe something by Zeppelin or Sabbath? But Dave had his shtick all worked out. Nah, he told 'em, and reeled off the titles of half a dozen Scream numbers he'd already memorised. Still not entirely convinced, Franz played along then stood slack-jawed, chewing a cigarette and marvelling at how good the kid was. Franz laughs as he recalls the scene. 'Our first record was like twenty-one tracks or something like that? And we just proceeded to blow through every one of those tracks – like that! I was just like, "Fuck!" The first thing I did was call Pete and say,

"Dude, this Dave guy, we just fucking jammed and he's it! We don't need to find anybody else!" This skinny gangling kid who lied about his age.'

The Stahl brothers offered Dave the gig on condition he was ready to commit totally, immediately, no pussying around. Dave acted cool, like no biggie, then fretted all the way home about how he was going to convince his mother it was a good idea for him to take off in the back of a battered old Dodge Ram van with these battered older punk guys. It was not an easy sell. Virginia hadn't worked her fingers to the bone trying to get her only boy through high school to have him drop out and leave home with some band. Ever the shrewd, Dave enlisted the support of his father, but James was even less keen. Dave recalled his father making it clear he would rather his son enrol in the army than drum in some no-hope band of misfits. But Virginia eventually came to the rescue and gave him her blessing. 'She said, "All right. Well, you better be good at this." I'm like, "I'll try."'

As learning curves go, becoming the drummer in Scream was a doozy. Once they'd started touring, 'There were a few clubs where Dave would have to sit outside until it was time for us to play, because he was obviously underage.' Dave was unfazed, though, determined to stick with it. 'I've always seen Dave as being a really strong character,' says Anton Brookes, the innovative young PR who would become first Nirvana's, then the Foo Fighters' London publicist. 'From his punk rock background and everything that he's been through, I've always seen him as really strong and he's always been driven.' Forcing his way into contention for the drum stool in Scream was early proof of that, says Anton. 'He'd just gone from high school, being some punk rock kid, going to the 9.30 Club to watch bands. Then he graduated up to Scream. That shows Dave's drive and ambition. That was part of his evolution.'

Looking back years later, Dave would romanticise the experience. 'The feeling of driving across the country in a van, stopping in every city to play, sleeping on people's floors, watching the sun come up over the desert as I drove, it was all too much. This was definitely where I belonged.' He would rhapsodise about learning to survive on seven dollars a day, living on cheap cigarettes and whack Mexican weed. Burger and fries was a banquet, mostly it was just fries.

Then there were the chicks. The cool chicks would buy you a Taco Bell and a beer then take you back to your Dodge Ram and give you head. The uncool chicks would just blow you, after they'd blown the other guys first. It soon became clear that Dave was going to be the eternal newbie. 'When Pete found out my real age and that he was ten years older than me, he became my father figure,' said Dave. Franz also took the young drummer under his wing, showing him guitar licks and enlightening him on the brutal methodology of Iggy Pop and the Stooges, or the herbal spiritualism of Bob Marley and the Wailers. It was, admitted Dave, a real crash course for a would-be raver who had 'never been past Chicago'.

'He was always kind of farting around with [guitar],' says Franz now. 'I would show him stuff when he wanted to learn something, just like I would show Skeeter: "Hey, I got this riff" and we would jam on that. But Dave was always kind of fiddling around with guitar and coming up with stuff, although he didn't really write anything until later on.'

The only one Dave couldn't quite figure out was the band's dreadlocked bass player, Skeeter Thompson. Skeeter played bass like most people smoked bongs – with deep, heavy breaths. He was a black guy who liked to put blond streaks in his hair. A stone cold dude who always had a million girlfriends all looking out for him but somehow always managed to find himself in places no one else knew existed. He smoked bundles of herb and endless packs of cigarettes, and he liked coke. A lot. So much so he soon graduated to freebasing. So much so he then turned to smoking crack. So much so he was soon pawning his bass guitar and other bits of band equipment to keep up his habit. So much so he ended up so far over the rainbow nobody thought he would ever come back. (He did, eventually, and now lives the quiet life, clean and sober.)

Franz sighs. 'Skeeter is an infamous character, a loveable guy, and an insanely great bass player and musical mind. He's the kind of guy you could go into any city in America and go, "You know Skeeter?" "Oh, fuck, yeah, I know Skeeter!" He's that kind of guy. We would be in Amsterdam doing shows, and we would lose Skeeter for a day and he would come back in completely new clothes! "Oh, I hooked up with this chick, she bought me all these clothes." Just a great guy; extremely good-looking. Me and Skeeter were very tight.' They would sit around listening to Black Flag records, followed by the O'Jays, Parliament, Bootsy Collins, 'all this crazy shit. He was like part of my musical education.'

Dave, who had also taken to putting flashes of blond in his dark hair, also tried hard to find a way into Skeeter's mind. They were, after all, the rhythm section of the band. But Skeeter had his own ideas, and at first would tease and torment the newbie, pinning him down on the ground and sticking his smelly feet in his face, or deliberately going his own way onstage. When things got really bad Skeeter would simply drop out of the band and they would hurriedly move to find a temporary replacement. At his worst, Skeeter was impossible. But when he held himself together long enough to actually *relate*, he was the man, good-hearted, funny, more genuinely punk than the rest of the Scream team put together. The only problem was that by the time Dave was in the band, the Skeeter stories were becoming less funny with each new misadventure. It seemed only a matter of time before the whole shithouse went up in flames. And then one day it did.

Dave was young enough, though, not to care. Not while Scream was able to still make albums and tour. The first record they made with Dave in the band was *No More Censorship*, released in 1988 on the RAS (Real Authentic Sound) label after Dischord decided they'd done all they could. The fact that RAS was a reggae label, formed by Doctor Dread – real name Gary Himelfarb, a reggae producer of huge renown who had actually been born in Washington – only added lustre to the label's name, the way the Stahl brothers saw it, reflecting both their own occasional forays into raw-edged reggae and the historical link between punk and reggae as exemplified by their idols, The Clash, and, more recently, the inspirational Bad Brains.

Scream had done a relatively big deal with the label, which gave them a budget of $20,000 to make the record and put them in a big studio, Lion and Fox, in Washington. It was supposed to be Scream's big break, their first real shot at the big time. But they overreached, took it too seriously, and tried too hard to please too many people. At a time when the biggest band in America was Def Leppard, whose *Hysteria* album was all about textures, finesse, balance, a sophisticated blend of sweet pop and hard rock, RAS were looking to get in on the action, using Scream as a mast around which they could build their own rock roster

These days, Franz recalls 'keyboards and acoustic guitars, pianos, it was just one big fucking vomit of ideas. And it really never meshed out. There were some good tracks but it was like where have we gone, what are we doing?' It didn't help that 'a lot of crazy shit was going on at the same time, there were lots of drugs going around . . . We were never happy with it. We were never sold on the songs. At one end it was very metal. Then there were some nice pretty songs, very dramatic. But we didn't know what we were doing or where we wanted to go.'

Listening to it now, the only one on the album who really sounds like he knows what he's doing is Dave, whose obsession with John Bonham reaches its apotheosis on tracks like 'Hit Me', then cheerily morphs into passable imitations of Rat Scabies on 'Fucked without a Kiss' and Motörhead's drummer, 'Philthy' Phil Taylor, on 'No Escape'. Nobody in the band could really take this grudging step towards mainstream acceptance seriously, though. When Dave and some of the guys went to see the Monsters of Rock festival show at the RFK Stadium in Washington, other than Metallica they found the rest of the bill – starring the Scorpions and the headliners Van Halen – nauseously perplexing. But then Dave was tripping on some especially powerful acid at the time. He later said he spent the whole time veering between laughing and feeling sick. 'It was a fucking comedy. Like, "Why is this person leaping around in ballet slippers with bandanas around his microphone? What the fuck is that all about?"'

All Dave could see at the time were the shiny new advance copies of the *No More Censorship* record with his name on the back cover: 'Dave Grohl – Drums'. That it would be several months before it was actually released hardly mattered. The plane ticket to Amsterdam, where Scream had begun their first European tour that year, in a bid to spread their flickering fame across yet more beer-and-butt-stained carpets, made up for that. Dave could not believe his luck! Getting on a plane with a band and flying to Europe to tour! Come on! What more proof did you need than that that you'd finally made it, were really going someplace; were sprouting real wings and beginning to move with both feet off the ground? Even if it meant you had to crash-land at the other end of wherever it was you thought you were going? Even if it meant you never came back at all?

Dave and the band found Amsterdam itself to be beyond their wildest dreams. It didn't matter that they spent most of their time crashing at strangers' pads. Pot was *legal*, man. That's right, motherfucker! You could just stroll into one of the many coffee houses situated among the endless winding canals and buy whatever you liked: heavy black hash, sticky green weed, opium-streaked Nepalese Temple Ball . . . They'd even sell you tobacco and the rolling papers. Give you a chessboard to sit and relax with, or a book, or a hooker. And they never closed. If you had the cash you could just sit in one of these magical places for the rest of your life, right Skeeter?

The gigs themselves paid next to nothing but the band would soon be surrounded by new girlfriends willing to spring for a burger, or a beer, so that was all right. New best friends would welcome them in like long-lost punk brothers. It was the same wherever they went in Europe. At one gig in Turin, Italy, they arrived to find the gig was in a squat where they were burning mattresses because they were infested with scabies. 'You walk in with your gear,' Dave recalled, 'and they're still trying to figure out how to steal electricity from the building next door. And someone's building a stage. That's how it was every night.'

Touring Europe became a badge of honour for Dave and Scream. Back home they might have been slipping down the ladder in terms of recognition. But in Europe they were still regarded as the authentic voice of American hardcore. Over the next two years they would complete three European tours, the last of which, in the spring of 1990, found them playing 23 shows in almost as many days. There was little that was triumphant about these final appearances, though. After one show in

Germany, they discovered someone trying to steal their T-shirts from their stand. As the band generally made more money from tee-sales than they did the gigs, this was viewed as a hanging offence and the band hastily ejected the joker from the venue. Then afterwards, as they went to load up the van, they discovered the same guy, 'banging on the windows of the van and I just had a total loss of control,' admitted Dave. 'I just beat the shit out of his face.'

So much for being the nice guy of the band. The fact was, the novelty was wearing off, for all of them – even in Amsterdam, which had become a second home for Scream, as the sheer grind of travelling and playing with little pay, less food and just an endless stream of cheap drugs and increasingly faceless wannabe friends and groupies to sustain them.

One typical anecdote was later immortalised by Dave in the track 'Just Another Story about Skeeter Thompson', on which he tells the story, in spoken word against a comically gruff punk riff, of how the band were staying at the apartment of one of their Dam friends named, simply, Toss. Skeeter had begun an affair with the hot-looking girl that lived next door. 'I guess she had a lot of money,' Dave recounts in the song, 'Cos she was constantly buying him clothes.' Clothes and weed and wine and whatever else Skeeter wanted, baby. Until one day Skeeter walked in, dumped his stash bag on the table, pulled out his dick, squeezed the head of it, and asked Dave to take a look at it. 'He said, "Does that look like pus to you?"' says Dave in the song. 'I said, "No, I think it's lint."'

The track ends there so it's not known whether Skeeter was reassured by the reply or decided to get a second opinion. But the next time the band came skidding and careening through Europe, Skeeter was out of control. He didn't even bother to try and conceal his bags of weed as the band went through customs, crossing another border. Then, halfway through the dates, he bailed out completely. Pete called a friend back home, J. Robbins, singer-frontman of fellow DC rockers Jawbox, to fly out and help them finish the dates. But you knew things must be bad if even Skeeter couldn't take Europe any more. By the end, they were all glad just to get home in one piece – or several pieces, as it turned out, though that wouldn't become entirely apparent for a few more months yet.

Two live documents exist of Scream's foreshortened European career: two albums taken from either end of their tours with Dave. The first, *Live at Van Hall – Amsterdam*, which came out on the independent Dutch label Konkurrent, at the end of 1988, captures Scream still trying to find a middle ground between the outright punk of 'U Suck A / We're Fed Up' and the mainstream rock-lite of 'Walking by Myself'. The second, *Your Choice Live Series Vol. 10*, comes from one of their last shows in Germany, in 1990, and veers a little more towards the original punk sound that made them once so nearly famous. The most stand-out features now though are the drums, which are brilliantly explosive while sacrificing none of their rhythmic dexterity, and the guitar, which Franz is now so skilled at it's as if he is having to dumb down his playing in order to make what he's now capable of fit into what Scream are still gnawing away at.

Still, the dream dies hard when you're still under 30 and people keep telling you how good you are and how big you would be if only the world would wake up and recognise your talent. When they came back from the *No More Censorship* tour, Franz was still so upset with the album he immediately began working on new material. 'I wanted to write something straightforward, rocking, fast, and I grabbed Dave and we went into the basement and we kicked out this whole record': a brutal ten-track mini-masterpiece that would eventually become Scream's fifth and final album, *Fumble*. 'We wrote that whole record, just Dave and I, basically, regardless of what anyone else says. They were mainly all my ideas but Dave and I were like, "Let's do these riffs. None of these fucking keyboards and acoustic guitars, let's just do something really hard and solid." And we did.'

They also tuned down 'for half a step' – a trick that would become a signature of the grunge bands that were now hovering on the musical horizon – 'which, sonically, made it very heavy. Because I heard Metallica was doing that. So I adopted that idea.' At the same time he and Dave were listening to a lot of stuff by a Canadian progressive thrash metal band, Voivod. 'That was in the mind-set, too.'

The irony was that just as Scream were shape-shifting into something which anticipated the darker corners that rock would start to explore more fully in the Nineties, it was becoming harder to get anyone to take them seriously. When, in the late summer of 1990, Scream set out on their fifth American tour since Dave had joined the band, they did so still believing they were just one lucky shot away from stardom. Dave, though, was already having other ideas about where he went next. In the gaps between Scream tours he and a friend, Barrett Jones, had spent time together at the Laundry Room Studio, where Jones was helping another local act, named Churn, make a demo.

Barrett was a talented singer-guitarist in his own right, and owned his own four-track recording set-up. He was happy to show Dave how to make his own rough demos, laying down the drums on one track, the bass and guitar on two other separate tracks, leaving the vocals for the fourth. Dave later recalled how Barrett had helped him lay down three tracks in one quick-fire session, Dave hurrying over the guitar and vocal parts lest anyone should actually come in and see him play-acting at being a frontman. 'These were no epic masterpieces,' he insisted, 'just a test to see if I could do this sort of thing on my own.' Pleased with results, he said it was 'the beginning of a beautiful relationship' between the two men. One that would have lasting repercussions neither man could possibly have foreseen.

So confident was Dave in what he'd accomplished on his own, he persuaded the band to record one of his demo tracks, 'Gods Looked Down', on *Fumble*. He also talked them into allowing him to sing it, though the results would not be heard until 1993, when *Fumble* was belatedly released, long after Scream had disbanded, but in the wake of Dave's newfound fame in Nirvana. Interestingly, the end result, with its Zep-like, boy-gone-wrong riff and contrastingly wide-eyed, faux-naïf vocal, sounds somewhat like how one imagines a cross between Nirvana and the Foo Fighters might sound.

Clearly, Dave was already thinking several steps ahead. Not just musically. When a local music biz figure named Glen E. Friedman decided to try and shop around for a new deal for Scream, based on the tapes of what became the *Fumble* album, later claiming to have sunk $10,000 of his own money into doing so, Dave was the one who stayed on his case, phoning him every few days, keeping the pot boiling, pushing hard to see what progress Friedman was making. 'Dave called me more than the other guys, and we became good friends,' Friedman would tell the Australian writer Jeff Apter in 2005. 'Everyone wanted it, but Dave *really* wanted it.'

Wanting it and getting it, however – at least with Scream – were proving to be two very different things. When, in the late summer of 1990, Skeeter bailed again, leaving the band stranded penniless in Los Angeles, it looked like the game was finally up, says Franz. 'Skeeter spins out of control and that's it. We're tired of trying to keep pulling it back together again. Just feeling like: what the fuck? Everybody had kind of had enough of it. Whether we would get back together later, at that point it was just like, forget it, whatever.'

Crashing at the Laurel Canyon house of Sabrina Stahl – elder sister to Pete and Franz – they phoned Friedman to beg for money but that wasn't the would-be entrepreneur's way. He wasn't in it to give them money, he was in it to find them a deal and make money. Clueless as to what to do next, still unwilling to give up on their dream, the Stahl brothers holed up at their sister's place and waited to see what happened. Dave, meanwhile, though he didn't make a big deal of it, had already decided he'd had enough. He kicked back at Sabrina's pad too for a while, which she shared with a couple of female mud wrestlers from the infamous Hollywood Tropicana, then found himself a cash-money gig working for a guy he'd met named Lumpy, who was building a coffee shop in nearby Costa Mesa. Dave still pitched in whenever he could, asking around if anyone knew of a half-decent bassist willing to hook up with the increasingly desperate Scream, but mainly he was thinking about his own future.

When he heard that the Melvins, fellow-traveller punk-metallists from Washington state, were coming through town, he phoned their leader, the singer-guitarist Buzz Osbourne, and asked if he could be put on the guest list. They had met some time before, when Scream had shared the bill with the Melvins at a show in San Francisco. Dave looked up to the band, especially their brilliant drummer, Dale Crover, and respected their opinion. Inquiring whether he knew of any bassists who might be willing to team up with Scream, Dave was disappointed but not surprised when Buzz said he did not. His ears pricked up again though when Buzz added that there was a band he knew, from Aberdeen, who he believed might be looking for a drummer. How serious was Dave about sticking it out with Scream anyway? Could he use another gig, maybe?

Dave decided he could. These guys from Aberdeen, asked Dave, did they have a name? Yeah. Nirvana. Buzz added that the Nirvana guys – Kurt the singer and guitarist and Krist the bassist – had already seen Dave play when they came along – at Buzz's suggestion – to a gig at San Francisco's I-Beam club some weeks before. 'I called Buzz and he said that Kurt and Krist had seen a Scream show in San Francisco and they really liked my drumming.'

Dave was intrigued but not yet sold. He knew there was a growing buzz about Nirvana on the underground hardcore scene and that they were working out of Washington state, and he recalled he'd probably checked out their only album, *Bleach*, recorded for just $600 (about £400) and released on Seattle's burgeoning indie label Sub Pop, somewhere along the line. But he hadn't been impressed enough by it to know whether he actually liked it. 'I thought it was pretty cool,' he did his best to enthuse, years later, not wanting to be a jerk, but conceded that he 'wasn't the biggest fan in the world'. The pedestrian drums were hardly likely to impress someone of Dave's bottled-lightning ability. The actual songs, though, they had something. 'I thought some of their songs were really great and some of Kurt's lyrics were really hilarious,' he said later, not entirely convincingly.

What mattered was that their album had come out on Sub Pop, the most happening new label in Washington state, and now, rumour had it, they were on the verge of signing a major label deal, though with which label exactly no one knew yet, least of all Kurt and Krist. There was just that feeling about them and Dave picked up on it instantly. They were also about to take off for a British tour, their second trip to London, the one place he had never been with Scream. Dave didn't need to know any more than that. He was also impressed when Buzz told him that the Melvins' drummer, Dale Crover, had played with the band for a while, too. Wow. If they were good enough for Dale . . .

Dave wrote down the number Buzz gave him but when he called that night and got Krist on the phone, the bassist, though friendly, told him it was too late, they had just hired Danny Peters from another local Seattle act, named Mudhoney. Too bad, man. But maybe Dave could come along and say hi when Nirvana were next in LA. Yeah, man, maybe . . .

Dave put down the phone, utterly deflated, and went back to watching TV with his mud-wrestling new girlfriends. Then out of the blue, a few hours later, Krist phoned him back. Dave was still smiling in astonishment as he recalled the moment a few years later. 'He said, "You know what, maybe you *should* come up here."'

'I wasn't surprised,' says Franz now. 'The nucleus of Scream were three guys that went to school together, lived close together. Dave was a little outside that circle, for obvious reasons: his age, his neighbourhood. So he probably always felt a little outside of the circle. And him being his age he's like, "I wanna keep playing. I gotta find something."' When Dave told Franz and Pete he was going up to Seattle 'to jam' with Nirvana, but that he didn't know if anything would come of it, that he would likely be back on Sabrina's couch the next day, Franz just nodded. 'He wasn't sure how it was gonna work out. But I did. For some reason, I knew: he's not coming back. Regardless of what happened to the band, I knew he wasn't coming back. I felt it.'

Dave was on the next flight up to Seattle, where Nirvana were doing a show they had invited him to come along to, then worried about what he was going to tell the Stahl brothers if Nirvana did offer him the gig. Franz and Pete were the ones that had taken a chance on him when he was just a kid: the guitarist who had shown him how to really play that thing and the singer who had become like a father figure to him out on the road, the guys who'd always had his back, lost somewhere between Amsterdam and Nowheresville.

But Dave didn't do what-ifs. He just went with his gut. It was a habit that would prove invaluable over time, but right now he just had a sick feeling inside, 'It was the toughest decision I ever had to make,' he said. Nevertheless, the decision made, he then moved quickly to implement it before he could change his mind. 'I got the hell out of LA,' he later recalled, feeling no pain, 'and there was no looking back.'

4. The Three Fires

Dave Grohl might have thought he knew what he was doing when he arrived to see Nirvana play at the Motor Sports International and Garage, in downtown Seattle, but he had no fucking idea what he was about to let himself in for. Caught completely off-guard by the size of the dank but spacious venue, which held over 1500 people – and by how insanely crowded the place was – he was also perplexed to witness how well Danny Peters played: powerful but percussive, inventive and sly. What did they need Dave for if they already had someone as good as Danny? It made no sense. For Dave, nothing in Nirvana ever would.

It was 22 September 1990, a warm Saturday night, and Nirvana were headlining over the Dwarves and the Melvins. It was easily their biggest gig yet, but Dave didn't know that. He just assumed it must be like that at all Nirvana's gigs now. 'When I flew up to Seattle I'd never seen them play before. We went down to the show and there were 2000 people there. It was amazing, because they weren't punk rock kids. Kurt would say, "This next song is called 'About a Girl'", and the place would just freak out.'

The other thing Dave didn't know was that Peters was just the latest in a long line of drummers that had passed through Nirvana in the three years they had been going. Danny was actually their fifth, but despite playing on their new single, 'Sliver', a track the drummer would also be given credit for helping inspire, in the spontaneous burst of energy that birthed it, Kurt had decided he wanted to try Dave out too. He didn't like the Scream guys, called them assholes, but after he and Krist had caught their gig in San Francisco earlier that summer, he had come away impressed by the loud sound of their young drummer. Dave didn't just play with a bigger kit – something Kurt had fixed on as an essential component in the new, more all-embracing direction he wanted to take Nirvana in – he played *bigger*.

And there was something else. Kurt was also a drummer. He could really play and knew exactly what he was looking for now. Someone like Dale Crover, ideally, who had drummed with Nirvana briefly, before returning to the Melvins. As a teenager, Dale had been in an Iron Maiden covers band, where he'd learned how to kick the shit out of his drums. Buzz Osbourne had talent-spotted him at 17 and invited him into the Melvins. The following year, Dale also got together with an 18-year-old Kurt Cobain to play bass and drums in a housecat outfit Kurt dubbed Fecal Matter, where they recorded a rough demo together with the entirely Cobain-esque title of *Illiteracy Will Prevail*, from which at least two tracks would later be reworked into early Nirvana songs. Nothing happened with the demo – few people saw any future for a band called Fecal Matter and the tape, made at Kurt's aunt's Seattle home, using her four-track tape-recorder, remained buried until after Nirvana became so famous people were eager to listen to anything Kurt had ever had the slightest thing to do with.

Instead, it was the Melvins who forged ahead, at least to begin with, releasing their first EP, *Six Songs*, in 1986 and their debut album, *Gluey Porch Treatments*, the following year. Kurt was such a fan he would hang out at their rehearsals, crouched behind Dale's drums.

'I met [Kurt] only a few weeks after I met [the Melvins],' Dale later recalled. 'Buzz said that I needed to meet this dude . . . They had a lengthy conversation on the bus regarding music. That weekend [Buzz] took Kurt to see Black Flag in Seattle. And that's how we hit it off. "You like this kind of music?" "Yeah!" I'd go hang at his place and he played me demos of his songs.' It was then, said Dale, that Kurt first started writing songs influenced by bands like Black Flag and the Butthole Surfers. Dark, twisted, propulsive music that put off more people than it attracted, but which Kurt found his own connection to, could identify with, like all the other outcasts.

Kurt called on his pal again not long after he and Krist Novoselic formed Nirvana, when Dale agreed to play on their now legendary, much-bootlegged first demo, in January 1988; a mini-masterpiece, nine of whose ten tracks would eventually be released in re-recorded or other form, including three on *Bleach*: 'Floyd the Barber', 'Paper Cuts' and 'Downer' – the latter originally found in primitive form on the Fecal Matter demo.

Dave would learn all this, piecemeal, over the coming months, as he tried to find his own place in the band. The bond between Kurt and Krist was clear. They both came from Aberdeen, Washington, a squat little logging town a hundred miles southwest of Seattle. The son of Croatian immigrants, Krsto and Maria Novoselić, Krist had actually grown up in a Croatian neighbourhood of San Pedro, California. The family had moved north to Aberdeen when he was 14, and his mother opened a hairdresser's there: Maria's Hair Design.

'The thing about Krist,' says Anton Brookes, 'is that Krist is one of the most easy-going people you're going to meet. Just so laidback, so down to earth, enjoys a drink, likes a laugh. He was like the ambassador of Nirvana. He took the pressure off Kurt.

Krist is very outgoing and he makes people feel at ease with them, even though he's this big lumbering six-foot-seven hulk of a man.'

Kurt Donald Cobain had been born in Hoquiam, on the outskirts of Seattle, in February 1967, the only son of Don, a garage mechanic, and Wendy, a secretary. The family moved to Aberdeen when Kurt was still a baby and these days everyone said the boy grew up in a settled, happy, typically American blue-collar household. That all changed, however, when Kurt was eight and his parents divorced. Kurt stayed with his mother, but when Wendy took up with a 'paranoid schizophrenic' (Wendy's own words) who seemed to resent having Kurt around, he turned inward, famously pinning a poem on his bedroom wall that read: 'I hate mom, I hate dad. Dad hates mom, mom hates dad.' Another concluded: 'I hate myself and want to die.' A wincingly horrible line he would later turn into a song – and a wincingly horrible prophesy.

Kurt told his friend Dylan Carlson that his mother's new boy-friend was a 'mean, huge wife-beater', and that he had decided to go and live with his father – which he did, until he was 11, and his father found his own new love, whom Kurt could not connect with either. Thus began a period of years during which the teenaged Kurt was shuffled from relative to relative, various aunts and uncles stepping in to offer him a home, but never for very long. At one point, Kurt lived under a bridge; at another juncture, he stayed for months at the home of a school friend, in a sleeping bag on the floor of the lounge.

Oversensitive, unsure of his sexuality, so thin he took to wearing extra layers of clothes just to make him look bulkier, he was quick-witted and sharp when you got him talking, but so withdrawn and socially inept he spent most of the time in silence, glowering out from beneath his dirty-blond fringe.

Beaten and bullied by the redneck school jocks, barely toler-
ated by the school geeks and potheads, the only thing Kurt had
going for him was his music. He still had the Mickey Mouse
drum kit his mother had given him when he was four, and the
bass his aunt Mary had given him for his seventh birthday.
And he would carry these things around wherever he went.
When his Uncle Larry gave him a cheap electric Lindell guitar
for his fourteenth birthday his future was set. You didn't have
to be the popular kid to write your own music and poetry.
These were the tools of the loner and Kurt held tight to them
like amulets.

If his trip with Buzz and Dale in 1984 to see Black Flag
proved to be his musical epiphany, as he got older Kurt would
also turn his cold blue gaze towards painting, drawing, collages,
sculptures. He liked to come up with Francis Bacon-esque gro-
tesques, figurative abstracts, disturbing, at their best, that is to
say, at their beautiful worst. When VCRs came in, he would
tape TV shows, not to view, but to scramble together, scenes
of one slashed together with scenes, half-views, from others.
And he liked to read. He loved Samuel Beckett and William S.
Burroughs because they wrote as he wished he could paint, with
their entrails, their innards exposed. And he was addicted to
Charles Bukowski, because in his stories of outsiders wandering
aimlessly across America's terrifying streets he thought he saw
himself.

As Kurt got older, he would later say, 'I felt more and more
alienated – I couldn't find friends whom I felt compatible with
at all. Everyone was eventually going to become a logger, and I
knew I wanted to do something different. I wanted to be some
kind of artist.'

His other big escape was pot, which he'd been smoking
since he was 14. But in Aberdeen, a town as depressed as its

bleak year-round weather, that was not unusual. Krist later expounded the theory that the very history of Aberdeen – dating back to its earliest incarnation as a well-known whorehouse for sailors and frontiersmen – had left the current-day residents 'a little ashamed of our roots'. That and the high rate of unemployment, out-of-control alcoholism and a suicide rate more than twice the already high state average. Aberdeen was the kind of place, Kurt recalled, where people owned guns they couldn't afford to load and guitars they couldn't afford not to pawn. When he and Krist first began forming bands together, the idea was simple: to get the fuck out of town as fast as they could. For which they would have to get good at their instruments. So they did.

By the time Dave Grohl joined them in this quest, his mission was clear, at least musically. Starting with his discovery of what all his predecessors in Nirvana had quickly learned: Kurt loved Dale Crover's playing. So much so, said Danny Peters, that 'if you're playing drums behind Kurt you're filling Dale Crover's shoes.' When the drummer who had played on *Bleach*, Chad Channing, left the band after repeated bad scenes out on the road – Kurt throwing bottles at the wall behind where he was playing; pouring a jug of water over his head onstage; continually trashing his drums – Kurt had once again turned to Dale to come and fill in temporarily during a short but important summer tour: seven shows in August opening for Sonic Youth. Kurt was deeply respectful of Dale's place on the stage, as if trying to seduce the drummer into staying on when the tour was over.

But Dale was a Melvins man through and through and as soon as the dates were done he went back to them. Instead, Kurt and Krist had ushered Danny in. He'd been playing with Mudhoney, a Seattle band building its own formidable local reputation, and with its own self-titled Sub Pop album, released some months before. But Nirvana were the ones with the growing rep who had already spurned the chance to do another album for Sub Pop, in favour of doing a major label deal, which everyone on the scene in Seattle now knew was just around the corner, and Peters had understandably seen the chance to join them as his shot at potential stardom.

There was something else about Nirvana, too, which made them different to Mudhoney, or indeed any other Seattle band at the time. As Anton Brookes recalls: 'I remember Jonathan Poneman, the co-owner of Sub Pop, telling me that if Mudhoney and Nirvana were to play on the same night in Seattle, at that time [before *Nevermind*], Mudhoney would probably get the bigger audience but Nirvana would get the bigger percentage of girls going to their show. From an early stage, Nirvana appealed to everyone across the board. Their music was like almost asexual.'

When Nirvana came up with 'Sliver' the first time they went into a recording studio with Danny, Kurt was convinced. 'The chemistry was definitely there with Danny, Chris and I,' he would tell Michael Azerrad. 'We could have ended up writing some really good songs together.' But for Kurt, a perfection-ist, despite his apparent lack of self-worth, 'It wasn't quite perfect.'

Could Dave Grohl do any better? It would be awkward find-ing out, but Kurt was determined to try. At the time, Nirvana were practising in Danny's own small rehearsal space, nick-named the Dutchman, on a rundown industrial estate in South Seattle. A lot of nascent Seattle bands ended up rehearsing there. It was barebones but it was cheap. You went in, did your thing, left again. Only this time when Nirvana went in it was without Danny.

Dave had to keep his mouth shut, though, until the band had got round to telling Danny. As it happened, a writer and photographer from *Sounds* magazine in London had just arrived to do what became Nirvana's first magazine cover story. A barbecue was organised at Krist and Shelli's place, at which was all of Nirvana – that is, the Nirvana with Danny Peters still in it – along with a new face who was introduced to the *Sounds* team as the band's new gear humper, driver and helper out: Dave. When the story later appeared in *Sounds*, it showed the Cobain–Novoselic–Peters line-up together on the cover, pictured at the barbecue.

By then, though, Kurt had already made an appearance on the local Olympia college radio station, KAOS 89.3, giving news of the band's latest recruit. Interviewed by the DJ Calvin Johnson, Kurt announced that Nirvana had a new drummer. He said he considered Dave a 'baby Dale Crover', who Dave was 'almost as good as' – the highest possible compliment in Kurt's book. They also dug it that Dave could sing, giving Nirvana the opportunity for vocal harmonies on stage for the first time – something Kurt was keen to explore, given the more poppy kinds of songs he was now writing. Only snag, he confessed on air: he and Krist hadn't actually told Danny Peters yet. Danny was 'a beautiful guy and such a beautiful drummer', Kurt said, sounding sad. 'But you can't pass up an opportunity to play with the drummer of our dreams, which is Dave.' It felt to Kurt, he added, that they'd been searching for Dave 'for like two years'.

Years later, Danny would insist his initial reaction to the news had been one of relief. Rehearsals with Nirvana had been 'sullen, tense' affairs, he said. Still, he could not disguise his understandable bitterness at the underhand way in which Kurt and Krist had dealt with the situation, allowing him to be photographed and interviewed for the *Sounds* story while, unbeknownst to him, his replacement stood just feet away.

'If they were honest with me and upfront with me,' Danny told the British writer Keith Cameron, 'I would have totally accepted it, but the way they went about it bummed me out, because they didn't have the balls to tell me. The last thing I wanted to do was look like a chump, and I looked like a chump.' This profound lack of good manners, of abdicating responsibility for their actions, no matter how much they might hurt others, characterised Kurt's way of dealing with things more as time went on. Then it became something Dave also struggled with in the Foos.

Initially, Dave had moved into the spare room at the small apartment Krist shared with his girlfriend, Shelli. Once he was a confirmed member of the band, though, Kurt invited him to move into his tiny shithole in Olympia. A one-bedroom apartment in which Dave slept on a small couch, his long legs dangling over the side. If sleeping on floors and in vans with the Scream guys had at least been fun, this was more like penury. 'Oh my God! That place was trashed,' laughed Krist Novoselic. Among other things, Kurt had 'defaced the hallway with pornographic cartoons'. He also kept toy dolls, which he enjoyed decapitating and painting Alice Cooper eyes and gluing human hair onto, then hanging them, limbless, from his window. Kurt saw it as part of his art. Some nights he would sit there in his filthy room with a little rubber monkey that he called Chim Chim perched on his shoulder. Kurt's gotta monkey on his back – geddit?

'The walls were just a montage of pictures, painting, statues, toys moulded into other things,' says Brookes. 'It was almost like walking into a cross between David Bowie's mind and Hannibal Lecter's flat. There's all these things on the walls. A lot of rock'n'roll stuff but a lot of just weird stuff too. You'd think, okay, step back a little bit from this . . .'

Dave's memories, though, centred more on the times when the two barely spoke, the days and nights that flitted by when, like vampires, they would crash out at dawn and not rise again until sundown; the boredom and mounting anxiety; the sheer bafflement and peculiarity. 'I don't think Kurt really spoke to Dave,' says Brookes. 'Kurt was quite insular, kept himself to himself quite a lot. On the other hand,' he insists, 'Kurt could be the life and soul of the party, very outgoing, very funny, very witty, very sarcastic, very humorous.' You could have fooled Dave. 'At the same time you could have really deep, philosophical conversations with Kurt too.' Or you could just get stoned and sit around watching TV. It was all as one to Kurt.

What neither Kurt nor Krist knew yet was that Dave now remembered them from times before. There had been a Scream gig in Olympia some months ago. One of the local scenesters, named Slim Moon, who would later go on to form the highly re- garded independent label Kill Rock Stars, invited the guys back to his pad for an after-show party. Among the typically Olym- pian Boho gathering there – which Dave described to Michael Azerrad disdainfully as 'total Olympia hot chocolate drinking Hello Kitty people' – was Kurt Cobain.

When one of the young women – a dark, imp-faced creature named Tobi Vail, later a founding member and guitarist of the self-styled 'riot grrrl' outfit Bikini Kill – presumptuously turned off the stereo, sat in the middle of the room, and began playing and singing some of her own songs, Dave and the Scream guys were silently appalled by what Grohl recalled as 'total bad teen suicide' music. He still didn't put the two together though until he recounted the story to Kurt late one night during one of their stunted small-hours conversations, and Kurt replied, 'Oh, yeah, that's my girlfriend.'

Dave hadn't even realised Kurt had a girlfriend until that moment. When Dave then started dating Tobi's friend Kathleen Hanna, who was about to become the singer in Bikini Kill, the four of them actually double-dated for a while. Strangely jolly occasions in which Dave and Kurt got to drunkenly talk about their favourite punk records while the girls feigned interest. Tobi and Kathleen had plans of their own. The boys were cute but then so were lots of other Olympia art-throbs. When, a few weeks later, Kurt announced that he and Tobi had broken up – that he had been looking for commitment but that Tobi, even younger than Kurt, most emphatically had not – the morose singer lapsed into a silence that went on for weeks. Dave began to question his own sanity. Was this normal? Was he the weird one, maybe, for thinking this was strange behaviour? No. Kurt the outsider was really just a homebody, a lonely boy in search of a mother figure. When Kurt finally spoke again, on the way home from rehearsal one night, Dave was like, 'Thank God!'

Dave's first show as Nirvana's drummer came at the North Shore Surf Club, a few blocks over from where he and Kurt lived in Olympia, on 11 October 1990. Tickets for the show had sold out the day they went on sale. Dave was so elated he phoned his mother and sister to tell them. When he hit his snare drum so hard he broke it, midway through the set, he feared getting 'the face' from Kurt. But the singer instead held up the broken drum and announced nonchalantly to the crowd: 'We have a new drummer who's very good.'

The second show the new line-up did together was a week later, again in Olympia: a short set at a dorm party at Evergreen State College. Five days after that they were in London, staying at the Dalmacia Hotel, decidedly downmarket digs in grimy Shepherd's Bush Road, Hammersmith, whose principal attraction was that they sold cheap triple rooms, which made it perfect for hard-up visiting bands like Nirvana.

Dave, though, loved it. Having got used to touring Europe with Scream, who could not afford to stay in hotels at all, this seemed like the height of luxury to the wide-eyed 21-year-old drummer, who discovered the joys of English breakfast tea, until he drank so much of it in one day he 'thought I was gonna have a heart attack'. Not that they were in London for long. Six shows in seven days meant they hardly had time to sleep. 'The first time we came to England, I thought it was great,' said Dave. 'We were playing places that held a thousand people, staying in nice hotels. When I was in Scream, we were living off five dollars a day, sleeping in the van, on floors. So to be playing in bigger places, having my own bed and being able to smoke two packs of cigarettes a day was a big deal to me.'

It was also Dave's first opportunity to gauge just how popular Nirvana were outside the US. As Brookes says, 'They may have been big in Seattle but everywhere else in America they were playing some nights to twenty people. In the UK, though, they already had the music press behind them and were getting played on the John Peel show. Among that sort of student audience there was a real buzz about them.'

Sizing up the band's new recruit, Anton says he was astounded at just how good a drummer Grohl was. 'Dave came in and solidified Nirvana's sound. He brought it together and he added to it. He made it a lot tighter and stronger and gave Kurt a platform to build his songs upon.' Anybody else, he thinks, 'would have struggled but here you've got two punk rock kids from Seattle who don't have a pot to piss in, just have a load of great songs. One good thing about Dave – and I think he learned that from moving between different bands – he just came in and adapted and got on with it.

'The first time I met Dave I just liked him straight away. He was such a nice, kooky guy. He was funny. He was constantly just bouncing off the walls, just full of personality. But, more than anything, anybody who saw him drum and saw the change in Nirvana – he took Nirvana to a different level . . . he completed that circle and gave it something that it didn't have before. And that allowed Kurt to stretch his talent. Kurt and Krist were joined at the hip. They had their ups and downs but they were like brothers. Krist could read Kurt better than anybody. They'd spent so much time together over the years. They'd forged Nirvana out of the fires – the furnaces – of Aberdeen. Dave comes along and he's served his apprenticeship too.'

Headlining at the Astoria, in London, before a crowd swollen with music critics, other bands, tastemakers and music biz power brokers, for the first time Dave truly got what Nirvana were about, might yet become. The last time they had played there, ten months before, third on the bill to Mudhoney and Tad, Nirvana had been the epitome of punk rock alliteration; juddering rhythms and acned vocals; noise and incoherence; above all, angst-ridden authenticity. Now, with Dave in the band, and Kurt's new songs leaning over backwards towards a new kind of punk-pop sensibility, more Buzzcocks than Stooges, catchy as a meat hook yet light as laughing gas, it was clear the band had risen to a new plateau in their musical journey, away from the stunted growth of *Bleach*-era material like 'School' and 'Negative Creep' and up into the clouds with songs like 'In Bloom', 'Lithium' and 'Breed' – all songs that would appear a year later on the breakthrough *Nevermind* album.

'The Astoria gig virtually sold out just on word of mouth,' Keith Cameron recalled. 'No record to promote and the place was rammed. You knew something was happening. People were saying, "You know, one day, they might be as big as Sonic Youth."' Anton Brookes remembers Kurt telling him after the show that Nirvana were now writing 'pop songs – and these songs were going to be Top 10 songs. Back then, our idea of the Top 10 was being as big as Sonic Youth or the Pixies, or getting a gig at Brixton Academy and maybe selling it out. I didn't realise he meant it *literally*.'

Kurt, though, had much bigger plans than that. Six months, earlier, while Chad Channing was still their drummer, the band had spent a couple of days in Smart Studios, the Madison, Wisconsin, home of the producer Butch Vig. Little known outside underground circles, Kurt was a fan of Vig's work on the 1989 album *Twelve Point Buck* by psycho-noise-rock outfit Killdozer. Speaking on the phone to Vig for the first time ahead of the sessions, he told him: 'We want to sound as heavy as that record.' Butch promised him he would try to do just that.

It was at Vig's Smart Studio that they laid down six rough, early versions of tracks, including 'Lithium', 'Breed', and 'In Bloom'. The idea was to go in and bash out a follow-up album to *Bleach*, to be released again on Sub Pop. But when Kurt realised the potential of what he had, he began to backpedal. He didn't want the next Nirvana album to be on Sub Pop, he'd now decided. He complained that Sub Pop had not distributed *Bleach* well, that they had not given proper accounts to the band for its sales. In love with the idea of releasing his records independently, he had never stopped to consider the business realities of working with a small homespun label. He may have romanticised the idea of working with a little label, but his dreams had always been so much bigger than that.

When Sub Pop presented the band with a new, 30-page contract, Kurt was infused with anxiety, barely able to breathe. The money on offer, had he signed, though still modest, would have been sorely welcome. Kurt had recently applied for a job at a dog kennels, scooping up poop and hosing down dog piss – but didn't get it. He had also tried pawning some of the band's gear. Yet still he resisted the temptation to sign the Sub Pop contract. He knew what he had, in his new songs, was worth more than that, was good enough to tempt a major label, and he coveted that opportunity, even as he maintained the facade of not wanting to 'sell out'. As Nirvana's biographer Charles Cross later commented: 'I think he wanted a career in music, and he wanted to be successful. But ... had to figure out a way to both be successful and have it appear that it happened by accident.'

Meanwhile, as the summer wore on and bootleg copies of the demos began leaking out, the underground was abuzz with stories of how good the tracks were, how Nirvana were ones to watch. Desperate to set himself apart from the undergrowth of Sub Pop bands, Kurt turned to Susan Silver, manager of fellow Seattle leading lights Soundgarden. Silver took one look at the contract and told Kurt and Krist they badly needed to see a lawyer, and suggested some names for them in Los Angeles, but still they struggled to get meetings with most of them.

When Nirvana toured briefly with Sonic Youth that summer, their leader, Thurston Moore, an early advocate for the band, strongly advised them to sign with their own management team, Gold Mountain, who would provide them with all the muscle they needed to be taken seriously in the dog-eat-dog environs of the LA rock biz. Thurston told Kurt he should also think seriously about signing Nirvana to Sonic Youth's label, DGC – the shiny new independent wing of the giant LA-based Geffen Records label. Sub Pop, meanwhile, were using Nirvana's growing reputation, and tapes of their Smart Studios demos, to try and parlay their own distribution deal with a major label.

By the time Dave Grohl joined Nirvana, things were getting so complicated Kurt said he felt his head was going to burst. The stress had given him stomach ulcers, he said, the pain had become intolerable. He quit booze in an effort to fight his constant indigestion but when that didn't work he turned to less prosaic panaceas – first prescription painkillers like Percodan, then permanent killers like heroin.

Kurt told Krist he'd done it, as though describing a social experiment: a one-off exploration into what lay behind the locked basement door your parents told you never to open. Krist freaked out but knew enough not to make a big deal of it in front of Kurt. When Dave returned from a short trip to LA in November, Kurt told him too. Dave was appalled, yet tried to keep a straight face, play it cool. Like Krist, he'd learned by then that the worse thing you could do was tell Kurt he was wrong about something. What, Dave asked, was it like then? 'It sucked,' Kurt told him earnestly. 'It makes you feel gross and bad.' Yet when questioned about it by other, less important friends, Kurt defended his 'experiments', claiming the smack made him more sociable, better to be around. Just better.

By the start of 1991, paradoxically, just as Kurt's personal life was becoming more centred on injecting heroin, while attempting to keep it quiet from the rest of band, the pieces were finally starting to fall into place for Nirvana. On Thurston Moore's personal recommendation, Gold Mountain's John Silva had flown to Seattle to settle a management deal with the band. After that all the major label A&R teams descended on Nirvana gigs like clouds of flies. The band were simultaneously courted by MCA, Columbia, Capitol, RCA, Charisma and several others.

The winners in what Susan Silver later called 'a feeding frenzy' were the one label that had so far not been actively trying to sign Nirvana: DGC. Again, it was the Sonic Youth connection that helped broker the deal – for both band and label. 'I got turned on to them by Thurston of Sonic Youth,' explained Gary Gersh, then DGC's A&R director. The singer had passed on a copy of *Bleach* to Gersh. 'I listened to it and I just thought the songwriting was exceptional . . . [Kurt's] emotion was pretty special.'

'Kurt signed to [DGC] because Sonic Youth told him that we didn't interfere with bands creatively at the label and so he wouldn't be fucked with,' Chrissy Shannon, who would become Nirvana's first publicist at DGC, would later write. 'I know that I jumped at the chance to work with this indie band cribbed from Sub Pop because I was bored working with the second- and third-generation pop-metal bands [on Geffen].'

The deal included an advance payment on signature of $278,000, with Sub Pop getting $75,000 of the money, plus two royalty points on each of Nirvana's next two albums, as a way of extricating the band from their deal. Kurt, whose hard-bitten profile among the local Olympia cognoscenti as a stalwart of an independent label scene mentality that viewed all such major label deals as intrinsically foul and wrongheaded, maintained his integrity by pointing out that DGC were also 'independent'. (In fact, DGC was merely an imprint of Geffen, itself a subsidiary of the giant MCA, and the home of such corporate rock goliaths as Guns N' Roses, Whitesnake, Aerosmith and Cher.) That if the label was good enough for Sonic Youth, darlings of the 'alternative' Washington scene, they were certainly cool enough for Nirvana. And for a while people were happy to go along with that.

Deep down, though, as he lay there at night, smacked out of his brains and dreaming of whatever it was he supposed dreamers still dream of once they've hit the big time, Kurt could not have been more delighted. 'I want to sell a million records,' he would confide to friends, hugging himself. Then pretend he was joking about it. Dave Grohl and Krist Novoselic knew the truth though. They weren't fools. They wanted to sell a million records too. Who wouldn't, man? Be fucking serious . . .

5. Smells Like

The first couple of months of 1991 found Dave Grohl mostly sitting around smoking, drinking and twiddling his sticks. There had been an appearance at the No More Wars benefit gig back at Evergreen College in January, where Kurt gave an impassioned, if rambling, anti-Gulf War speech, then finished the set by smashing his guitar to pieces with a hammer. He was now sporting a dark beard and deep black eye makeup, a plaid shirt and ripped-knee jeans, his unwashed blond hair tangled like rope. Krist had also grown an unkempt goatee. By year's end, everyone in Seattle would be rocking their own version of this look, as both the music – stripped-to-the-bone rock with a more expansive lyrical edge – and the look – thrift store chic with declamatory beards and unminded hair – replaced the backcombed hair and extravagantly posed hair metal scene that had previously dominated. A year after that the whole world would be walking around in their 'grunge' clothes.

For now, though, being in Nirvana was all about handing over the reins to the business people, the new cats with their smart LA offices and cool connections. With Gold Mountain on-board things had moved fast. With Geffen, in the guise of DGC, sending them a list of producers and studios to consider for their first album with them, there were suddenly more important decisions to make than working up a set list for their next gig, which wasn't until March, at the 1000-capacity Zoo in Boise, Idaho.

There had also been the arrival of several key new songs during rehearsals. 'A good song is the most important thing, it's the only way to really touch someone,' Kurt told Keith Cameron in 1990, preparing the ground for the new, more overtly commercial material he had begun writing. 'You can have the most perfect ideals in the world and still can't get your point across unless you have good music.' That is to say: good sales.

Back in the rehearsal room, Dave watched, fascinated, as Kurt would start to strum the basic chords to whatever his latest masterwork was and expect the band just to pick it up intuitively, bringing their own thing to the job. 'With Nirvana,' Dave later observed, 'the process of making the music was so entirely simple, pure and real. Kurt was a great lyricist, he had a beautiful voice, and he wrote really simple songs. There were things that I learned about songwriting from being in a band with Kurt I don't think anyone else could have taught me.'

One new number in particular was starting to grab everyone's attention. 'I was trying to write the ultimate pop song,' Kurt later said of the song destined to become his signature tune. 'I was basically trying to rip off the Pixies, I have to admit it.' Adding: 'We used their sense of dynamics, being soft and quiet and then loud and hard.' The song was called 'Smells Like Teen Spirit', an extraordinarily catchy piece of high musical drama that was about to become the soundtrack of the 1990s. Ironically, given the iconic status it would later achieve under the Cobain imprimatur, 'Teen Spirit' was also the only track on *Nevermind* to be credited on the album equally to the three band members. Krist and Dave, numb with playing the simple singsong riff over and over as Kurt tried to complete it, decided between them to slow the verse part down, to their own metronomic beat. Suddenly the rest of the song just fell into place.

The title was even more coincidental. When Kathleen Hanna spray-painted 'KURT SMELLS OF TEEN SPIRIT' on the wall of his grotty room one night, Kurt assumed it was meant as some kind of revolutionary slogan. A salutation to his own indomitable spirit or some such. In fact, what Hanna meant was that Kurt smelled of the deodorant Teen Spirit, which his then girlfriend Tobi Vail wore. When, months later, after the song was a huge international hit, Kurt discovered the truth, it was just one more reason to feel morally ambivalent about his newfound, or as he saw it *fake*, success.

There had been talk of getting R.E.M.'s producer, Scott Litt, to do the Nirvana record, but by the spring of 1991 Litt was the most sought-after producer in the world, having just guided R.E.M. to the biggest-selling album of their career and first US No. 1, *Out of Time*. The idea that Litt – whatever his 'alternative' credentials – would make his next project an unknown band was unlikely, to say the least. Others were sounded out and considered but they were either unavailable (Don Dixon, who had produced the 1988 album by The Smithereens, *Green Thoughts*, a big favourite of Kurt's) or simply too cool for him to feel comfortable with (Gil Norton, who had produced *Doolittle*, the 1989 classic by the Pixies, on which Kurt was now basing so much of Nirvana's sound).

In the end, they plumped for using Butch Vig, who had recorded the demo sessions at Smart the year before. Vig might not be a 'name' but he had been fun to work with and he seemed to have an easy understanding with Kurt. Unlike all the other suggestions, Butch was also as hungry as Kurt to build a successful career for himself. He had recently enjoyed a career breakthrough as the producer of *Gish*, the much heralded debut album from the Smashing Pumpkins. But he had never worked on a major-label record before, let alone in LA, which in the early Nineties was now taking over from New York as the home of the American music business.

Arriving for a pre-production session in LA at the end of April, Butch immediately noticed the difference the addition of Dave's drums had made to the Nirvana sound. Kurt had called him ahead of time, giving him a heads-up about what to expect. Butch was out but Kurt left a message on his answering machine: 'Butch, we have the best drummer in the world. He's the greatest drummer in the world. I'm not kidding you. He's awesome, dude . . .' An opinion Vig instantly shared, he said, the moment the band lit into their newest song, 'Smells Like Teen Spirit'. He recalled with a smile how 'when it got to Dave's part' – bu-da-dung, bu-da-dung – 'it just floored me!'

It was the same throughout the making of *Nevermind*. The songs – every track an almost too perfect blend of feral angst, mathematically perfect melody, and sheer bloody-minded intransigence – came out rounded, whole, defiantly so. But while the guitars tended towards fizzy textures and a deliberate kind of blurriness, as opposed to the self-absorbed bugling of most rock guitarists, the bass a spongy force field, elastic and embracing, Grohl's drums were titanic, thunderous, playful and bold, the strong human bones around which the rest of Kurt's phantasmagorical images are projected.

Admittedly, Dave had a template to work from, faithfully replicating the bareknuckle punch of the Smart Studio versions Chad Channing had constructed for 'In Bloom', 'Pay To Play' (now retitled, 'Stay Away'), 'Lithium' and 'Immodium' (now retitled 'Breed'). But it was the extra precision and subtlety he brought to the new recordings that really distinguished his playing – crisp, clean and endlessly inventive – and basic recording was completed within days, leaving Kurt to work on his guitar and vocals. After which Vig experimented with vocal harmonies, overdubs and a whole arsenal of production techniques designed to smooth away the rough edges they had displayed like war wounds on *Bleach*, now transformed into the sleek sonic landscapes of *Nevermind* (originally called *Sheep*, until Kurt had a change of heart and came up with *Nevermind*, from the line in 'Smells Like Teen Spirit': '*I found it hard, it's hard to find / Oh, well, whatever, never mind*').

The only time Dave stumbled during the recording was when they came to record 'Lithium'. They went through several takes, but the track kept speeding up. 'It wasn't Dave's fault,' reckoned Vig, 'it was the whole band. But I said, "Have you ever tried a click track?"' A click track was a series of audio cues relayed to the drummer via headphones, a recent innovation in recording technology, inspired by the then new digital recording equipment that was becoming widespread. Dave went into emotional free-fall. Asking a drummer to use a click track was like telling a drummer he couldn't keep time. 'That was like a dagger in the heart for him,' Butch agreed. 'He went back to the hotel that night, freaking out a bit. He had a sleepless night then came in and slayed it in one take [without the click]. It was perfect.'

With recording of the *Nevermind* album completed by the end of May, DGC were looking at a total cost – including recording, mastering, and living expenses – of around $120,000 (approx. £65,000); 200 times more than *Bleach*, but still a relatively modest sum for a major label album by 1991 standards. The only bringdown was that nobody liked the initial mixes: not even Butch Vig, who was handling them.

It was the Geffen executive who signed them that had the inspiration of bringing in Andy Wallace to mix *Nevermind*. At the time, Wallace was 'the guy who mixed Slayer'. That is, the guy who had been the producer Rick Rubin's right-hand man on

Slayer's recent *Seasons in the Abyss* album, which *Rolling Stone* memorably described as 'music to conquer nations by', and had been their first to make the US Top 40. 'It was quite a ride getting to the point where [*Nevermind*] was finished,' Gersh would later say. He recalled walking into the Geffen offices with cassettes of the finished album, and being acutely aware that he was 'delivering a record that was so different to what was happening in the music business at that time'. But he'd already been working with Sonic Youth for over a year, they'd put out the wondrous *Goo*, so 'we already knew that there was this groundswell building. That people just didn't care for this stuff that was successful at the top level,' referring to what were then the rock giants of the American charts like Guns N' Roses and Def Leppard, Bon Jovi and Mötley Crüe.

Chrissy Shannon, at 24 the youngest member of the Geffen Records publicity department, would be assigned the task of handling the press for *Nevermind*. 'I vividly remember taking the advance cassette home that night in my car and popping it in as [my boyfriend] Steve and I were driving to dinner. 'Smells Like Teen Spirit' came crashing out of the speakers and where Grohl's drums kick in after the opening riff, Steve and I simultaneously reached for the volume knob to crank it! We just sat there in the parking lot, saying, "What the fuck is this?" To me it sounded like nothing I'd heard before, not even *Bleach*, really, because the songwriting and melodies had improved so much from that album, and me being more of a classic rock person than an indie girl, I hadn't heard much Pixies and all of that yet. But with that Lennon-like snarl and angst and those propulsive drums, it felt like a bomb going off.'

It *was* a bomb going off. There would be many casualties, very few survivors.

In June 1991, while still listening to various mixes of the album, Nirvana set out on a short American tour, opening for Dinosaur Jr. Franz Stahl, now living with his brother full-time in LA, was hired at Dave's recommendation as their roadie for the tour. 'Just me and the band,' says Franz now. 'I was their only roadie. The whole time we were travelling we were listening to these mixes of *Nevermind* on cassette. I was like, this fucking thing is gonna be huge. But nobody knew it yet. Nobody even knew about *Bleach*. They were playing to 200 people a night. But on this tour I could see it all happening. I could see it cos I wasn't in the band and I could step back and watch it. They were *crushing* it. Places would be packed. Nirvana would come on and play, be done with the show, then 75 per cent of the people would leave. And Dinosaur Jr. would be playing to small portions of that initial crowd.' Nirvana seemed to be playing each show as if it were their last, he says. 'I would be wiping down Kurt's guitar every night. There would always be blood everywhere.'

On 14 June, when the tour reached the Hollywood Palladium, a local band of LA misfits named Hole were added to the bottom of the bill. It was not the first time their singer, Courtney Love, who resembled one of Kurt's broken panda-eyed dolls, had met the Nirvana singer. That had been the year before, when Nirvana had played at a dingy little dive called Satyricon, in Portland. Courtney had teased Kurt that he looked like the Soul Asylum singer Dave Pirner, and Kurt had play-wrestled her to the floor (something he liked to do with girls). When, several months later, Dave Grohl had begun going out with Courtney's friend Jennifer Finch, Kurt's name came up again and Courtney, three inches taller than Kurt and several lifetimes more street savvy, nicknamed him 'Pixie Meat', a double joke on his height and his devotion to the music of the Pixies. Courtney had her sights fixed on him, though. The 'Sliver' single had done it for her, especially the B-side, 'Dive', which she described as 'sexual, and strange and haunting'.

When Courtney discovered Kurt wasn't currently seeing anybody she sent him a heart-shaped box with a miniature porcelain doll inside, a toy teacup, some shellac-covered sea-shells and three dried roses. Kurt was mesmerised. He placed the doll on a shelf next to his growing collection of toy dolls, and wondered what it would be like to fuck someone like Courtney, who was clearly on a different wavelength to the other girls he'd known. At the Palladium, she had told him how her band had just finished recording their debut album, *Pretty on the Inside*, co-produced by Sonic Youth's Kim Gordon. Impressed by this further connection, Kurt was even surer of their entwined destinies when Courtney, noticing Kurt gulping from a bottle of cough syrup (his latest 'stomach-remedy' of choice), pulled out her own, much stronger cough syrup from her handbag. Before the show was over they had swapped phone numbers. It was the start of a beautiful relationship, they were both sure. But one that would have to be kept secret for now, as Courtney was still sharing an apartment with Hole's guitarist, Eric Erlandson, still hurting from the breakup of his own affair with Courtney a few months before. She was also still carrying on an on-off-on-again relationship with Billy Corgan, frontman of Smashing Pumpkins. Kurt said he didn't mind. Whatever Courtney wanted. It would become his credo throughout their relationship and eventual marriage. Even when whatever Courtney wanted threatened to drive a wedge between the members of Nirvana, or help drive Kurt to his fateful end.

In the weeks leading up to the release of *Nevermind* in September, the band found themselves back in Britain and Europe for a series of festival dates and smaller concert appearances.

The highlight was their appearance at the Reading Festival, in England, on Saturday, 23 August.

Speaking from his home in Brighton, Anton Brookes recalls the occasion with great warmth, and no little astonishment, even after all these years. 'They were in a respectable mid-table spot on the bill, and they went on and it was a real coming of age. All the cool music journalists were waiting for them to come on, all the cool bands. The audience was also like über-fans, the kind that listened to John Peel. It was almost like a pilgrimage. Then they came on and Kurt was wearing his *Sounds* T-shirt and they just absolutely destroyed Chapterhouse, the band who had to follow them afterwards. It was like they'd gone and just nuked Reading Festival. Then afterwards that's all anybody was talking about.'

Dave Grohl later admitted: 'I had never been so scared in my life' before going onstage. You would not have known it from his demeanour, though. With Kurt in a typically monosyllabic mood, barely making eye contact with the audience, far less addressing them directly, Dave took it upon himself to make the first verbal contact, before the band had begun playing, when he announced that they would be joined onstage that afternoon by 'a very special guest. His name is Tony and he is . . . *an interpretive dancer!*'

'Tony' was Antony Hodgkinson, then the 23-year-old drummer of a British rock band, Bivouac. Also signed to Geffen, Tony was a pal of Nirvana's London booking agent, Russel Warby, and had become friends with the band, offering to pick them up from the airport and generally hanging out. When Dave joked that Tony should come onstage at Reading with them as their dancer, he took the bait, following them on wearing 'clown's trousers', and braces over his naked torso. Warby scribbled the words, 'Lose weight now / Ask me how' on his chest; Kurt wrote: 'God is gay'.

During a gap for tuning between two of the new, as yet unreleased numbers from their new album, 'Drain You' and 'Smells Like Teen Spirit', Dave took it upon himself to address the audience again: 'We asked someone how much ... admission was ... and they told us it cost ... you had to bring a forty pound squid ... and we were like ... no way ... and we thought ... then we, then we ... and then Krist, and then, and then Kurt was like ... and then Krist just sorta ... you know ... and then Krist was just sorta ... you know and then Kurt just kinda did this ... fuckin' ... it was weird cause it was uhhh ...' The crowd laughed and applauded his goofy incoherence while Kurt merely waited for Dave to stop before nonchalantly chopping out the opening lines to 'Teen Spirit', while Tony returned to the stage to start flailing around again.

Not yet the climactic moment of the set it would soon become, 'Teen Spirit' was largely overlooked in the reviews that followed the show in favour of the real climax of the set, another as yet unknown number called 'Endless Nameless'. As Krist threw his bass into the drums at the end – and Dave picked it up and threw it back at him – Kurt walked backwards to the lip of the stage then ran full pelt and swallow-dived straight into Dave's drums. Meeting over. Cue huge applause from the crowd, Kurt walking off waving shyly to them, retrieving his can of beer from behind a stage monitor on the way, still not actually talking to them, but getting his message across loud and clear all the same.

At the time *Nevermind* was released, on 24 September 1991, Nirvana were completing a two-night stand at the Axis club in Boston, part of a 24-date North American tour that would see them graduating slowly from the clubs to the smaller theatres. Though they were now getting almost daily phone calls telling them how much the album was selling, the band was still blissfully unaware of the sheer scale of the excitement now building around *Nevermind*.

Before the album was released, Gary Gersh said, 'I felt like if we kept our heads down and worked really hard, and got a little bit lucky, and the band didn't implode, that maybe over the course of time, we could sell maybe 500,000 records. Like really a successful first major-label record.' Initially, however, Geffen decided it would only be shipping 30,000 copies to retail outlets. When Gersh objected that the figure was too small, the label's president, Eddie Rosenblatt, bet him $1000 the album would not sell the 30,000 in a month.

Determined to win the bet, Gersh decided his best strategy was to simply start passing around pre-release cassettes of the album to as many people in the business as possible, from music critics to radio programmers and DJs, record store managers, regional managers and distribution chiefs, and promotional staff across the US. 'We made more pre-release tapes of [*Nevermind*] than anybody had ever made and we gave it to everybody.' No fears of it being leaked online in those days. In fact, they *wanted* these tastemakers to pass it around and share, word of mouth being the surest marketing technique of all. 'People started talking and people started telling other people,' says Gersh. 'We could feel it happening.'

The morning of *Nevermind*'s release, Gersh got a phone call from Rosenblatt. 'He said, "The record has sold out everywhere in America – and it's eleven o'clock in the morning and the West Coast hasn't even opened yet." He goes, "I think you were right."' By the end of that first week DGC had shipped 500,000 copies throughout the US – and sold over 400,000 of them. 'It wasn't because the record was on the radio,' said Gersh. 'The video had [just] broken on MTV but it wasn't because of that either. It was because people were just telling other people that it was great. And you couldn't stop it.'

Meanwhile, Chrissy Shannon in LA and Anton Brookes in London had gone seemingly overnight from working hard to simply get the album reviewed, to fielding calls from major magazines and newspapers for interviews and pictures. 'It was a little hard for [the band] to initially get that it was getting so huge, so fast,' says Shannon now. 'They were playing the same damn circuit every rock band plays around the country and visiting little indie record stores on the way, so it was really hard for them to grasp that they had gone gold in a couple of weeks.'

Chrissy says she remembers the first time they came into the publicity office 'and Kurt was like a little kid' spinning around in her boss Lisa Gladfelter's big leather chair. She laughs. 'I remember telling him that I was so glad that I could work their album and not be stuck only in the hell of Don Dokken-land and him giving me a pitying look . . .'

Almost a year to the day exactly since Dave's first gig with the band, Nirvana played another landmark show in Seattle, at the 2000-capacity Paramount Theater. Mudhoney, who had just released their own new album, *Every Good Boy Deserves Fudge*, on Sub Pop, were originally billed as headliners. But by the time the tour had reached Seattle it was clear who the ticket-buyers would be coming to see. 'Every club we walk into, every fucking club we hear "Smells Like Teen Spirit",' recalled Danny Peters. 'We're like, "Holy shit, this record's everywhere!"' Arriving six weeks into their own tour to hook up with Nirvana in Portland, Peters asked them: '"Hey guys, how's it going?" And they said, "Our record just went gold today." Ah . . .'

As if to underline their newfound status, the band had agreed to have the Paramount show filmed by a large professional film crew. The set consisted of almost all of *Nevermind*, a few crowd-pleasers from *Bleach* – and one new track that nobody quite knew what to make of yet: 'Rape Me'. Kurt prefaced the song onstage at the Paramount by saying, 'This song is about hairy, sweaty, macho, redneck men – who rape.' In fact, it was an insulting swipe at the record industry that was about to make all of Kurt's and Krist's and Dave's maybe-one-day dreams come true. And written, in spite, to the very same chords as 'Teen Spirit' – an incredibly prophetic gesture considering the single was still riding the crest of the charts. But like a cancer victim going under the knife, Kurt already knew what the expected outcome would be for him. At the same time, there was something incredibly disingenuous about Kurt having written a song called 'Rape Me', it coming from the same guy who just weeks before had told Keith Cameron: 'I think denying the corporate ogre is a waste of time. You should use them, rape them the way they rape you. I don't believe in closing off options to make your own world seem more important.'

Three days after the Paramount show they were back in Britain, for another tour, again upgraded from previous visits, this time to concert halls. In the three months since their Reading appearance, Kurt had become emboldened in a way only a hit record can make you. But there was something else too: he had finally consummated his relationship with Courtney. Making their UK television debut, playing live on the late-Friday-night show *The Word*, then the hippest music show on British TV, Kurt began by telling the audience: 'I want all you people in this room to know that Courtney Love, the lead singer of the sensational pop group Hole, is the best fuck in the world!'

According to Jo Whiley, then working as one of the researchers on *The Word*, now a BBC Radio Two presenter,

'I was dead keen to get them onto *The Word*. I was saying to everyone, "We've got to have them on", but nobody had particularly heard of them. We discovered the song ['Smells Like Teen Spirit'] was really long [and] for the show it had to be under three minutes. I was told, "Tell them to do an edit!" I'm going, "You don't understand, we've *got* to have them on the show, they're more important than [that] . . . This was the one time I thought, "Fuck it, I'm not being a TV researcher here, I'm a fan." I stood down the front for when Kurt said, "Courtney Love is the best fuck in the world." Then it kicked off and it was so exciting.'

Three weeks later Nirvana made their debut on *Top of the Pops*, not the hippest music show but the one with the biggest mainstream audience on British TV, where they were asked to mime to 'Teen Spirit'. This, of course, was frowned on by the brutally cred-conscious trio, who proceeded to send the whole thing up, not bothering to pretend to play their instruments, while Kurt, offered the chance to at least do his vocal live, made a mockery of the process, changing the opening lines to 'Load up on guns and kill your friends', while singing in a preposterous baritone, then practically swallowing the mic. Afterwards the staid BBC production team inquired whether Kurt would 'mind doing that again?' Kurt's deadpan reply: 'No, I'm happy with that, thanks.' London-based Geffen Records executives watched in disbelief, certain that it would kill the record's sales stone dead. But nothing could stop the momentum of that song, and 'Teen Spirit' went even further up the UK charts the following week.

But Nirvana weren't quite done with subverting the UK TV viewing audience. When they were booked to appear on the Jonathan Ross chat show *The Last Resort*, in December, they had agreed to perform live, not 'Teen Spirit', this time, the band was relieved to learn, but 'Lithium' – the track, in fact, that had originally been earmarked as the lead single from *Nevermind*, before the band came up with 'Teen Spirit'. Except, in a fit of extra would-be punk aplomb, Kurt, who had only shown up an hour before broadcast, changed his mind and – much to the producers' alarm – they ripped into 'Territorial Pissings' instead. Ross made the best of it, as the band trashed their gear and stumbled off amid ear-splitting feedback, telling the folks back home, 'I hope we didn't wake the neighbours.' But it was clear this was not all fun for the band. As Dave Grohl trooped off he looked exasperated, wasted. Nirvana had done over 70 shows in the past three months, plus an ever-increasing number of press interviews, record store appearances, and TV and radio slots. Their eyes were dusty; their emotions dumbed down.

The next night they appeared on the bill at the Transmusicales open-air festival in Rennes, France. This was to have been followed by more shows in Spain but they were all exhausted, in bad shape, none more so than Kurt, who had been doing heroin again. Because he missed Courtney, he said. Because it made him sociable, he said. Because his ulcer pains were back and worse than ever, he said. When he said anything at all.

The Spanish shows were cancelled; the festival in Rennes would now be the last stop on the European tour. Kurt could barely make it to the stage, so Dave and Krist improvised a ramshackle version of The Who's 'Baba O'Riley' with Dave on vocals, coyly putting the blame for the band's disarray on the band's ridiculously busy schedule, changing the payoff line of the song to: 'It's just a *major label* wasteland.' At the end, as was becoming tediously predictable, they trashed their gear, as though never intending to use it again. Then, as the feedback whirred in the wind and the crowd cheered for they knew not what really, Krist leaned over and picked Kurt up off the floor where he lay, as though unconscious, and carried him off as though carrying a sleeping baby.

Dave Grohl looked on and said nothing. Just thought it.

6. Dodgy Kebabs

And that was it. It never really got any better for Dave Grohl in Nirvana after those last few months of 1991, when 'Smells Like Teen Spirit' was becoming the world's favourite song, and Nirvana the world's newest coolest band. By the time *Nevermind* had replaced Michael Jackson's *Dangerous* album at No. 1 in the American album charts, in January 1992, the world had already become aware that the game had changed, maybe for ever.

The only ones still in denial about it were the band themselves. 'When Nirvana knocked Michael Jackson off No. 1, I was there when they got the champagne,' says Anton Brookes, 'but it was so anti-climactic. I was excited because it was punk rock. Nirvana knocking Michael Jackson off of Number One – that is punk rock history in the making! But they were all really flippant about it.'

Taking their lead from Kurt, they were too self-conscious, too uptight about not being seen as rock with a capital 'R', that they didn't really know how to react. Kurt didn't do high-fives. Dave and Krist did, but not while Kurt was watching. Says Anton: 'They weren't gonna be jumping up and down, and going like, "Yeah!" That's not their way. But it was *such* an anti-climax; it almost went like . . . it didn't seem to register. Nobody seemed to be taking much notice of it.'

Nobody wanted to be uncool, at least not while Kurt was around, frowning. 'It was the same with things like limousines,' says Anton. 'If the record companies or promoters hired limos to pick the band up, the band would get in a taxi. It was all kind of like that. They never wanted to be seen as selling out, or that mentality. But then they were learning the game. They were holding back and not giving too much away. I think they learned quite quick that what they would give away people would grasp on to. They were still very cautious.'

Cautious and inhibited and, in Kurt's case, increasingly, it seemed, just plain fucked-up. A feature published the same month in the high-profile San Francisco magazine *BAM* wrote of Kurt 'nodding off in mid-sentence', and described him as sitting there with 'pinned pupils, sunken cheeks and scabbed, sallow skin', pointedly suggesting there was 'something more serious than mere fatigue' about the emaciated singer.

But if becoming, as *Rolling Stone* noted in April, 'the world's first triple-platinum punk rock band' was spacing out Kurt, it was having the opposite effect on his two band mates. 'Dave's just psyched,' Nirvana's friend and new fan-mail coordinator, Nils Bernstein, was quoted as saying. 'He's twenty-two, and he's a womaniser, and he's just: "*Score!*"' Krist, who was about to get married to Shelli, may not have been a womaniser, but he *was* a drinker. So much so, Bernstein suggested, he had recently gone on the wagon, to try and bring himself back down off the cloud he'd been riding since *Nevermind* changed everybody's minds. He'd also recently bought a five-bedroom house in one of Seattle's more salubrious neighbourhoods. When one of his pals from back in the day remarked that the mortgage payments must be crippling, Krist had shrugged: 'What payments?' He'd paid for the house in cash. '[Krist] and Dave have had to pick up a lot of Kurt's slack,' said Bernstein. Krist and Dave 'were close before, but now they're inseparable'.

In fact, when Dave wasn't on the road with the band, or

hanging out in Seattle, where he was looking to buy a house, he was hurrying back to Virginia, to spend time with his mother and sister and old high school pals. Despite the now out-of-control media blitz surrounding the band, Dave was the only one of the three who could still walk around without drawing a crowd. Everyone now recognised Kurt's whey-faced visage, all distraught blond hair and big blue crybaby eyes; everyone knew Krist as 'the other one', who always accompanied Kurt onstage, this huge, pogoing loony with the horse face and giraffe legs. Dave was the only one in Nirvana nobody ever really recognised offstage. The only one who could still show up at a Mudhoney show and no one would even notice. Shit, Dave could show up at a Nirvana show, some places, stroll through the crowd, and no one would notice. At least, not at first . . .

Chrissy Shannon says one of her favourite memories from this period 'was of Dave calling me to bitch about having to leave his hotel room in the middle of the night and go sleep on soundman Craig Montgomery's floor because Courtney had joined Kurt on the road and they were fucking in the other bed! He's hilarious when he's bitching.

'Another fun moment was Gary Graff from the *Detroit Free Press* wanting an interview with Kurt that never happened, so I finally set up a phoner with Dave. Dave apparently was not in the mood to talk, so he put [stand up comedian] Bobcat Goldthwait on the phone with Gary, who did the interview straight up as Dave. It went to print that way and when Dave spilled the beans later, Gary and the *Detroit Free Press* were not at all amused.'

By the time *Rolling Stone* ran its first cover story on the band, in April 1992, it was already all over. Kurt had married Courtney in February (she signed a pre-nup, which she later in-sisted was *her* idea), two days after the band's last date of their current tour, she being three months pregnant at the time of the wedding. Both were determined, they said, not to replicate their own experiences of coming from broken homes, and to ensure their child grew up with a married mother and father. A couple of weeks later, the writer Michael Azerrad showed up at their newly rented two-bedroom apartment in Los Angeles's low-key Fairfax district. In his piece, Azerrad describes Kurt lying around in striped pajamas, his toenails painted red. The place was littered with records and ashtrays and his dolls and teddy bears. Kurt makes much of 'a long-standing and painful stomach condition . . . aggravated by stress and, apparently, his screaming singing style'. The fact, as he tells Azerrad, that he has hardly eaten 'for more than two weeks' obviously hasn't helped either. What he makes a point of *not* telling Azerrad is that he has been doing smack with Courtney on a virtually day-to-day basis, which has also contributed to his 'gaunt and frail' appearance.

When Azerrad asks about the couple's recent marriage – on the idyllic island of Waikiki, in Hawaii, on the way home from Nirvana's first tours, in January, of Japan and Australia, Kurt describes their relationship as being 'like Evian water and battery acid'. He was joking but you know what they say about jokes. Azerrad wasn't to know that yet, though. He could only take what Kurt told him at face value. So that when Kurt had given Krist a kiss on a recent *Saturday Night Live* performance of 'Teen Spirit', it's because they knew 'it would piss off the folks back home – and everybody like them'. Cos Kurt is such a rebel, see?

Later in the piece, when Azerrad rides in Kurt's car with him to go get some money out of a cash machine, Kurt explains how dumbfounded he is to take $20 out only to find his balance is now in excess of $100,000. So he's still poor, at least in his own mind, and he's still misunderstood. Kurt is worried that 'Smells

Like Teen Spirit' will become a latter-day 'Born in the USA' – that the millions of kids buying it don't really *get it*. That they might lump Nirvana in with all the other bands from Seattle now being gobbled up by major-label deals, with Pearl Jam, whose debut album, *Ten*, had actually been released a month before *Nevermind*, coming in for special treatment.

Having gone out of his way to label them a 'corporate, alternative and cock-rock fusion' in an interview with *Musician* magazine, Kurt had since made clear his disdain for fellow-travellers like Alice in Chains, whose own major label debut, *Facelift*, had been released a year earlier but had been marketed initially as a cross between Guns N' Roses and Metallica, both of whom were too macho for Kurt to take seriously. Alice in Chains 'used to be a glam-metal band', reckoned Kurt, like that said it all. 'They're obviously just corporate puppets that are just trying to jump on the alternative bandwagon,' he ranted in an interview with *Flipside* in May 1992. Only Soundgarden, whose career on the Seattle scene preceded Nirvana's, and who were also now enjoying mainstream success with their third album, *Badmotorfinger*, released just a week after *Nevermind*, escaped Kurt's withering junkie gaze. He may have disapproved of them touring with Guns N' Roses but he knew where they were coming from, could see the links. (Jason Everman had even been their bassist briefly.)

As Anton says, 'That one album [*Nevermind*] came along and it was a complete game-changer on every level.' Mostly, though, Kurt despised the new 'scene' that had sprung up around Nirvana like poison ivy. They called it 'grunge' like it was an organic fungi native to Seattle. For Kurt, 'those bands have been in the hairspray/cock-rock scene for years and all of a sudden they stop washing their hair and start wearing flannel shirts. It doesn't make any sense to me. There are bands moving from LA and all over to Seattle and then claiming they've lived there all their life so they can get record deals. It really offends me.'

Ironically, the only other musicians suffering along with Kurt at the advent of grunge were the bands whose careers the all-conquering success of Nirvana had virtually ended: the 'hairspray' bands like Bon Jovi, Def Leppard, Mötley Crüe, Poison and Whitesnake. Van Halen's former singer David Lee Roth later blamed Kurt Cobain personally, claiming he ushered in an era in rock when 'fun just wasn't fun any more'. Or, as Anton puts it, 'Kurt vanquished a race of bands overnight. As soon as Nirvana broke through, suddenly the poodle bands were non-existent. These were huge, established stadium rock bands. They just came along in a Nirvana-esque way and just vanquished everything that lay in front of them, by default, not by design.'

Even the ones who eventually managed to swim to safety, like Bon Jovi and Guns N' Roses, did so with their sales intact but their credibility in tatters. The latter, arguably, suffered most by the comparison, releasing two double albums simultaneously – *Use Your Illusion I* and *Use Your Illusion II*, seen as the very limit of pompous rock star over-indulgence – just a week before *Nevermind*. So that by the summer of 1992, when Guns N' Roses now toured the stadiums of America with a hugely overblown stage production, the highlight of which found their prickly singer, W. Axl Rose, sitting aloft a gigantic Harley Davidson motorcycle-styled piano, they looked even more preposterous when set against the stripped-naked stage set Nirvana were still touting like a badge of honour.

When Axl Rose wore a Nirvana baseball cap in the Guns N' Roses video for their single 'Don't Cry', Kurt was beside himself with embarrassment. Axl even told one journalist how much he'd love to hear Nirvana do a version of the Guns N' Roses hit 'Welcome to the Jungle' – 'their way, however that is'. He even put in a request to have Nirvana perform at the thirtieth birthday party he was planning in February 1992, an invitation Kurt dismissed out of hand. When Axl then offered Nirvana the opening spot on their huge summer tour co-headlining with Metallica, Kurt ran a mile. 'We're not your typical Guns N' Roses type of band that has absolutely nothing to say,' Kurt was quoted as saying in an interview with *Seconds* magazine at that time. 'Whether we're proficient in saying what we want to say doesn't matter, it's just the fact that we're actually trying to communicate something different, something those cock-rock bands don't.'

'I remember being with Kurt and him getting upset about all the kids turning up to their shows in Guns N' Roses T-shirts,' says Anton Brookes, 'and he found that really difficult, because I think the people he had in mind for his songs were *not* of that ilk. But they would also turn up in Sonic Youth T-shirts, Black Flag T-shirts, Mudhoney T-shirts, the purity and the message encapsulated within the songs, it just seeped out. It just went everywhere, and a lot of people who didn't own a Stooges album or The Ramones or The Clash, for some reason Nirvana ignited something within their soul.'

Maybe so. According to Chrissy Shannon, though, it was around now that Kurt began to lose his own soul, or as he saw it anyway. 'I know that Kurt did not want everyone to like him and love his band,' she says. 'That's what he couldn't take. He wanted to manage who his audience was. He was there for the misfits, the bullied, the freaks. He did not want the asshole frat boys, who beat him up in high school, to buy his records, but they did and the whole thing suddenly felt very out of control. I know that's when he started slipping away.'

The first time Chrissy realised just how bad things had got, in terms of Kurt's heroin use and his consequent isolation from the band, was during the video shoot for the 'Come As You Are' single, in LA in 1992. Though she didn't know it at the time, it later transpired that Courtney was now pregnant, and that the two of them had checked into a Holiday Inn for three days while a 'rock'n'roll doctor' – a self-styled specialist in speedy heroin withdrawal – had been called in to hurriedly wean them off the gear. Courtney accompanied Kurt to the shoot, the couple hiding out in their own trailer. Kurt was still in such bad shape that he insisted there be no close-ups of his face in the video, forcing the director, Kevin Kerslake, to extrapolate from the *Nevermind* cover, as Kurt's face becomes obscured by images of a baby swimming underwater and the sight in slow motion of a sinking revolver.

'That was after things had taken the negative turn with Kurt,' remembers Chrissy. 'Krist and Dave were affable and lovely. In fact, Dave took me by the hand and led me around their elaborate set – he was really glad I was there to see it because it's so hard to explain to people what they want it to look like.' Later, they were all sitting around a picnic table set up with food for the band and crew, 'shooting the shit, while Kurt was holed up – pun intended! – with Courtney in his trailer. Then all of a sudden he was with us at the table. Careful to sit as far away from the food as possible, but was hanging out for a bit. He looked like Brian Jones did in those last [Rolling Stones] films, translucent and like he was already in the spirit world. He didn't stay long as the trailer door flew open and in her foghorn voice Courtney bellowed "KURT!" and he went back in with her shortly. That night I called my mom crying because I told her I thought he was going to die. Of course, I had thought it was going to be from the heroin . . .'

It was also during this period that the band performed live

for the first time on *Saturday Night Live* – 'Smells Like Teen Spirit' and 'Territorial Pissings'. Kurt looked wan onscreen, his face shaved clean, his hair dyed a dull copper red, his cardigan hanging off him. Charged up at the thought of appearing on what was still one of America's hippest TV shows, though, he at least puts some energy into his performance, even if his pained facial expression never alters. Nor was the tension surrounding Nirvana restricted to the stage. Back at the DGC publicity office, in LA, Chrissy Shannon was being hauled over the coals for sending limos to take the band to the show.

She explains: 'When Nirvana was going to play *Saturday Night Live*, their manager, John Silva, called me and said, "Chris, when you book the cars, don't send a limo for Kurt, he hates them." Fine, so I call Music Express in Seattle and order regular cars to take the boys to the airport. At this point Kurt and Courtney are living out of a hotel. The car company had run out of regular cars and unbeknownst to me, sent a limo to pick Kurt and Courtney up. They refuse to enter the limo claiming it's not "punk rock" to do so.

'While I'm desperately trying to book another car company, Silva's calling me saying, "Chris, you fucked up!" So Kurt misses his plane to New York and *Saturday Night Live* is on the horn to Lisa Gladfelter freaking out. So now I have to re-book [Kurt's] flight as well. Lisa meanwhile flies to New York to pick him up and deliver him personally to [producer] Marci Klein at *SNL* and Courtney has just scored them heroin off the street somewhere in New York. Lisa picks up Kurt and puts him in a cab personally to make sure he makes it to *SNL* and he pukes on her!'

In fact, far from stressing about limos and his punk credibility, Kurt had been out on a prolonged bender with Courtney, as revealed to the writer Lynn Hirschberg in an interview that went on the cover of the September 1992 issue of *Vanity Fair*, in which Courtney was quoted as saying, 'We went on a binge. We did a lot of drugs. We got pills, and then we went down to Alphabet City and we copped some dope. Then we got high and went to *SNL*. After that, I did heroin for a couple of months.' Elsewhere in the same story, Hirschberg quotes 'a business associate who was travelling with them at the time' as saying, 'It was horrible. Courtney was pregnant and she was shooting up. Kurt was throwing up on people in the cab. They were both out of it.'

It was now that the whole over-the-top public persona of Courtney Love – and her Sid-and-Nancy-esque relationship with Kurt Cobain – threatened to overshadow anything Nirvana did next. The details and anecdotes began to fill up the pages of the gossip press, like bilge in an overflowing sewer. Courtney's dad was a drugged-up hippy; Courtney's mum was a rich girl gone wrong. Poor Courtney had been shuffled off to boarding school, yet somehow ended up stripping in Taiwan. Courtney lived in England, in Liverpool of all places, where she had flings with Teardrop Explodes' singer Julian Cope and others less famous. Courtney fled back to America and ended up in Seattle, where she fucked more wannabe rock stars and took lots of Percodan. Courtney first took coke when she was 19 and had dabbled with smack on and off ever since. Courtney really loved Billy Corgan but Billy didn't love Courtney so she settled for Kurt. These days any half-decent Google search will tell you a lot more than that and some of it is almost certainly true. But in the internet age, who doesn't have a chequered past, a dysfunctional *histoire*, a few bodies buried somewhere? Nobody worth listening to with the lights out, that's for sure, right, kids? Back in 1992, though, this was very hot stuff. Less Nancy, more Yoko – but with *bite*. Nobody in the media was gonna get away with running this gal out of town, right, dude?

Except they nearly did. By the time the *Vanity Fair* article broke, Courtney had given birth to her and Kurt's baby daughter, Frances Bean. When the public realisation that her self-confessed heroin 'binge' overlapped with her early pregnancy became national news, the baby was taken into temporary child custody. Courtney would never forgive the writer for that, later making the astonishing claim that Hirschberg 'deserves most of the blame' for Cobain's death.

In another, less sensational but equally telling part of the *Vanity Fair* story, when Kurt returned from a lengthy phone call from Dave, Hirschberg reports the following exchange: 'Dave is upset,' Kurt says after hanging up. 'So,' Courtney says, 'why don't you start a new band without [him]?' Looking upset, Kurt says, 'But I want Dave. He's the best fucking drummer I know.' Courtney signs off by telling Hirschberg, 'The worst thing is when people say Kurt's helping me to make it.'

'Ah, the delicate flower that is Courtney,' sighs Chrissy Shannon. 'For a while she made life pretty miserable for Lisa and I. At first the Sid and Nancy thing was kinda funny, if creepy, and the phone calls from Dave spelling out his opinion on Kurt's choice of girlfriend were hilarious . . . but as they descended into their addiction . . . it started to get ugly.

'Then the infamous *Vanity Fair* article on Courtney came out and all shit hit the fan . . . When Child Protective Services went after them what did they expect? Dumb, dumb, dumb move and we had nothing to do with it.'

Both Kurt and Courtney had gone 'ballistic on Lynn Hirschberg', she recalls, 'threatening her with bodily harm'. Then, 'Courtney got obsessed with the unnamed sources quoted in the article. She was convinced that they came from inside Geffen for a while and so she set me up. She called me once claiming to be a writer from a fanzine and asked me a bunch of questions about herself to see what I would say about her. It was so lame and juvenile – she had another friend on the line listening, just like people do in junior high to their "enemies"! And, honestly, does anyone else on the planet sound like Courtney Love?'

Back on tour in Australia, earlier in the year, Kurt had been withdrawing so heavily it looked like they would have to cancel shows. Dave, future nicest man in rock, did what he was getting used to doing at times like this and looked the other way. What else was he supposed to do? It wasn't really his band. Maybe things would get better once Kurt was 'well' again. 'The first time Nirvana came down [to Australia] in January, 1992,' Dave recalled disingenuously years later, 'we were there for a few weeks and I had never been there before. I was just blown away because it was the best of both worlds. It almost had a European feel to it, but it was a little too friendly and sunny and beautiful to be considered European.'

It sounds so nice. It was not. The only way Kurt got through the tour and the subsequent dates in New Zealand and Japan was after a Sydney doctor prescribed him what turned out to be methadone pills. When the writer Dave Cavanagh joined Nirvana's latest UK tour, in Belfast, in June, for a piece in *Select*, he was aghast at what he found. 'There was quite a mood of fear. On the plane over, Anton said to me, "I'd really like you to just talk about the music with Kurt." I was like, "What else am I supposed to talk about? Are there any other subjects?"' In the event, Cavanagh interviewed Kurt for an hour or so, and found him to be 'a nice guy, sweet, cute, dry and self-depreciating', dressed in 'grubby clothes, a second-hand watch . . . He looked like his entire life had cost about ten quid and he was deliberately eating the worst food he could buy, while everyone around him was becoming a millionaire. That's how it seemed to me.'

The following morning, however, Cavanagh was awoken early

and told to hurry as everyone was leaving early for the airport. 'We were all being shepherded away from the hotel because, we later found out, Cobain had run out of methadone. He'd started withdrawing and paramedics had had to be called. When we rang up to ask more about this a couple of days later, we were told, "Oh, he had a dodgy kebab" or something.'

Anton Brookes sighs heavily at being reminded of such horror stories now. 'When Nirvana came to town there was like a dark element that followed them. The junkie chic would latch on to them and these people would turn up and they were, basically, the walking dead. Zombies: just the colour of their skin, their eyes in their sockets. The way they dressed. It's like, "Nobody understands us. We're rebelling against whatever we've got to rebel against. And we're cool but you're not, because you're not doing heroin."

'It was kind of like a little club. They'd be stood on one side of the dressing room and everybody else was on the other side of the dressing room. It was like poisons in the room. All these people like friends of Kurt and Courtney. You just want to go up and kick them out and go, "Fuck off!" But you can't. And if you do, you're not helping the situation, you're making it worse. Suddenly you're not a friend any more. It was a fine line trying to help and hinder, if that makes sense.'

Nobody was in a more difficult position than Dave and Krist, both of whom now found themselves on the wrong side of Nirvana's dressing room. 'There's no denying that, to be honest,' says Anton. 'You could see the pain and the anguish etched on their faces every time you saw them and spoke to them. It was very self-evident. For a lot of us, it was the first time anything like this had ever happened.' He pauses then goes on: 'You add heroin into any situation – look at the whole history of rock'n'roll – it changes everything.'

How did Dave deal with this, as the new guy, the outsider? As the young guy parachuted into this situation, who always brings his best game to the show, now having to put up with all this horrible negative death-ray stuff going on? 'I think he was quite worried,' says Anton, simply, 'and quite scared. He's gone from punk rock kid, to working his way up into this really successful band, having an absolutely fantastic time. Then suddenly you wake up and the shit has hit the fan. We were all basically kids. We'd never experienced anything like this.'

When Nirvana arrived in Britain for their second successive Reading Festival appearance – this time as Saturday night head-liners – in August 1992, they did so under a cloud. Kurt's heroin use was no longer a secret and there was open talk that the band would either cancel the show or make an announcement that it would be their last. When Keith Cameron joined the tour in Bel-fast, 'everything had changed beyond recognition,' he later said. 'All the talk was of heroin; the gigs almost seemed a diversion. They seemed static and distant from each other. I imagined that selling a lot of records might empower them. Success seemed to make Nirvana powerless.'

'There was just a tidal wave of questions at Reading,' recalls Anton. '"Are Nirvana playing? Are they splitting up?" People knew that Dave and Krist were on-site, they'd watched a few bands on the Friday night, but people were still saying that they wouldn't play. Yes, there was turmoil in the Nirvana camp, but at the time you have to deny it.'

When Kurt arrived onstage in a wheelchair, dressed in a surgi-cal gown and long, blond wig, it seemed like the joke was on the media. 'Kurt got up from his hospital bed just to play for you,' Krist deadpanned to the audience, as Kurt pretended to drag himself out of the chair by clinging to the mic stand. Then the joking stopped and the band leaned full tilt into 'Breed'. Tony the 'interpretative dancer' was back for a second year running too but that was where the fun ended. Despite the celebratory air among the rain-soaked crowd, the driving 18-song set was as grey and glowering as the weekend skies, the atmosphere coming off the stage as muggy and grim as the knee-high mud the audience was forced to wade through just to be there, at what would prove to be Nirvana's valedictory UK show. They would not be back, you sensed it somehow, in the way Kurt couldn't even be bothered to remove his 'comical' surgical gown, nor speak much to the thousands who now believed all the guff about him being the spokesman of their generation. Sensed it in the way Kurt felt the need to tell them, 'This isn't our last show.' Sensed it in the desperate way Kurt shared the fact that 'Courtney is beginning to think everybody hates her', urging the crowd to chant: 'Courtney, we love you!' even though no one there really cared either way. They just loved Kurt and would do or say whatever it took to keep him onstage with them, sensing this was the end. When Kurt then dedicated a new song, 'All Apologies', to Courtney and their 12-day-old daughter, Frances Bean, the words rang horribly true, as he hollered: 'Married!' Boom-a-boom-a-boom-ba-ba. '*Buried!*'

Even the six-song encore seemed as though it was concocted as a taunt, almost, to the fey tropes of traditional festival-going. 'Territorial Pissing', always a cue for onstage havoc, lent itself to the biggest auto-destruct yet, as Dave and Krist spent the next several minutes absolutely destroying anything they could get their frustrated hands on, while Kurt, his hospital gown flapping in the stinking wind, did a mocking, shocking version of Seattle's other prodigal left-handed son, Jimi Hendrix, doing the 'Star-Spangled Banner', as if to underline the fact that this was *not* Woodstock. 'An ironic soundtrack for generational pain' is how the review in *Rolling Stone* later described it. But that was

Scream. L-R: Dave Grohl, Peter Stahl, Skeeter Thompson and Franz Stahl. Franz was Dave's guitar mentor and was in Foo Fighters – before apprentice turned master and fired him. (Corbis)

'Kurt could sleep anywhere!' Nirvana during an interview in 1991. (Getty Images)

Go towards the light: Kurt's dark glamour would soon be replaced by Dave's bright tomorrow. (Stephen Sweet /REX Shutterstock)

Opposite, from top left: Nirvana do zany for the cameras at the 1992 MTV Video Music Awards. (Getty Images)

Dave and Krist join Red Hot Chili Peppers' Anthony Kiedis (left) and Flea (right) in some cross-dressing 'antics'. (Getty Images)

By 1993 being in Nirvana wasn't fun anymore, even if Dave still put a brave face on it. (Stephen Sweet /REX Shutterstock)

Nirvana on the In Utero tour, 1993. (Getty Images)

According to Courtney Love, 'Kurt hated Dave'. (REX Shutterstock)

Original Foo Fighters line-up, 1995. L-R: William Goldsmith, Pat Smear, Dave Grohl, Nate Mendel. (Corbis)

Not such a nice guy. By the end of the 1990s, Dave had asserted his leadership of Foo Fighters. (Getty Images)

(Left, above) The ill-starred Franz Stahl years. 'I cried,' says Stahl, when Dave sacked him. (Getty Images)

(Left, below) Foo Fighters arriving at the 1998 MTV Video Music Awards. (Getty Images)

Guitarist Chris Shiflett (back) joined the Foos in 1999, but didn't actually play on any of their albums until 2002. (Getty Images)

being kind. This wasn't irony on display any more. This was just pain. Not generational, but specific and of the moment.

The fandango now surrounding Nirvana wherever they showed up continued in September, at the MTV Video Music Awards show, broadcast live from the Pauley Pavilion at UCLA. Having agreed not to perform their newest number, 'Rape Me', Kurt then strummed the opening chords, before cutting into 'Lithium', throwing the production team into a major spin, as MTV's vice-president, Judy McGrath, was about to order the director to cut to a commercial break.

In the event, Nirvana ran through 'Lithium', as planned, but as the number ended Krist threw his bass into the air, as he'd done a thousand times before, but mistimed his catch, the bass catching him square in the jaw, knocking him down onto the stage. Kurt then tried to stab his guitar right through the amps while Dave kicked over his drums and stumbled to the mic to call out, 'Where's Axl? Hi, Axl! Hi, Axl! Hi, Axl!' over and over to the general confusion of everybody – except Guns N' Roses' singer, W. Axl Rose, who knew exactly what was going on.

It was the latest instalment in the Kurt-hates-Axl row that had been simmering for months. Round one had occurred the year before when Axl and GN'R's guitarist, Slash, had gone to see Nirvana play at the Palace in LA. Courtney later recalled in the press Axl standing next to her at the side of the stage, 'doing that dance he did in the "Sweet Child o' Mine" video.' She claimed that after the show Axl had told Kurt: 'You're everything I could've been.' Kurt did not know what to say. For him, Axl Rose was everything he would never want to be. As Axl was 'obviously a racist and homophobe'.

For Kurt Cobain the idealist, Axl Rose and Guns N' Roses represented everything he claimed to most abhor about rock stardom, seeing them as unforgivably self-indulgent and out of step with the times. No matter that Kurt and Axl actually had a lot in common: both contrarians never happier seemingly than when cutting off their noses to spite their faces; both from highly dysfunctional families in which the son had essentially run away from home, fending for himself on the streets since his teens. Both of whom had finally found a twisted kind of self-validation through forming mega-successful rock bands; and had fallen for the rock star lifestyle clichés, including sex and drugs and deliberately going against the grain. But Kurt had underestimated the personal animus Axl could bring to bear on anyone who crossed him, including his closest friends and band mates. When Kurt's public rebukes of Axl and his band hit the press in 1992, Axl was bent on revenge, telling one audience: 'Right now alternative – the only thing that means to me is Kurt Cobain and Nirvana, who basically is a fucking junkie with a junkie wife. If the baby's born deformed, I think they both ought to go to prison, that's my feeling. He's too good, and too cool, to bring his rock'n'roll to you, because the majority of you he doesn't like, or want to play to, or even want you to like his music.'

Kurt responded in kind, telling the *Advocate*: 'I can't even waste my time on that band, because they're so obviously pathetic and untalented. I used to think that everything in the mainstream pop world was crap, but now that some underground bands have been signed with majors, I take Guns N' Roses as more of an offense', adding, 'They're really talentless people, and they write crap music.'

The only thing he had in common with Axl, Cobain told his biographer, Michael Azerrad, was that they both came from small towns. 'His role has been played for years. Ever since the beginning of rock'n'roll, there's been an Axl Rose. It's just totally boring to me. Why it's such a fresh and new thing in his eyes is obviously because it's happening to him personally and he's such an egotistical person that he thinks that the whole world owes him something.' This from the guy who now shut himself away from his own band and management before shows so he could shoot heroin.

When both Nirvana and Guns N' Roses were booked to appear at the 1992 MTV awards, it was an accident waiting to happen. Elton John had agreed to join Guns N' Roses on piano and backing vocals for their number, 'November Rain'. As a childhood fan of Elton's, Axl was in a deep swoon over the occasion, yet the show is now recalled for very different reasons. The trouble began when, as he left the stage, Kurt spat on the keys of the piano he believed belonged to Axl, but which actually belonged to Elton. Then when Kurt and Courtney were sitting backstage with baby Frances in Courtney's arms, as Axl walked by with his then girlfriend, the model Stephanie Seymour, surrounded by his usual retinue of bodyguards, Courtney called out, 'Axl! Axl! Will you be the godfather of our child?' Embarrassed, Axl strode over and jabbed his finger in Kurt's face. 'You shut your bitch up,' he snarled, 'or I'm taking you down to the pavement!'

To which Kurt replied, sarcastically: 'What? What are you going to do, you're going to beat me up?' Axl glared at him. 'You better keep your wife's mouth shut. You embarrass everybody. You embarrass your wife, you embarrass your old man, you embarrass me.' At which, Kurt turned to Courtney and wagged his finger: 'Shut up, bitch!' Then burst out laughing.

In a desperate attempt to try and smooth the situation, Stephanie asked Courtney: 'Are you a model?' Courtney sneered. 'No. Are you a brain surgeon?'

Furious, Axl stormed off. Then later in the show a posse from the GN'R camp pushed their way into Nirvana's trailer, and a brief but pointless scuffle broke out, quickly extinguished in a kind of music industry stand-off as executives from Geffen – to whom Nirvana and Guns N' Roses were both signed – intervened to calm the situation. The incident was reported around the world, with Kurt coming out of the story as the frail hero, Axl the screwy-eyed monster. Later, when the media dust settled, Axl told friends that Courtney had actually been attempting to do more than just rile him. She was actually trying to *possess* him. 'He believes people are always trying to find a window through to control his energy,' said a friend. Axl's way of dealing with it was by 'controlling the people who have access to him'.

The harsher reality, though, was that Courtney had already taken possession of Kurt's soul, and, by extension, that of Nirvana. And the only other people Kurt was now allowed access to were their heroin dealers.

'I'd go backstage to get him,' Anton Brookes recalls, 'and you'd knock on the door and, "You can't come in! You can't come in!" Because he was shooting up before he goes onstage. It's just kind of like . . . it's just no fun. All the fun has been sucked out of what a few months previously was such an exciting, absolutely brilliant time.' Anton adds, tellingly: 'I could be naïve here but I think it's wrong to blame Courtney for all of that. I think in any relationship you have to accept a certain amount of responsibility for your actions. Kurt was his own man and Kurt was doing heroin before Nirvana became big. He was doing heroin probably before Nirvana even started. But he didn't have the money to be able to sustain a habit.

'Once you get more money, it becomes easier to get it and the ways to get it become . . . simplicity, really, isn't it, after a while? Junkies attract junkies.' Before that, 'Kurt was a laugh. People are shocked to hear that now but it's true. He was a funny fucker! Kurt was a good person – a very nice, caring, charming person. But you throw heroin into that and the nicest person at times can be a bastard . . . I didn't used to get the full brunt of it but you can bet your bottom dollar management did on a daily basis.'

Not to mention Dave and Krist, who were now beginning to think seriously of a life beyond Nirvana. Could such a thing exist? They would soon be forced to find out.

7. Where Did You Sleep Last Night?

Things just got worse and worse and worse. As they always do with junkies. 'I feel like people want me to die, because it would be the classic rock'n'roll story,' Kurt was quoted as saying at the end of 1992. But nobody wanted Kurt to die. Least of all Dave Grohl, who would put his own career on the line by eventually telling Kurt that he wasn't prepared to play in Nirvana any more unless Kurt stopped taking heroin and got himself the fuck together. Not that that worked, either.

The last 18 months of Nirvana's career were just horrible. When Kurt wasn't injecting heroin he was injecting speed, when he wasn't doing that he was taking Percodan and methadone, or Valium or any other super-strength tranquilliser and opiate he could get his hands on, legally prescribed or simply bought off the street. Courtney, freaked to the bone by the temporary removal of Frances, had sworn to stay off drugs. But she was always falling off the wagon. Sometimes they would be using the same drug dealer but without telling each other, constantly lying to each other about what they were or weren't taking, and how much or how little. Both would go through various stages of detox, but many around the band found Kurt even harder to deal with when he was off drugs than when he was on them.

Dave Grohl and Krist Novoselic might have decided they must be the ones on drugs though when they received written notice of some amendments Kurt now insisted on being made to their existing band contracts. Spurred on, many believed, by Courtney, Kurt, through the band's own lawyers, was allegedly demanding 90 per cent of all songwriting royalties, leaving Dave and Krist to split 10 per cent between them. Moreover, this new agreement was to be made retrospectively, covering the songs on *Nevermind*, too. Thus putting Dave and Krist into a position where they had to actually pay Kurt back millions of dollars.

Grohl's future biographer Paul Brannigan recalls the pair's bitter reaction to this latest development. 'Kurt's own latter history rather overwhelmed any decision that was made at that point. But certainly at the time, I think, both Dave and Krist were close to walking away from the band. "Like, *really? Fuck you!* I thought we were all in this together!" Even as much as it was Kurt's vision that was driving the band, and Dave was a late arrival onto that album – seven of the songs on *Nevermind* had been demoed without him, in pretty much exactly the same form – initially there was a hostile reaction. But then, later, Dave said something to me like: "At some point you just think, well, shit, I've got my house. I've been able to look after my mum. I've got more money now than I ever thought I was gonna have two years ago. So, in a sense you go, right, well, that's the way it is then."'

He goes on: 'In pragmatic terms, I can imagine that there's a sense of ego where you just wanna just throw your toys out of the pram and go, fuck you, this is not what I signed up for. Then another part of you thinks, right, well, so this is how it is then, I guess. We know the rules now. We know this isn't all for one, one for all. And you deal with it. This is business. This is life. So suck it up. Yeah. It's something of a rewriting of history. I know Dave's, legally, not allowed to talk about it. They had to sign a nondisclosure thing when they did it. But it was backdated to one point in time, I'm not exactly sure when. It wasn't just that in future they weren't gonna get the same money. It was that Dave and Krist actually now *owed* Kurt money. You can imagine it being a bit of a kick in the balls.'

When asked for his memory of events, Anton Brookes says now that he has 'no idea how much the split was, but when it did come along, I got the impression, because Kurt wrote the lyrics, and chiefly the songs, even though the band developed them, I think [Dave and Krist] were quite happy with it ... I think that was more to do with Courtney, more than anything.' He pauses, then adds: 'I only saw that, when it happened, as Courtney looking out for her husband. Looking out for his interests and everything.'

Somehow, in the middle of all this, Nirvana managed to record one last great album, *In Utero*, released in September 1993, and another multi-platinum smash, even though it was as far removed from the sugarcoated punk-pop of *Nevermind* as it was possible to imagine. The original title Kurt wanted for the new album was *I Hate Myself and Want to Die*. Everyone else shuddered at the idea, not least DGC, which had everything riding on this next release. With *Nevermind* on its way to 30 million sales worldwide, this was no time for pathetic junkie jokes. Kurt was adamant, though. It was only after Krist put the case to Kurt that such a title would open the band up to endless lawsuits from parents of kids whose deaths had potentially been inspired by listening to the album that Kurt finally saw the light. (Both Judas Priest and Ozzy Osbourne had recently faced lengthy and expensive high-profile court battles over two such cases.)

Then Kurt wanted to call it *Verse, Chorus, Verse*, a marvellously prosaic title that again met with frowns and much shaking of heads. In the end, Kurt came up with *In Utero*, a phrase lifted from a poem he admired by Courtney, and which was enigmatic enough – most Nirvana fans would have no idea what it actually meant – to work for everyone else in the band and their management and record company. Harder to swallow for 'the grown-ups', as Kurt called them, however, was the music itself: 12 tracks of such unremittingly bleak power that they amounted to a refutation of everything Nirvana had achieved with *Nevermind*, including that album itself, and most of all its totemic single, 'Smells Like Teen Spirit'.

The uncompromising Steve Albini, once of Big Black, now renowned as one of the most anti-establishment producers in the business, with his distrust of digital technology, his insistence on 'old school' recording techniques, cutting bands live to tape, their 'pure sound' captured by the placement of microphones around the room – much as the early Zeppelin albums had been recorded by, as Jimmy Page put it, 'moving the air around in the room' – was exactly what Kurt was looking for to return Nirvana to the vanguard of punk.

In a letter Albini sent to the band prior to taking the album on, outlining his own ideas, Albini wrote: 'I like to leave room for accidents or chaos. Making a seamless record, where every note and syllable is in place and every bass drum is identical, is no trick. Any idiot with the patience and the budget to allow such foolishness can do it. I prefer to work on records that aspire to greater things, like originality, personality and enthusiasm.'

He also underlined his own freethinking philosophy when it came to payment for his work. 'I explained this to Kurt but I thought I'd better reiterate it here. I do not want and will not take a royalty on any record I record. No points. Period. I think paying a royalty to a producer or engineer is ethically indefensible. The band writes the songs. The band plays the music. It's the band's fans who buy the records. The band is responsible for whether it's a great record or a horrible record. Royalties belong to the band. I would like to be paid like a plumber: I do the job and you pay me what it's worth. The record company will expect me to ask for a point or a point and a half. If we assume three million sales, that works out to 400,000 dollars, or so. There's no fucking way I would ever take that much money. I wouldn't be able to sleep.'

All of which endeared the maverick producer to Kurt in a way that went beyond money. Whatever this album was going to sound like, its primary focus, as far as Kurt was concerned, was that it not sound like the slickly produced *Nevermind*. Now, in Albini, it seemed like they had found someone who could do ragged justice to the subject matter of the album's cornerstone tracks – ranging from Kurt's 'teenage angst' that has 'paid me well' on 'Serve the Servants' to his longing to 'eat your cancer when you turn black' on 'Heart-Shaped Box', his open love-hate letter to Courtney (originally titled 'Heart-Shaped Coffin'), to promising the world that now judged his every move to 'kiss your open sores' on 'Rape Me', or, most moving of all, to cooing about distilling 'the life in me' on 'Pennyroyal Tea', a drink once used to induce abortions.

Other tracks, like 'Milk It', 'Radio Friendly Unit Shifter' and, most especially, the vicious 'Tourette's', are sheer fury, fired like a gun in a crowded room, not caring what tender parts their bullets might hit. While still others appeared to belie the whole sense of the album as one long howl of rage, realigning it to something much more poignant and frail: the touching 'Dumb', with its lonely midnight cello, reminiscent of wistful mid-period Beatles; the hypnotic 'All Apologies', with its callused call-and-response lines about wishing 'I was like you, easily amused . . .' and its signature switch from feather-light guitar to thunderous rock avalanche.

Full of recycled riffs from older Nirvana songs – most notably, the vampiric 'Rape Me', built on the same once-charming chords as 'Smells Like Teen Spirit' – and pieces that don't end so much as collapse in a heap when they can run no more, the tracks on *In Utero* smelled like nothing so much as burnt shit and warm blood, seeping through old bandages encrusted with the broken shards of yellowed syringes. Baffling even to believers; beautiful only to the already dammed. Like Kurt and the woman he wrote most of the songs to, Courtney.

'The first time I heard it I didn't get it at all,' admits Anton Brookes. 'There were a couple of stand-out tracks like "All Apologies" and "Heart-Shaped Box", but you go back and listen now and it's still completely different, only now it makes *sense*. They did a complete U-turn, encapsulating their sound but pointing into a different direction [and] Dave's role in that is superb. His drums just explode, yet they're one of the most subtle things about the album.'

Talking about the album on the twentieth anniversary of its release, in 2013, Dave summed up most people's reactions first time around to *In Utero* when he told *Rolling Stone*: 'There are a few ways you can look at it. You can describe it as a remarkable achievement', or 'as a really fucked-up time'.

DGC saw it more as an *under*achievement, rejecting the final Albini mixes and bringing in Scott Litt to remix the tracks earmarked as the album's future singles: 'Heart-Shaped Box', 'All Apologies' and 'Pennyroyal Tea'. Litt did not disappoint the executives who had hired him, taking Albini's 'pure sound' tapes and adding a reverb to the drums, extra vocal tracks as bedding, fading out certain rhythm guitars here and bringing further up into the mix a jangly lead guitar line there . . . adding fairy lights to the dark clouds Albini had so adroitly helped Kurt capture.

Recorded in just 12 days, the end result delighted Kurt, and Dave and Krist too. Mostly, though, Dave was just glad to get the hell out the claustrophobic atmosphere in the studio. 'That was a weird thing,' he said in 2013. 'We're sequestered in this house, in the middle of the snow, in February in Minnesota. Recording with Steve – he would hit "record", we'd do a take, and he'd go [*claps hands*], "Okay, what's next?" Wait, is it okay?' He went on. 'We blazed through *In Utero*. I was done after three days. I had another ten fucking days to sit in the snow, on my ass with nothing to do. Once we were finished with all of the instrumentation, it was time for Kurt to do his vocals and overdubs.'

The worst moment for Dave occurred – as with *Nevermind* – when the producer expressed over-concern about the drummer's ability to keep a straight tempo, in this case on 'Heart-Shaped Box'. But whereas Butch Vig had suggested using a click track – 'Not cool, man!' – Steve Albini made the radical suggestion of using a strobe light to cut Dave in on the beat. 'I sat there for a take or two with this fucking strobe light in my face until I practically had a seizure. I said, "Can we just play? A little ebb and flow. Don't worry about it."'

Once the sessions were complete, Nirvana did . . . not much else until it was released six months later. They averaged around one gig a month for much of 1993, arenas now, usually, or festivals, but being on the road was by this time a familiar grind. The only thing anyone knew for sure was that Kurt would be out of it. Either good out of it, as in making the gig a better one, which he could still do on those nights when he wasn't bugging out about something else. Or, more often, bad out of it, as in the day of their supposedly 'more intimate' show at the Roseland Ballroom in New York, in July, when Kurt nearly killed himself.

Anton Brookes, who had flown in a party of journalists from London, was the one who found Kurt, in his words, 'slumped behind the toilet of his hotel room in New York'. Anton had gone over to visit the band at their hotel the day before the interviews were set to take place – the first serious round of UK publicity for the forthcoming *In Utero* album. All was going to plan, with Dave and Krist on their usual good form, when Anton caught sight of someone he immediately recognised as one of Kurt's drug dealers also in the hotel lobby.

'You knew what was happening,' said Anton, 'and you knew what that guy was there for and you knew what the outcome of that would be. The next day was when we were supposed to do press, and it was just a nightmare from start to finish, really.' Things got worse when Kurt and Courtney began to fight. 'I was upstairs,' Anton recalled, 'and suddenly the screaming, or the arguments, changed.' Alerted by the sudden calm, 'We realised we should go in. We went rushing into the bathroom and slumped behind the toilet was Kurt with a syringe in his arm, blue.' For all his private and public determination to avoid rockstar clichés, Kurt had fallen for the biggest of them all: shooting smack much stronger than he was used to. 'Hence the reaction,' said Anton, 'virtually ODing.'

Still wincingly unsure of the commercial potential of their new album, when *In Utero* was released on 13 September 1993, almost two years to the day since *Nevermind* broke the mould, DGC decided to take what it told America's leading music biz trade magazine, *Billboard*, would be a 'set things up, duck, and get out of the way' approach. So unconvinced was the company by the album's commercial potential, DGC didn't even release a single from it in America, issuing a video of 'Heart-Shaped Box' to MTV and sending the sparkly new Litt-mixed version to college and 'alternative' radio stations, but omitting to send anything to mainstream Top 40 radio stations in the US.

Adding to the impression that the album was a non-starter in the 'real' world, both Wal-Mart and Kmart, the two biggest retail chainstores in America, refused to stock it, objecting, they said, to the 'controversial' album artwork, specifically the back cover, a reproduction of one of Kurt's collages, this time of the tangled bodies and bones of several babies, both in and out of the womb, which he was quoted as describing as 'Sex and woman and *In Utero* and vaginas and birth and death.' There was also consternation about stocking an album on which one of the tracks was titled 'Rape Me'. DGC eventually reissued the album with a heavily edited version of Kurt's collage, and with 'Rape Me' relisted on the cover as 'Waif Me'. Kurt felt both justified and vilified by the news. He was mortified, though, when 'a spokesperson for Nirvana' explained in an official press release that the band had decided to edit the packaging themselves because as kids Cobain and Novoselic were only able to buy music from the two chain stores; as a result they 'really want to make their music available to kids who don't have the opportunity to go to mom-and-pop stores'.

None of which prevented *In Utero* from debuting in both the US and UK charts simultaneously at No. 1. It would eventually sell less than half the 30 million copies *Nevermind* had sold worldwide, but it was still one of the biggest-selling albums of 1993. Again, Kurt felt both justified and nonplussed. He needed a fix.

The rock press didn't care either way. They just wanted to make sure they were still welcome to the party. *Rolling Stone* in its review called the album 'brilliant, corrosive, enraged and thoughtful – a triumph of the will'. *Time* magazine's Christopher John Farley went further, stating: 'Nirvana hasn't gone mainstream, though this potent new album may once again force the mainstream to go Nirvana.' But it was David Browne's needlepoint review in *Entertainment Weekly* that really nailed it. 'The music is often mesmerising, cathartic rock'n'roll,' Browne wrote, 'but it is rock'n'roll without relcase.' While in Britain it was John Mulvey in the *NME* who came closest to really grasping what *In Utero* represented, when he wrote: 'As a document of a mind in flux – dithering, dissatisfied, unable to come to terms with sanity – Kurt should be proud of [the album]. As a follow-up to one of the best records of the past ten years it just isn't quite there.'

To help launch the album in America, the band were booked for their second appearance on *Saturday Night Live*. A show with a self-aggrandising tradition of 'controversial' performances, it agreed that Kurt should be allowed to perform 'Rape Me', in defiance of the cringe-making new album cover DGC was preparing, as well as the band's new 'alternative-only' single, 'Heart-Shaped Box'. A bigger surprise to Nirvana fans watching back home, however, was the unannounced inclusion of a new, fourth member: the guitarist Pat Smear.

That Kurt had wanted another guitarist in Nirvana was no big secret. He had been talking about one from the start, but after Jason Everman was let go in 1989, no more had come of it, at least not publicly. In fact, Kurt had sounded out Eugene Kelly of The Vaselines 18 months before. Kelly had been in the middle of recording his first album with his new band, Eugenius, at the time. 'There were loads of messages from their tour manager to call them,' he later recalled. 'I phoned them up in Los Angeles and . . . Kurt said to me, "We're having a three-month break, then I want you to come over and write songs, maybe join the band." I was like, yeah, definitely, but I've got to finish this record first. After that I never heard anything more. I'm kind of glad it didn't work out because I'd have come along and hit them with happy, poppy tunes, and *In Utero* wouldn't have happened.'

That last sentence seems highly unlikely, and may in part explain why Kurt never got back in touch. His days of including 'happy, poppy tunes' in his material were long over. Instead he turned to Pat Smear, whom Courtney had first met some years before, and who Kurt became casually acquainted with in the early Nineties when the largely unknown guitarist was working at the SST Superstore, selling punk rock vinyl and CDs.

Pat – real name: Georg Albert Ruthenberg – had just celebrated his thirty-fourth birthday when he got the phone call from Kurt that would finally, after 15 years of trying, make him a star. A native of Los Angeles, Georg had a bloodline which was an unusual blend of African American and Native American on his mother's side and German immigrant on his father's. Pushed into taking classical piano lessons as a child, he insists he'd never even heard any rock music until he was at high school. 'My parents didn't allow rock music in the house,' he once explained. 'I actually didn't even know it existed until I was probably eleven years old.' That changed when his parents bought his older sister three albums: the Beatles' *Sgt Pepper* and *Abbey Road* and George Harrison's *All Things Must Pass*. 'She just played them over and over and over . . . I just thought there was the Beatles – and everything else!'

By the time he met a 19-year-old high-school dropout named Paul Beahm, in 1977, Georg had taught himself to play guitar, taking inspiration from Brian May of Queen and Mick Ronson of Ziggy-era David Bowie. Latterly, he had also become obsessed with the British punk scene, obsessed with the intersexual look as much as the spastic-elastic music. His new friend Paul, who had recently changed his name, in true punk fashion, to Darby Crash, shared similar tastes in 'outrageous music', although Darby was more inclined to the Sid Vicious school of ultra-violent onstage action than he was the razor-sharp attitude of a Johnny Rotten. Both, though, had a love of Queen and Iggy Pop and it was on this common ground that they found their place together. With Darby as singer and Pat as guitarist, they would form the band that was to become the start of a musical journey which seemed doomed to failure.

Darby came from pain: an older brother, Bobby Lucas, who had been murdered in a drug deal gone bad, and a stepfather, Bob Baker, who had also checked out badly three years earlier. Brought up by an abusive single mother with her own mental health issues, Darby outlined to Ruthenberg, whom he now renamed Pat Smear, what he thought of as his five-year plan to make himself immortal. First off, form the most outrageous band ever. Next record just one great album. Then kill himself, thus ensuring his legend would live for ever.

Pat listened to all of this and thrilled to the thought. British punk rock had already arrived in Southern California, but it was only ever a second-hand version, based on out-of-date British music paper stories and pix, and simple word of mouth. The Sex Pistols, who they worshipped, never did play live in LA, and The Clash, whom they found too straight by comparison, didn't get there until 1979, when they headlined a sold-out show at the Santa Monica Civic. Instead, LA punk was like a sleazier version of original Detroit garage rock groups like Alice Cooper and The Stooges, with hot flushes of Bowie-as-Ziggy and Queen-as-Freddie-Mercury-plaything thrown in.

That was what Darby and Pat were aiming for anyway when they formed their group, Sophistifuck and the Revlon Spam Queens. Half boy, half girl (they advertised for 'two untalented girls', recruiting the bassist Lorna Doom and drummer Belinda Carlisle, whom Darby renamed Dottie Danger, but who soon left to form the Go-Go's), all amateur, none of the band, aside from Pat, could actually play when they did their first gigs. But that was beside the point. They changed their name to The Germs because it fitted better on T-shirts than Sophistifuck and the Revlon Spam Queens, and their shows were essentially triggers for full-on punk riots, with Darby, often tripping on stage, or simply high on anything anyone gave him, from booze to dope to speed to downers, throwing himself around the stage and among the audience, slashing open his chest with broken bottles and mangling lyrics to songs like 'Sex Boy'. Key line: *'I like it anywhere any time that I can / I'm the fucking son of superman!'*

'Whatever we were going to be, we were going to be the most,' said Pat. 'If we're gonna be punk, then we are gonna out-punk the Sex Pistols! If we are gonna be the worst band ever, then we are gonna be the fucking worst band ever!' It was a pledge they more than lived up to. Their only album, *(GI)*, aka *Germs Incognito*, was released by local LA punk label Slash Records in October 1979. Produced for peanuts by the former Runaways star Joan Jett, idolised by Darby and Pat, its 17 tracks recorded in a matter of days, the comparative clarity of the tracks, as opposed to the totally chaotic live performances, where Darby would deliberately not sing into the mic for half the show, lifted the band's reputation out of the punk gutter and into the pantheon of all-time LA punk classics. It even got reviewed in the *LA Times*, which described it as an 'aural holocaust'.

There was an extra element to what The Germs did, too, that some have theorised since may have had to do with Darby's closeted homosexuality. Was that inward-turned rage really just another expression of punk rock? Or was the boy railing against something more specific? Pat, too, liked to flaunt an androgynous allure that may have had more to it than just punk 'front'. Interviewed in the classic Penelope Spheeris movie documentary, *The Decline of Western Civilization*, about the LA punk scene of 1979–80, Pat cheerfully tells the camera: 'I'd probably hit lots of girls in the face. I don't like girls very much.' Not because he was a tough, butch guy. As he says, 'I've probably punched out everybody I know at one time or another. But I've always run afterwards because I can't fight.'

The question of Pat Smear's sexuality has been shushed and tutted over ever since. Darby eventually became much more open about his homosexuality, or bisexuality, as he saw it. Pat, despite his heavy makeup, loud clothes, black nail polish and generally effeminate mien, has never been so bold, at least not publicly. And why should he? What does it matter as long as his guitar playing is up to scratch? Yet it seems likely that it was this extra aspect of his personality that helped endear Pat to Kurt, as much as his musicianly abilities. Kurt also liked dressing up in feminine clothes and wearing outré makeup and nail polish. Lived to blur the masculine–feminine, in his music as much as his life. When asked about his love affair with Courtney by Michael Azerrad, he suggested it didn't matter whether his soulmate was a man or a woman as long as there was real love there on both sides. Or as he sang in 'All Apologies', one of the most affecting tracks from the *In Utero* album: '*What else should I say / Everyone is gay.*'

Less triumphal was the tragi-comic way Darby Crash eventually died. As good as his word, The Germs had split up in the months that followed the release of their 'one great album', dispirited by the near-impossibility of getting gigs (their reputation for leaving venues wrecked having turned off almost all of LA's club owners) as much as Darby's five-year plan for self-destruction. Then, out of the blue, a Germs 'reunion' show was announced for Wednesday, 3 December 1980. The venue was a packed Starwood club, on the corner of Santa Monica Boulevard. It was, typically, a chaotic affair, with Darby telling the crowd at one point, 'We did this show so you new people could see what it was like when we were around. You're not going to see it again.' On the night, it was interpreted as a literal farewell from the band. But Pat would later recall how in the run-up to the show, Darby had confessed to him: 'The only reason I'm doing this is to get money to get enough heroin to kill myself with.' Pat had heard stuff like that from Darby so many times over the years, though, he shrugged it off. 'He'd said that so many times I just said, "Oh, right", and didn't think about it any more.'

Four nights later, Darby and his then girlfriend, Casey Cola, were sitting on the floor of a backroom at her mother's house and shooting up $400 worth of heroin. Darby shot Casey up first, then himself, then held her in his arms while the lights went out. But Casey didn't die. Instead, she came to hours later to find a dead Darby in her arms. Blue at 22, he had kept his promise. But fate, always an unreliable witness, foiled his scheme, robbing him of even minor punk immortality when news of John Lennon's assassination by another painfully deluded young American hit the airwaves.

Pat Smear didn't know whether to laugh or cry, when he heard the news, he was too in shock, too afraid for his own future. Too busy chewing on a cigarette and hanging by the telephone. Three months later he had joined The Adolescents, Orange County's reigning punk rock kings. But left soon after when he decided he didn't want to tour with the band. The Germs had never left LA. The thought of being stuck in the back of a van with a bunch of laughing, farting smart boys was probably too much for the hypersensitive guitarist.

Pat spent the rest of the 1980s living off the fumes of an assumed outlandish past. There had been short-lived new wave bands like Twisted Roots, with Black Flag's former bassist Kira Roessler as vocalist, who were considered ultra-cool but too late out of the gate to get a deal; 45 Grave, with whom he recorded a single, 'Black Cross', before he split; a stint playing with punk-witch-queen Nina Hagen's live band; and two solo albums – *Ruthensmear* (1987) and *So You Fell in Love with a Musician* ... (1991), both released on the independent SST label, founded by Black Flag's Greg Ginn and early home to bands like Sonic Youth, Hüsker Dü, Meat Puppets and Soundgarden. Between times Pat had also built up a CV as a bit-part player in various movies and TV shows, starting as an extra in an episode of *Quincy, ME*, then appearing as a 'background artist' in *Bladerunner*, *Breakin'* and *Howard the Duck*. It was during this period he first met a teenage Courtney Love, whose lead part in Alex Cox's so-bad-it's-good cod-Western, *Straight to Hell*, also starring Joe Strummer, had been noticed by Pat and his one-day friend Kurt Cobain.

Cut to the summer of 1993, and after several weeks of to-ing and fro-ing about who to ask to join Nirvana as second guitarist – 'We talked about Steve Turner, we talked about Buzz Osbourne,' Dave Grohl later revealed, 'but of course we didn't want to break up Mudhoney or the Melvins' – Kurt suddenly decided to phone Pat. It had been what seemed like a lifetime since Pat had been in The Germs, but Kurt the punk-historian revered the story of Darby Crash. No matter that Pat's most recent claim to fame was an occasional appearance as a lisping fashion consultant on MTV's *House of Style*, starring the supermodel Cindy Crawford, as a guitarist he carried all the credibility that Kurt sought for himself.

'I'd read an interview with Kurt, where he said that Nirvana was meant to be a four-piece, and I thought that I could be that fourth member,' Pat later recalled in *Clash*. 'I was looking to search them out, to ask them about joining. And then I got the call – it was a big, crazy coincidence.' Before then, he'd been 'calling friends, asking for Courtney's number. I'd not had her number for a while, as she was always changing it. But the story

I heard about the call was that Kurt and Courtney were just sitting around, talking about potential second guitarists to bring into the band, and The Germs were playing in the background. And then Courtney says, "Hey, I know *this* guy . . ."'

At first, he'd thought it was a prank call. Then realised it really was Kurt Cobain on the phone. 'At the time I was working at a punk rock record store, not really thinking about playing music – I was kind of bored and sick of it and then this came along. It was all such a whirlwind . . .' According to Dave, speaking to *Mojo* in 2013: 'What Pat added more than anything was an injection of life and happiness to those last months of Nirvana . . . One of the first rehearsals, we were trying to figure out [David Bowie's] "The Man Who Sold the World" and the three of us just couldn't do it. Pat said, "Actually, it goes like this." I thought: "There's a musician in the band now!" Having Pat changed things dramatically. Kurt and Courtney were on that side of town and Krist and I were on this side of town, and Pat definitely bridged us back together for a while.'

But only for a while. In truth, Pat would always be more of a friend to Kurt and Courtney than to anybody else in Nirvana. For now, his debut appearance with the band on *Saturday Night Live* introduced a refreshingly kooky atmosphere to their per-formance. Just as Kurt begins to look all washed out and Krist's pogoing takes on a desultory, broken-willed aspect – Dave the only one left of the three still apparently giving his fiery all on the drums – Pat's angular old-school punk un-dance adds life to what is increasingly becoming a kind of musical wake for a de-ceased ideal, overexposed and undermined, cheaply surrendered.

It was a similar story for the now famous MTV *Unplugged* performance they filmed at the Sony Music studios in New York in November. The 22-date US tour they had completed between the two TV appearances has obviously beefed up the band's musical muscularity, everything suddenly coming easier for them now. But there is still an undeniable air of gloom pervading everything, as though conducting a public post-mortem, a sense of overwhelming ennui not helped by the deliberately tomb-like setting of flickering black candles, half-dead flowers, all bathed in hazed purple lighting, and an almost tangible feeling of having the dust settle onto you like a frost. Meanwhile, Pat, effeminate, half-caste, outcast, street cred to the max but no visible means of support, sits at the back *grinning*.

'We were really scared shitless about doing the *Unplugged* thing,' Dave said. 'We really had to sit down and think, "What are we going to do?"' Rehearsals had not gone well. Few Nirvana songs really fitted the all-acoustic format, forcing them to decide on a range of cover versions, comprising almost half the 14-song set. 'We thought, "Oh great, we're going to go out there and make fools of ourselves." But we got up and did it, and for some reason, it turned out okay. It was kinda nice cos it was the show that wasn't supposed to work,' he laughed. 'We were really looking forward to it sucking hard.'

Musically, though, *Unplugged* proved an unexpected triumph, even though the largely maudlin choice of songs – from their own decidedly downbeat versions of stuff like 'About a Girl' and 'Come as You Are' to brutally skull-and-bones versions of Bowie's 'The Man Who Sold the World' and the Vaselines' 'Jesus Doesn't Want Me for a Sunbeam', to positively ethereal versions of three Meat Puppets songs: 'Plateau', 'Oh, Me' and 'Lake of Fire', with the brothers Kirkwood, Curt and Chris, joining the band onstage to help out – turned the event into something more resembling a requiem than a celebration.

'Looking back at MTV's *Nirvana Unplugged* I view it, in retrospect, as [Kurt's] public suicide note,' says Chrissy Shannon. 'There is a point at the end of, "Where Did You Sleep Last

Night" where you see in his eyes a moment of absolute, searing pain. It's as if for a moment you witness him glimpse the other side and it's scary as fuck.'

During a lengthy local cable TV show interview in Minneapolis in December, when Pat was asked how playing in Nirvana compared to playing in his 'previous group' – meaning The Germs – Pat grinned and said, 'It's kind of the same.' Kurt, seated on the opposite side of the couch, his pinpricked eyes hidden behind plastic blue sunglasses, glances over and says in a comic voice, 'You mean you calling me Darby?' Pat, his hair now dyed blond, his eyes weighted with blue eye shadow and long, spider leg mascara, drawls, 'No [but] he's got the same problems.'

'Oh gee, I hope not,' says the interviewer, but the implication is there for all to see, Dave and Krist chuckling along nervously.

8. Death is a Call

When the end finally came, that cold, bloody day in April, a single blast from a 20-gauge Remington shotgun removing the top of Kurt's head and what was left of his mind, Dave Grohl – no matter what he said later – was deeply shocked but no longer really surprised. How could he be? As Charles Cross says now, 'He was Kurt Cobain's roommate and at one point one of his best friends.' By the end, though, 'he's an estranged band mate on a ship that's gonna hit an iceberg and neither he nor anyone else can stop that from happening.'

The European tour at the start of 1994 had been one long cold turkey. Without the regular supply of smack that he could get in the States, Kurt had hooked up with one of those London-based 'Doctor Feelgoods' familiar to music and movie stars of a certain celebrity status, who loaded Kurt up with prescriptions for enough opiates and tranquilisers to get him through the three-month tour. But still Kurt wasn't happy, fighting on the phone daily with Courtney, who was busy gearing up for the promotional campaign for the April release of the next Hole album, *Live Through This*. Falling out with Krist, whom he begged to let him cancel the dates, complaining of bad stomach pain and nausea, which Krist and Dave now routinely shrugged off, seeing it for what it was: Kurt's endless yearning to retreat to some darkened room where he could obliterate himself on heroin.

Adding to his misery while he was on the road in Europe was that he was now convinced that Courtney was having an affair with Billy Corgan of the Smashing Pumpkins. He knew the two had been an item in the past, sensed that Courtney had never really got over Billy, and was freaked out to find the Smashing Pumpkins were doing four dates in London during the last week of February, and that Courtney had been on the guest list for them all. Not only had she missed Kurt's twenty-seventh birthday on 20 February, but she was still in London for their second wedding anniversary four days later. As if to make Kurt even more paranoid, Courtney told him matter-of-factly that Billy had invited her to take a vacation in Paris with him. Stories would later emerge that Courtney *had* secretly gone with Billy to Paris, where the Pumpkins were booked to make an appearance on national TV, but these were later denied.

Whatever the truth, within days Kurt had called his lawyer in America and told her he wanted a divorce. He also found a German doctor willing to write him a medical note explaining he could no longer continue touring because of a mystery voice problem – finally getting his way when the next two weeks of European dates were cancelled. Dave and Krist, who knew exactly what kind of 'voice problems' Kurt was experiencing, flew home the next day. They knew when they weren't wanted. Kurt had stopped hanging out with them anywhere but on stage long ago. Dave and Krist didn't find Kurt funny any more. Not even on a good day. Pat still did. 'That's one reason Kurt liked Pat,' says Charles Cross. They shared the same twisted sense of humour. 'Kurt had a friendship and a kinship with him. Kurt never told me that personally but Courtney Love told me that. She said that towards the end of Nirvana, Kurt and Pat were closer than the other members of the band. Just based on that sense of humour.' Now, though, Kurt made his position even more clear to the rest of the band, relieved to see Dave and Krist go home, but persuading the guitarist to travel with him to Rome where he had arranged to meet Courtney.

'The longer things went on it seemed to get more and more personal,' says Anton Brookes. 'It just seemed to be more them two – Kurt and Courtney – against everybody else. I remember sometimes I'd been out with them and stood with management and the tour manager, and they'd go: "Do you mind going to get Kurt?"'

By the time Courtney, with baby Frances in tow, arrived at the luxurious Excelsior hotel in Rome on 3 March, he had apparently changed his mind about leaving her and bought her several reconciliatory gifts, including a dozen red roses, some rosary beads from the Vatican, a pair of three-carat diamond earrings – and a bottle of the heavy-duty tranquilliser Rohypnol ('roofies', in drug parlance, which would become more famous as a 'date-rape drug') from one of his London doctor's special prescriptions. But when Courtney said she was too tired that night to make love, for Kurt it was the last straw.

'Even if I wasn't in the mood I should have laid there for him,' Courtney later confessed to an American writer, David Frieke. 'All he needed was to get laid.' Too late. When she awoke the next morning, she found her husband's body unconscious on the floor, dozens of empty Rohypnol blister packs and over $1000 in cash by his side, and in his left hand a suicide note.

According to Charles Cross, who would become Cobain's most authoritative biographer, and who knew him well from his days as editor of Seattle's best-known local music paper, *The Rocket*, Kurt had tried to get clean in the weeks leading up to the European tour by checking into the Canyon Ranch, a luxury American health spa and wellness centre. There he had been told by one of the centre's physicians, Dr Baker, that the time had come for him to continue his addictions – that is, allow himself to die – or get clean, i.e. choose to live. A dead-eyed Kurt had replied: 'You mean, like Hamlet?' referring to Shakespeare's tragic hero.

In his Rome suicide note, Kurt wrote: 'Dr Baker says that, like Hamlet, I have to choose between life and death. I'm choosing death.' According to Cross, the rest of the note made reference to the fact that 'Courtney didn't love him any more', accusing her of sleeping with Billy Corgan. Over the coming weeks Kurt and Nirvana's management company, Gold Mountain, would all deny it was a suicide note and that Kurt's overdose had merely been accidental – like all his other recent overdoses. But given what happened just five weeks later, that now seems an absurd claim.

Rushed by ambulance to the nearby Umberto Polyclinic Hospital, Kurt had his stomach pumped of what was later reckoned to be over 50 of the pale green Rohypnol pills and at least half a bottle of champagne. But he remained in a coma, doctors warning Courtney that he might die, or, worse, wake up a vegetable, or, who knows, make a full recovery. They would have to wait and see. 'He was *dead*, legally dead,' Courtney later claimed. Kurt was then moved to the Rome American Hospital, where he very slowly over the next 24 hours regained consciousness, his first words to Courtney, upon partially awakening: 'Fuck you.'

Dave, like Krist, now back home in Seattle, claims the first he knew of what had happened was when he turned on the TV and 'Kurt was being wheeled away in an ambulance.' Years later, being interviewed for the Foo Fighters' film documentary, *Back and Forth*, Dave appeared to buy into the accidental-overdose theory. Kurt, he reckoned, had 'just made a mistake', took some pills, drank some vintage champagne, and got carried away with the razzmatazz of being in Rome. But that was Dave in

17-years-later, nicest-man-in-rock mode. Dave who'd by then had so many legal battles with Courtney he was extremely wary of inadvertently opening up any more cans of worms with her name on them.

The Dave Grohl of 1994, however, was frankly appalled, freaked out, ashamed and worried for his own future. Like, *what the fuck, dude*? We gave you the time off, *now this*? The day the news broke, CNN actually interrupted their regular broadcast to announce that the Nirvana singer had in fact died in a Rome hospital. Krist got a phone call at home from Gold Mountain confirming it. But that news proved false. Instead, Kurt flew home a week later with his wife and child, to his new $1.1 million mansion in Lake Washington, the most beautiful and exclusive part of Seattle – and a new kind of drug-induced hell.

The next few weeks found Kurt Cobain walking around as though he was already dead. He refused to return to Europe, where promoters had hoped Nirvana would play some re-scheduled shows. He even turned down a reported $8 million for Nirvana to headline that summer's Lollapalooza tour. He didn't want to rehearse or talk to Dave or Krist. As far as he and Dave were concerned, 'The band was broken up,' said Krist. 'It had sort of split off and it just got really weird,' said Dave. 'I don't do drugs [and] there were drugs around and there was like the people that did the drugs and the people that didn't do the drugs. And I didn't do the drugs and so I was just out of that world.' When you're a junkie, he shrugged, 'You don't care about anyone but yourself, at that point. That's how it works.'

When Courtney banned drugs from the house, Kurt checked into a sleazy motel and didn't even bother to use an assumed name. Just paid in cash and began shooting up again. Back at the Lake Washington mansion, his fights with Courtney became so out of control that police were summoned to the place more than once. The second time was because he had locked himself in one of the bathrooms with a load of guns, revolvers and shotguns and was threatening to kill himself. Courtney called 911 but Kurt put on his simple sweet face when they arrived, promising them he was not suicidal. 'He was *so* fucked up,' Krist would tell Charles Cross. 'He just wanted to die.'

There was an attempt at 'intervention' by a professional rehab counsellor just two weeks before Kurt finally did what he'd been threatening to. Courtney and several people from his record company and management office were there. Pat Smear was also there, the only member of Nirvana to be invited. Kurt ranted and raved and called them all hypocrites. At the end of it, Courtney got into a car, taking her to the airport and from there to LA, where she, too, was checking into rehab. The next day Kurt's mother, Wendy, made plans to fly down with Frances, so the toddler could be near her mother. And Kurt dived off the ledge into the big black hole below, never to return.

When news broke on the morning of 8 April 1994 that Kurt Cobain, singer of grunge superstars Nirvana, had committed suicide at his home in Seattle, loosing off a 20-gauge shotgun into his face, once again Dave Grohl was deeply shocked but very fucking far from surprised. 'I knew that he had gone,' he said, 'but I didn't know how to feel.' He added: 'I don't think Kurt wanted to become a huge fucking rock star, and I don't think he could handle how complicated it had all become.'

Seeing the shitstorm that was coming – the endless clichéd headlines written by people who had never even heard a Nirvana record: 'Tortured Grunge Icon', 'Slacker Poet' or, most frequent and appalling of all, 'Voice of a Generation' – Dave dropped right out of sight of the media. The day Kurt died, not knowing what else to do, he and his partner, Jenny, and several other close friends had gone over to Krist's house. 'It was such a weird time. We were kids. So it was strange . . . I couldn't listen to music. I *couldn't* listen to Nirvana. I'd turn on the radio and hear "All by Myself" [by Eric Carmen] and start crying. It was terrible.'

A couple of days later he simply pulled down the blinds and yanked up the drawbridge. Ran away and hid. Who could possibly blame him? Not even Dave though could imagine the endless river of shit he and Krist would be forced to wade through as the years went by and more and more stories emerged about Kurt's last days, how he'd hated Dave by the end, for daring to speak out about his appalling drug abuse, how he'd even fallen out with Krist, screaming in his face before running off to his drug dealer's apartment; more and more theories about how Kurt was murdered, by Courtney, by drug dealers, by accident, that he would never have killed himself, even though he'd both threatened and attempted it repeatedly in the weeks leading up to that final, successful attempt; more and more lies about what really was going on by the end of his life and what it really meant for the rest of us. People say it was the same when Jimi Hendrix died, when Jim Morrison died, when Elvis Presley and Sid Vicious died. And so it was in terms of conspiracy theories, of friends and lovers and band mates and fans left behind to wonder what *really* happened that night – because it was always night – and why?

In the case of Kurt Cobain though, unlike those other mythological rock stars, his death was a deliberate, pre-planned, suicide – the saddest, most tragic, most unforgivable kind of death, and the hardest to understand. Hence, to a large extent, the endless crazy stories that swirl around it to this day. Hence, too, the feelings of anger and betrayal that, in 1994, bedevilled those closest to Kurt in his lifetime, whom he'd now abandoned without even a goodbye.

That last year, says Charles Cross, 'there were times where the joy was gone. Then there were other times, even in the last few months of Nirvana's career, where there was an incredible amount of joy. I mean everybody loved *In Utero*. Dave loved it. He loved to play those songs. They were much more emotionally rewarding for him to play, the *In Utero* songs, than the *Nevermind* songs had been. Some of which, you know, the story that Dave told me repeatedly, on *Nevermind* there are some of those songs where he felt – I don't want to say *fraudulent*, but he was playing parts that Chad Channing had created.

'But there's a point where once the band became sort of Kurt's dictatorship, after the publishing deals were renegotiated and it was clear that it was gonna be Kurt calling all the shots, Dave shifted in the band. Both financially, emotionally, and I think things shifted in their friendship. They still had a friendship. They still had a kinship *but*, you know, Kurt at that point was a train wreck headed towards a wall and nobody could stop him, whether you were his band mate or his friend. Whatever role Dave had, whatever role Krist Novoselic had, which was always far deeper and a longer connection to Kurt, nobody could stop it.

'So, yeah, that last year was hell for everybody. The relationships were already frayed . . . [When Kurt died] essentially Nirvana was inches away from being broken up anyway. If Kurt would have lived or not, Nirvana was in all likelihood over. What the band had been was already lost. Even before Kurt died, the Nirvana that people knew and loved on *Nevermind* was already gone. And Dave sort of knew that and in some sense that's the beginning of Dave's solo [career].'

Even before Kurt had died, says Anton, 'The general feeling was that Nirvana had burnt out . . . It seemed like every other month or week there was a new "Kurt's dead" rumour.

I remember [the day Kurt died] all too well – it was a Friday afternoon, I was sat in the office and it just became a flood of calls. In your heart of hearts you're still clinging on to that hope that everything will be fine, it's just another false alarm. And then their tour manager called me up to say: "He's dead."'

Chrissy Shannon, who the same week had left behind the publicity department at DGC to work in A&R, was still tracked down by several journalists looking for a quote. 'One of them asked me how I felt about it and I couldn't believe they were asking us such stupid shit . . . I was devastated and, to make it worse, people kept printing that he couldn't handle the fame and I had done my best to get him there, so I actually felt really guilty for a while!

'Was he murdered? I don't think so. I think he was miserable and in a lot of pain and tied to a crazy woman and he took what he thought would be the fastest route out. I know he loved Frances and I have a sad feeling that due to his bleak outlook on the world and his addiction he felt like he could only be a bad dad. But, who knows, I've also read that he had contacted a divorce lawyer and had been talking to Michael Stipe about working on something together in the future . . .'

No one would ever really know. Not even the other members of Nirvana. Krist was so devastated, not just by the suicide, but by the whole journey to the end of night, that he would never work full-time in a band again. According to Pat Smear, 'Kurt passed on and my life went back to how it was. I went inward and was a hermit for a while. I didn't play at all until Dave [Grohl] came by – he was in LA – and dropped off a tape. It was the Foo Fighters album. It was the first thing that got me interested in music again.'

But that was months later and in the immediate ghastly aftermath of Kurt's death, Dave found himself in a place he'd never been before: a strange, shadow world where for a long time 'nothing made sense'. Nor would it ever again. Not when he would look back on his time in Nirvana. It's the main reason why he was not prepared to indulge in those games of 'what if?' that journalists are so fond of. Dave didn't know why Kurt killed himself any more than you did, not really. Dave didn't know what would have become of Nirvana had Kurt not blown his brains out, other than to recall how the band had in reality already fallen apart long before Kurt took it upon himself to make it official. Like the rest of us, Dave could only guess. The only thing he knew for sure when it happened was that he had been out on his own for a long time before that. That, really, his plans had never changed. Would never change. Another Dave – Bowie – had once famously sung of kicking it in the head when he was 25. But that was never this Dave's trip. He still saw a future for himself. Of course he did. Why wouldn't he? Unlike Kurt, who always agonised over silly shit like what the cool punk crowd made of his rock star success, Dave embraced it. As he laughingly told *Rolling Stone*, 'I was lucky, because I went back to Washington, DC, and had all my heroes tell me they were proud that I became a fucking corporate rock star! That weight was lifted from my shoulders, right out of the game. I never worried about that.'

Dave now strove hard to put as much distance between himself and the tragic mess of Kurt's life and disgusting death as he could. He refused to visit the funeral home where Kurt's body lay prior to his cremation, and made plans instead to escape home to Virginia, and so-called normality. His two and a half years being the drummer in Nirvana had been the longest, hardest, most extraordinary and rewarding of his life. But now Kurt was dead, the dream was over, only the nightmare remained. What *was* he to do?

The morning after Kurt's funeral, Dave would later recall, 'I woke up and I thought, "Holy shit, he's gone and I'm still here. I get to wake up and he's gone." And then my life completely changed for ever.' As if to reaffirm his own contract with life, to show to himself how much he still wanted to live, Dave married his long-term girlfriend, Jennifer Youngblood.

He wondered if he should reactivate his long-ago teenage dream of becoming a simple session musician, a hired gun paid top dollar to come in and do his sweet thing. And, at first, that's what he seemed to be gravitating towards. Having played drums on the soundtrack to a new Beatles-related movie, *Backbeat*, which was released with unerring inappropriateness – at least for Dave – the week following Kurt's suicide, later that year he agreed to act as Tom Petty's drummer for an appearance on *Saturday Night Live*. It was no secret that Petty was so impressed – and Dave so at ease with the rest of the band, so different to the febrile atmosphere surrounding Nirvana even at the best of times – that an invitation to sign on full-time was issued and contemplated for several days. Before Dave finally said no. Then wondered what the hell he'd done.

'It turned out that [Tom] and the other guys in the band were really big Nirvana fans,' Dave remembered. 'So then I was worried that maybe they had watched MTV *Unplugged* and they didn't know that I actually played really loud. I agreed to do it, of course, because Tom Petty is an incredible guy, and spent a week with them rehearsing and played on the television show. Within that week and a half, they had managed to make me feel like I was part of the band. And it was the first time I had that feeling since Nirvana. It was just awesome, to have friends you can play music with, to be happy with, you know, to go with to the bar and talk and then go back and play some more. It was just amazing. I was really this close to doing it.'

There was also talk around the same time of Dave joining Pearl Jam. Dave bridled at the rumours but never actually denied them. Same deal with more loose talk about a collaboration between Dave and former Misfits frontman Glen Danzig, replacing Chuck Biscuits, whom, ironically, Dave had revered as a young drummer. Ultimately, said Dave, 'I didn't want to be a drummer for hire at twenty-five. By the time I was forty I would've been on the Jay Leno show. I was really torn.' But Dave was already looking beyond that, having his own big ideas. 'It was play drums with Tom or do something I had never done before. I thought I might as well try something new while I'm young.'

That something new would entail going back and redoing something old. Back in 1990, not long after he'd joined Nirvana, Dave had hooked up again with his friend Barrett Jones to record – 'for fun!' – a six-track demo in Barrett's eight-track studio. These were tracks all written solely by Dave, with Dave playing all the instruments – including the original version of 'Just Another Story about Skeeter Thompson'. The following summer, he went into WGNS Studios and recorded four more tracks. Again, ostensibly 'for fun', though it's impossible now not to look back on these sessions as Dave's way of doing something on his own without the extra pressure of thinking they might be of any use to Nirvana.

When the combined cassette tape found its way into the hands of fellow Washington-based indie rocker and arts activist Jenny Toomey, she suggested releasing it on her own small independent label, Simple Machines. By now, Nirvana had hit the big time and Dave agreed on the proviso it only came out as a cassette tape, and absolutely not under his own name, but that of Late!, a name chosen, he said, 'because I'm an idiot and I thought it would be funny to say to everybody, "Sorry, we're Late!"' Titled *Pocketwatch*, what's most striking about these tracks now is both the similarity to Nirvana – the signature downtuned guitars and rocket-fuelled drums and deadpan vocals on rockers like 'Petrol CB', as well as the same lo-fi, cigarette-lit ballads on tracks like 'Friend of a Friend' – and the future echo of how the Foo Fighters would sound, on slightly more sophisticated, melodic rockers like 'Throwing Needles'.

'I always tried to keep them sort of a secret,' Dave would later explain. 'I wouldn't give people tapes. I always freaked out about that. I have the stupidest voice. I was totally embarrassed and scared that anyone would hear them. I just wanted to see how poppy or how noisy a song I could write. It was always just for fun. You could do anything you wanted.' It stopped being 'just for fun', though, the day Kurt walked in on Dave at their shared Olympia apartment and caught him noodling around on a tape recorder with the vocals to another track destined for the *Pocketwatch* tape called 'Colour Pictures of a Marigold'. 'We sat there and played it a few times,' Dave said. 'I would do the high harmony, he would do the low harmony. It's funny writing songs with other people – sitting face to face with someone, that's another trip. I don't know if he had ever done that either. It was like an uncomfortable blind date. "Oh, you sing too? Let's harmonise together."'

When Steve Albini also later heard the tape, he suggested they include 'Marigold', as the new Nirvana take was to be known, on the *In Utero* album. 'I was terrified!' laughed Dave. 'No, no, wait! It was that famous joke: What's the last thing the drummer said before he got kicked out of the band? "Hey, I wrote a song."'

In the event, Nirvana would place the track on the B-side of the 'Heart-Shaped Box' single. 'To be fair, "Marigold" is quite a throwaway song compared to a lot of the songs Dave has written now,' Anton points out. 'It didn't really give much indication to his prowess as a songwriter.' What is less well-known, according to Anton, was that both Kurt and Krist were aware that Dave had 'written some other songs, which Kurt was gonna use on the next Nirvana album. Kurt wasn't that keen on some of the lyrics. But he liked the songs. And I think that was part of Dave's learning curve, as a lyricist. He had been behind the master', and that informed everything he did next 'as a musician, as a songwriter, as a lyricist and as a performer'.

In fact, some years after Kurt had died, Dave finally fessed up to the fact that he had played Kurt a handful of his own songs, two of which would actually end up on what became the first Foo Fighters album. Speaking on the *Howard Stern Show* in New York, he said: 'I played him tapes of stuff and there were a few songs that Kurt liked a lot and wanted to turn into Nirvana songs but for some reason never did. The song "Alone + Easy Target", Kurt really liked that song a lot. He liked the chorus a lot and I think he wanted to make the chorus into something.' Hardly surprising, as the chorus sounds like a typical Nirvana move. 'And then there's a song called "Exhausted", that apparently – he actually never said it to me – but he liked the song a lot. He just wanted to write his own lyrics to it. I think he was afraid to ask me if we could do the song but with his lyrics. Which I would have said, shit, sure. Fine. That would be great.' Dave didn't push it, though, because how could he when he was in a band with Kurt Cobain, now being hailed as being up there as a revolutionary songwriter alongside John Lennon and Bob Dylan. Nor did Dave exactly broadcast the fact that he was now writing his own songs outside of Nirvana, 'because I was nervous about it'.

Charles Cross reveals, however, that the band, minus Kurt, actually rehearsed a selection of original Grohl material, at the final Nirvana recording session, in Seattle's modest Robert Lang

Studios, in January 1994, where the last known Nirvana track, 'You Know You're Right', was also demoed. 'I think there's a seminal turning point here for Dave,' he says now. 'Nirvana has three days, four days, five days of sessions booked. Where they're gonna begin working on new material. And Kurt does not show for the entire first day. So you have Novoselic, you have Grohl. I think Pat Smear was there. You have these guys just sitting around basically doing nothing. And they worked through some of Dave's stuff. So that's when Dave first worked on some of his material.

'Then of course Robert Lang's is where Dave [later on] does almost all of the recording of the first couple of [Foo Fighters] records . . . So that was really a huge turning point. Suddenly Kurt not showing up, Dave is both probably rethinking his career but they're also just trying to fill time. And Dave began a friendship, a kinship, with Robert Lang, who ran that studio and out of that we get the first two Foo Fighters records, mixed and recorded.

'If Kurt would have shown up and Nirvana would have continued, maybe it would have gone the other way. Maybe Dave's solo project would have never have been released. Or maybe it would have been released on a tiny indie label, which was part of his concept for him putting it out. I very vividly remember him telling me he wanted to put it out as a cassette-only release on a tiny punk label. Then Kurt dies and suddenly the whole landscape changes.'

Pat Smear, who more than anybody in Nirvana would play a significant role in helping Dave find his next level as a songwriter also later recalled how, 'There was one day, after a Nirvana practice, before we'd begun the *In Utero* tour, where we were sat in Dave's car, and he played me some of his solo stuff. I guess they were early demos for what would be that first Foo Fighters album, but I can't be sure. But they blew me away. These were amazing songs, and I remember saying to him, "Man, you should be doing these properly."'

First though, says Anton, would come a great deal of soul searching. Dave knew it would not simply be a case of just carrying on as though nothing had happened. 'Look at Krist, God bless him,' sighs Anton. 'Krist has never recovered from what happened to Nirvana. When [Kurt] died a big part of Krist died. And Dave could have gone the same way. But even though Dave was close to Kurt he wasn't as close as Krist. They had grown up together. The three of them were brothers, to an extent. But Kurt and Krist were almost like twins.'

By the late summer of 1994, however, Dave Grohl had made up his mind. 'Whatever he did next, he knew he was never gonna win,' says Anton. 'He knew because of the cult surrounding Kurt there would be people who said, "How dare Dave get on with his life and try and salvage something from the train wreck which was Nirvana." But when Nirvana went down, Dave retrieved the black box and got on with his life. He licked his wounds and just got on with it. Every so often we'd just look at each other and go, "What the fuck happened?" Even now, you know? None of us really understand what happened and how it happened and how Kurt is dead and he's not with us. All Dave knew was that, really, he had no choice, he had to carry on.'

9. Grunge Ringo

In the depths of his depression, Dave received a postcard from the members of another Seattle band. One named 7 Year Bitch, not nearly as famous as Nirvana but who had, nevertheless, faced a similar experience when their 24-year-old guitarist and co-founder, Stephanie Sargent, died of a heroin overdose in June 1992. 'Basically, it said, "We know what you're going through, we went through it too, we know that you're feeling like you never want to play music again, but that will change." And it did,' he recalled in a moving 1995 interview with the foremost Australian DJ and music journalist, Richard Kingsmill. 'I'm for ever in debt to them for that,' said Dave. 'I've been touring in bands since I was seventeen years old and there is not much else that I know as well as playing music. It's like kicking a nasty habit. I just don't think I would be able to do it. And that is when I realised there is no way I am going to be able to stop doing what I've done for ten years. I can't stop . . . plus I knew it was good for me to keep going, just to keep moving.'

It was on his honeymoon with Jenny in Dublin that Dave bought the mini electric guitar that he wrote 'This is a Call' and 'Wattershed' on, both destined to become cornerstone tracks on the first Foo Fighters album, and both so good even Dave recognised it. This was the next important step towards finding a future he could truly see for himself. Looking back, he admitted he had fallen 'immediately in a depression' when Kurt killed himself. He saw it as the end of his career, something he was never going to be able to come back from. To battle those feelings he agreed to see a therapist, which 'was good', he said. But he still 'didn't know if I ever wanted to play drums again. Just sitting down at the drum set just reminded me of Kurt, reminded me of Nirvana and it was just sad . . .' Writing those two new songs in Ireland appeared to him to be a sign – of life after death; of renewal. Above all, of being given a fighting chance to somehow survive what seemed until then utterly impossible.

He knew what he had to do; it was just finding a way to actually do it. The easiest – and hardest and stupidest – thing to do would have been to simply get a new singer in. The way Van Halen had done, for example, just a few years before, replacing the until then 'irreplaceable' David Lee Roth with the on paper more staid but ultimately much more popular and, for Van Halen, even more successful Sammy Hagar. Or, closer to home, the way Pearl Jam's Stone Gossard and Jeff Ament had replaced their original singer, Andrew Wood, in their hotly tipped-for-success previous Seattle outfit, Mother Love Bone – going on to even greater success with Eddie Vedder. Or the way so many earlier classic rock acts from the Seventies had done, like Deep Purple, Black Sabbath or Bad Company.

But that would have been a joke, and one in very poor taste. The thought of forming a band with Krist and getting a new frontman in was something they never even *tried* to talk about. That would have been '*way* too heavy', Dave said. 'We've *never* talked about that. Ever. It's twenty years and we still haven't talked about it.' In fact, Dave and Krist had explored the possibilities of at least playing together again, jamming together in secret. 'Yeah, we thought about it,' Dave admitted a few months later. 'But when it came to actually making Foo

Fighters a band, I'm just not sure that Krist wanted to start up and be a bass player right away again. It just fizzled and we forgot about it.' He added, 'There weren't any harsh feelings or anything at all. I think we were both really happy to do our own things.'

There was another reason, though, why Dave didn't want to become involved in trying to build something new with Krist: his absolute need to move as far away from the Nirvana narrative as possible. He knew he would never be able to step out of the shadow of the band completely, but he was damned if he was going to willingly allow himself to be trapped there for ever. Dave also knew, though he would never come right out and say it, that any group he might put together with Krist would be a partnership, at best, and that in any partnership with his former Nirvana band mate there would be only one real equal and that sure as shit wasn't going to be Dave. Krist, four years older and several lifetimes deeper, had always been Dave's senior in Nirvana. That would not change now just because Nirvana had gone. Dave may not have known yet exactly what he was going to do, but one thing he was sure of, it would have to be something that was all about him. No one else.

In the end he simply told himself he would have no plan, just go into the studio with his old pal Barrett Jones and make some music, just like the old days. He had enough songs, nearly 40, he reckoned, if you included all the scraps and half-starts. Swearing everyone to secrecy, he discreetly booked a week at Robert Lang studios in October. Didn't even bother to bring in any extra musicians, would just lay down a demo, playing and singing everything himself. Just to see. Just to know. Just to do . . . something.

The previous month he and Krist had been involved in overseeing the mix of Nirvana's live *Unplugged* sessions, which

DGC were preparing to release as a stand-alone album. 'I re-member . . . that was extremely difficult,' he said. 'That's the album that it's most difficult for me to listen to. Just because it's so eerie and stark . . . It's just so bare-boned.'

He told himself that going in with Barrett would be different, that he was doing this 'for fun', not as his attempt to build a bridge to a future without Kurt and Nirvana. Yet he recorded the tracks in exactly the order they would later appear on the first Foo Fighters album, beginning with 'This is a Call', a sym-bolic choice with its chorus of, *'This is a call to all my past resignations . . .'* Dave would later tell journalists that 'This is a Call' was a song 'just basically thanking and paying respects to everybody that I have ever been close to . . . Whether it was friends, or previous bands.' But everyone knew that was a lie. That it was about Kurt and Krist and the life they had now been denied, and that Dave was free to now look back on and allow the distance to grow and be felt properly.

As if to prevent him from overthinking what he was doing, Dave raced through the recording process. 'This is a Call' set the pace: two takes, total playing time just under 45 minutes. 'It became this little game,' he later told *Alternative Press*, 'I was running from room to room, still sweating and shaking from playing drums and pick up the guitar and put down a track, do the bass, maybe do another guitar part, have a sip of coffee and then go in and do the next song. We were done with the music in the first two days.'

Although Dave would later employ the production team of Tom Rothrock and Rob Schnapf, who'd recently hit the big time with their work on Beck's *Mellow Gold* album, to mix the tapes – to lift them out of that sludgy home-recording vibe and onto a level where college radio, at least, would be comfortable playing them – the finished cassettes that he now started fanning out to anyone who wanted one was the template for everything the Foo Fighters would become famous for over the next three years. Twelve mainly rifftastic songs that got in, did their thing, and got out again – fast. There were no guitar solos, few real lyrics, and lead vocals so low down in the mix they effectively became another texture to the overall sound. The fist-tight rhythms were as brutal and as inventive as anything from the *Nevermind* period of Nirvana, but it was the sugar-shocked vocals that really did the job, where all the melody lay, all the catchiness. So that when tracks like 'I'll Stick Around' – one of four major highlights alongside 'This is a Call', 'Big Me' and 'For All the Cows' – were pilloried in the rock press for sounding too much like Nirvana, it hardly mattered. This was punk done with a bright pop sheen, unencumbered by the bloodied tendrils that had trapped so much of Nirvana's latter-stage material.

As Anton Brookes puts it, 'To an extent the Foo Fighters are Nirvana-lite, aren't they? It's not as intense. It's not as dark . . . Foo Fighters songs are not ugly-beautiful. But they have passion. It's just that the Foo Fighters [music] is sleek and it's well drilled and it's got diversity and everything. But the Foos' songs are completely different [to Nirvana's]. I think, to an extent, a lot of Nirvana's songs can be a little *too* heavy, mentally, for people to digest. It's like listening to Joy Division or something. Where the Foo Fighters is . . . and I'm not dumbing down here or anything . . . but you can put the Foos Fighters on and it's more enjoyable. It's more of a good time. Nirvana was never a good time . . .'

Buoyed by the good reactions his cassettes were getting from friends like Krist Novoselic and Alex Macleod, Nirvana's tour manager, Dave now sent a copy to Gary Gersh, Nirvana's A&R guru at DGC, now running the ship at Capitol Records, along with a hope-ya-like-it-no-biggie note. Leaving as little as possible to chance, though, he also sent a copy to Gersh's successor at DGC, Mark Kates. 'That's when things started getting a little crazy,' Dave later remarked disingenuously.

It's since become part of the Foo Fighters orthodoxy that Dave Grohl more or less fell accidentally into starting his own 'band'. That he'd made this tape 'for fun' that he'd really never intended releasing, slapping the made-up name 'Foo Fighters' onto it to disguise the fact it was actually the new thing from the drummer in Nirvana. That as the goofy smiley one of the group he simply didn't have that kind of shrewd, street-level suss to really know what he was doing.

In fact, the 'craziness' he spoke of was exactly what Dave had been banking on. His timing, as ever, was impeccable. It was no coincidence that the same month Dave began talking to both Capitol and DGC about a solo deal, the final 'real time' Nirvana album, *MTV Unplugged in New York*, was released, going straight to No. 1 simultaneously in Britain and America and topping the charts in six other countries. Less than three weeks later, on 19 November, Dave appeared with Tom Petty on *Saturday Night Live*. With his profile sky-high again and the most commercial-sounding album Nirvana never made under his belt, he was not short of offers to start again, but this time entirely on his own terms.

But this is where he really showed his hard-won street smarts. Instead of signing directly to either Capitol or DGC, or indeed any other major label, Dave Grohl, on the advice of the same Gold Mountain management team behind Nirvana, as well as the same lawyers, formed his own label, Roswell, and fashioned a production deal for himself, whereby he would retain control of all decisions pertaining to the Foo Fighters, while at the same time receiving the not inconsiderable benefit of the distribution,

marketing and promotion that only a major label could provide. He also rightly decided to eschew renewing his business
relationship with DGC in favour of sticking with Gary Gersh,
the man who not only signed Nirvana but also helped steer it
through its greatest commercial success with *Nevermind*.

Having spent his whole career, until then, prey to the whims of
others as the last to join groups whose destinies already seemed,
in some way, preordained, having spent, most perniciously, the
past two years being the victim of a singer whose horrendous
personal life had eventually nearly destroyed his own, Dave
Grohl was determined never to be put in that position again – by
anybody, friend or foe.

'One of the key things about the Foo Fighters that so few
bands have got is that they own their own masters,' says Paul
Brannigan. 'Roswell is Dave's record label and they license the
records to a major. Dave's attitude is, I *am* the record company,
so I never have to take orders from anyone else again about how
things work. I don't think he's got an axe to grind against the
major-label world, because of what happened with Nirvana. But
his upbringing was in DIY punk rock and that was how things
operated among all his friends in Washington, so it wasn't a
unique concept to him, either.

'So when the opportunity presented itself, I think, basically,
he sat down with his lawyer, and his lawyer said, you can sign
to a record label, or you can be the record label and you can
just license these records. It was probably the smartest decision
he ever made. It allowed him autonomy over everything. It
allowed him never to have to answer to anybody's whims but
his own, particularly as things became so successful from the
start.'

Quite so, but there were still more moves for Dave to make,
the small stuff that he knew from experience would make the

big difference. Like recruiting the right band. Now that he had his new record deal in place, Dave was ready to think about that. Secure in the knowledge that he would be in charge this time, that he already had an album in the can awaiting release, and that he had his own label, lawyers and heavy-duty management behind him, he switched back into simple-muso mode and went about persuading people it was a real *band* he was looking to put together.

That was how he put it anyway when he first spoke to Nate Mendel and William Goldsmith. Nate and Will had been the bassist and drummer, respectively, in Sunny Day Real Estate, a good-not-great, second-rung Seattle band that had conveniently just split up when Dave first called. Dave had caught them live a couple of times as they toured promoting their debut Sub Pop album, *Diary*. It's hard to believe he found anything much to like about the songs – although Sunny Day Real Estate would posthumously be tagged as one of the seminal 'second wave' Emo acts, with their single 'Seven' receiving generous after-hours MTV play, their whole mien was so earnest they were a tough act to really love – he was impressed enough by the rhythm section of Mendel and Goldsmith to make a move when he found out they were available.

Once again, his timing was spot on. Will and Nate were at a 'low point', the former told *Alternative Press*. 'I was just thinking, "What the hell am I going to do?" That was all I had pretty much been doing. I had finally focused on one band and now that was over.' Then a friend of Dave's wife Jenny passed on the cassette and told them to wait for a call. 'We listened to the tape and we liked it a lot, but we didn't know what would happen next,' said Will. But to their relief and surprise, 'It was a great phone call. He was like, "Oh, so your band's in the shitter?" I told him yes. He said, "All right. Let's play."'

Getting Nate in too was just a bonus, to begin with. Finding a competent bass player was never going to be that hard among the overflowing gene pool of Seattle talent. At first, Nate admits, he had a problem 'playing in front of people'. When he told Dave and suggested that maybe he shouldn't do it, Dave told him that was exactly the reason he should do it. Neither man really knew what that was supposed to mean, but it sounded non-judgemental enough to placate nervous Nate and he went ahead with the job.

Dave's main focus now though was on finding someone he felt comfortable with to play the drums – almost mission impossible, given how Dave was now regarded as one of the best drummers in the world. He did his best to play down the role, though.

'I went into it with the attitude that I'm not going to hand someone this tape that I just recorded and say, "Learn all these drum parts backwards." I want them perfect but there is no way I'm going to go to someone and say that because the record is just the way *I* would have done it. I tried to find a drummer that had enough feeling to go and put himself into it. William can do everything that I can do.' Dave told him, 'Just learn the arrangement of the song and then I don't give a fuck what you do with it after that.' Will, he insisted, 'is an amazing drummer. When I saw him play with Sunny Day Real Estate, then heard that they were breaking up, it was like I had won the lottery.'

Dave, of course, had already won the lottery when he joined Nirvana. He would leave very little to chance in the Foo Fighters. That said, even Lucky Dave felt like the cat who'd got the cream with his next move – getting Pat Smear to agree to sign on. 'I didn't expect Pat would want to play with me,' he insisted. Nevertheless, it didn't stop him slipping Pat a copy of the by now much-vaunted cassette while having a drink with him one night in LA.

When Pat got back to say he'd been listening to the tape and really liked 'For All the Cows', Dave got up the courage to ask him if he might be interested in . . . maybe . . . if he had nothing else to do . . . maybe . . .

Pat said he'd think about it.

'For the next couple of weeks I thought he was just being nice and wasn't really one hundred per cent into it,' said Dave. 'Until I called him and said, "What are you doing?" He said, "I'm getting my guitars ready for the tour." I said, "Who are you going on tour with?" And he said, "Us, man!" I swear to God, I thought he was too cool for it.'

The fact that Pat lived in LA – and not Seattle, like the other three – made him exotic, suspicious, 'other'. Definitely outside the comfort zone of Nate and William. But Dave needed Pat the most, the only one who really knew what he'd been through with Kurt and Nirvana, who could really relate to Dave's own outsider status in that band, which got worse and worse as Kurt's heroin habit did. Then once Pat started to play and the other two saw how easy Dave was around him, how much Dave needed someone who was more on his been-there level, the quicker they got used to it.

Still insisting to his new recruits that the Foo Fighters, though the first album was essentially a Dave Grohl solo production, was in every other respect a band of equals, Dave gave the go-ahead for his management to light the fire. A 'limited edition' 12-inch vinyl single of the album's closing track, 'Exhausted', was issued to college and alternative radio stations in January, and half a dozen tiny club dates were booked as warm-ups for a tour in late February and March. At close to six minutes, 'Exhausted' was the longest, least obviously commercial track on the album. It was also one of the songs that Kurt had expressed a liking for before his death. Therefore a strong choice as the track to introduce the Foo Fighters to what Dave implicitly understood would be largely the Nirvana audience, at least to begin with.

Sure enough, its bones-into-dust riff, wilfully distorted guitars and spaced-out vocals convinced enough to start a buzz about the new band, though the vibe was kept deliberately low-key, at least for now. 'I drove to a couple of their rehearsals with Dave,' says Charles Cross, 'and we're talking about a van loaded with crap. It's not only a van, it's Nirvana's van that Dave has kind of inherited.'

Their first show had been at a friend's house in Seattle. 'We bought a keg so everyone would get drunk and be like, "You guys are really good",' he later recollected with a smile. Their first officially billed show came a few days later at a small venue in Seattle's centre called the Velvet Elvis. Charles Cross was there for that one. 'There's no roadies. There's nobody else other than the members of the band. So their first show they had some other guy come in and help plug some guitars in while they weren't onstage. But there really wasn't a stage. We're talking a quad where you have to walk in front of the audience to get to the stage. It's a tiny, tiny place that literally held forty people. Dave very, very consciously at that point was trying *not* to make this a big deal. He wanted it to be an underground thing.'

Cross goes as far as to say he believes Dave 'didn't want it to be a big success'. He explains: 'I think it was a reaction to Nirvana. He wanted it small and he wanted it, ultimately, to be more of a democracy than it ended up. You have Pat Smear, you have the two guys from Sunny Day Real Estate, and I think his conception initially would be beyond his solo project, the idea of the band. Like this superstar group where these four guys are gonna play and everybody in the band has done something notable before. This is in Seattle, where egos don't matter. It doesn't matter that you're Dave Grohl and you're the drummer in Nirvana, you're still gonna be one of the members of this band early on. And that was the ethos of that first few months of the Foo Fighters.

'What changed, of course, was that the [first album] did better than anyone expected. Better, I'm almost certain, than Dave expected. That record got a lot of attention. Now he's obviously become something entirely different but my sense, truly, was that what he wanted [originally] with this band was to kind of wash his mouth out of all the bad taste of what Nirvana had become. How bloated, how gigantic, how unable to escape these demands on them . . . Dave wanted a band where he didn't have to play any Nirvana songs again. Where he could do something entirely different. And he had that for a very brief window of time. But early on, I'm absolutely convinced, from talking to Dave, from witnessing those first shows, from seeing the state of their van or their rehearsal studio, I'm absolutely convinced there was no idea that *anyone* had that they were gonna be this big. Nobody. Nobody thought that.'

Not for long, anyway. Released on 4 July 1995, *Foo Fighters* sold over 40,000 copies in the United States in the first week of release, lifting it to a debut position of No. 23. In the UK it did even better, rising almost immediately to No. 3. While around the world the album would reach the charts in half a dozen other countries. Boosted by the success of 'This is a Call', the first single proper released from the album, which made the Top 10 in nine countries, including the UK, where it reached No. 5 and America, where it went to No. 2 on the influential *Billboard* Alternative chart, the Foo Fighters didn't have long to be an underground band. They may still have been playing clubs by the time they'd begun their headline tour of the US, but they had also headlined their own much-hyped London show, at King's College, on 3 June, to which the entire London music scene appeared to show up, and made their first appearance on *Late Show with David Letterman*, then the hippest, most prestigious showcase on American television.

Watching the Letterman performance now, it's striking how much the Foos really do come across as a band, as opposed to how they would appear in years to come, as members came and went and Dave's confidence as a bandleader grew. The Mandel–Goldsmith combo looks on fire, locked together as closely as cogs in a wheel. Pat Smear is also at the top of his game, his hair dyed blond again, rocking on the balls of his feet as he blasts out the song. It's suddenly easy to see why Dave was so relieved to get Pat in the band. Yes, he's got the punk-cred and the grunge-cool, but he's got something else too. Pat's got glam. So that while the rest of the band – including Dave, in his nondescript white T-shirt and face hidden behind that curtain of hair – are workmanlike and sweaty, Pat is effortlessly cool. Just the hint of a smirk on his face, like this is all just too fucking easy, dude, you get me? Oh, yeah . . .

Everywhere the Foo Fighters went that first year they made friends, influenced people. Not least when they appeared at the Reading Festival in August, headlining the smaller *Melody Maker* stage, the day after Hole had opened beneath the Smashing Pumpkins on the larger main stage, and the setting three years before for Nirvana's last British concert. So much had changed since then, yet the ghost of Kurt hung heavy in the air. Many of the fans gathered in front of the stage for the Foos were in Nirvana T-shirts, some even yelled for 'Smells Like Teen Spirit', others not knowing what to yell for yet, just yelled anyway. The ones that came away most impressed, though, it seemed, were the ones merely curious to see what Nirvana's drummer was doing now – and were amazed to see how well he was doing it. Not just fans, but other bands, other media folk, other you-name-its attracted initially, no doubt, by the prospect of entertaining an actual living member of the sacred Nirvana, but just as easily hooked on the goofy-smiles of Dave and Pat and the happy-talk their music made, no matter how concentrated Nate and Will's grimacing became.

And this was important. In a year that saw big, multi-platinum album releases from other hot-right-now American acts like the Red Hot Chili Peppers (*One Hot Minute*), Alanis Morissette (*Jagged Little Pill*), Green Day (*Insomniac*), Pearl Jam (*Vitalogy*) and Smashing Pumpkins (*Mellon Collie and the Infinite Sadness*), Dave knew he could take nothing for granted. When *Foo Fighters* somehow found itself listed in both the *Rolling Stone* and *Spin* end-of-year best-of albums list, Dave couldn't believe it, wondered if it might ever happen again.

Or as Anton Brookes puts it: 'I think everything the Foo Fighters is, is everything Nirvana wasn't. And I think that's deliberate. Okay, as many doors opened for Dave because he was in Nirvana, as many doors closed for him too. He had to *earn the right* to be on stage. He was given a chance with the Foo Fighters, people gave him enough rope to literally hang himself – and Dave went on to prove his worth. Dave could have gone on to just drum every so often with someone, produce someone. Live off Nirvana royalties. Live off his Foo royalties and have a very comfortable life. But he chose not to.'

In Britain, he found himself having to fight a different battle, though. With the nation then in thrall to a new music phenomenon called Britpop and anything remotely grunge-oriented relegated to what Oasis's singer, Liam Gallagher, had deemed 'the smelly shorts and beards brigade – not having it!' Dave worried that the Foo Fighters would not be able to find a place at the top table in the way Nirvana once had. Somehow, though, in the middle of a year dominated by game-changing album releases from newly dominant British acts like Oasis (*What's the Story Morning Glory?*), Blur (*The Great Escape*), PJ Harvey (*To Bring You My Love*), Tricky (*Maxinquaye*), Radiohead (*The Bends*) and Pulp (*Different Class*), the Foo Fighters were still deemed worthy enough to get the music press, unlike today still a force of nature in the British media, in a lather over them and *what it all meant now Kurt was gone.*

Anton Brookes recalls early discussions with Dave about how to try and control the overflow of interview requests, knowing the main reason so many writers wanted to talk to him would be to ask about Kurt. Neither Dave nor Krist had given any interviews at all since Kurt's suicide, this would be the first opportunity the press had to try and get their hands on what was still the most burning question in rock: why did Kurt kill himself?

'Dave knew what the score was as soon as he put his head above the parapet and decided to do the Foo Fighters,' says Anton now. 'Obviously you try between management and yourself to protect him as much as you can. You know they've got to ask Nirvana questions. But it was always done with the proviso that they talk about the Foo Fighters too. And the best way to talk about Nirvana with Dave was *not* to talk about Nirvana, because every experience Dave Grohl had for the first three years of his Foo Fighters career, all roads lead to Nirvana.

'Virtually every experience he'd ever had as a successful musician was about Nirvana. But if you asked a question about Nirvana he was never gonna answer it. You don't ask about Nirvana. But he'll talk about Nirvana all day in a roundabout way. You've just got to be bright enough to see through that, because all his experiences were with Nirvana. What else is he going to talk about? What else has he got as a reference point?'

Fortunately, says Anton, 'Dave's never been anybody's fool. Dave's a very shrewd, very intelligent man. He's very driven. He's ultra-loyal to people. People say he's the nicest man in rock and he is! But the thing is, he's had to work at that. He's not . . . It's probably more by default than design but that's just the way Dave is. The smile and the cheeky goofiness and campness . . . There's a lot of that and Dave doing interviews . . . he gives the people what they want. Dave always knows what they want and he knows what to give, and where he's comfortable. He's never prostituted himself and chased after press. It's always come to him. But after Nirvana it wasn't an easy ride. Stepping out of the shadow of Nirvana under the guise of Foo Fighters, a lot of people were like, okay, impress us. A lot of people had the knives drawn for him too. Like, how dare you?'

One wag dubbed him the 'grunge Ringo'. Sooner or later everyone that came, ostensibly, to interview Dave about the Foo Fighters got around to Nirvana and Kurt's death, and Dave would wave them away like a bad smell. 'I don't talk about it and I don't want to talk about it because I feel like I have so much respect for that situation that I don't really want to share it with anybody' was his typically brusque response in the *NME*. 'It's like meeting someone for the first time and within the first fifteen minutes of meeting them you ask them how their father died and what was it like. You don't do that, that's fucking rude.'

What he did feel the need to try and explain were the next two most burning questions in 1995. The first – was the toy space gun pictured on the front sleeve of the *Foo Fighters* album some kind of warped reference to Kurt's suicide? – was easy to brush off. It was simply a play on the fact he'd named the band Foo Fighters – the nickname given to UFO sightings by fighter pilots in the Second World War, he explained over and over. This wasn't a picture of a smoking shotgun, for chrissakes, this was a *ray gun*. 'To me it's a toy,' he told *Rolling Stone*. 'It has nothing to do with anything. I love kitschy forties and fifties space toys. I thought it would be a nice, plain cover, nothing fancy [but] people have read so much into it. Give me a fucking break.'

Much harder to deny, though, was that one of the album's pivotal tracks, 'I'll Stick Around', dealt directly with Dave's feelings about Kurt's death, Courtney's own mental state, and his determination to ride out the calamitous fallout and somehow make good again. Feelings all borne out in fierce relief by the repeated snarling stanza, *'I don't owe you anything!'* As if to rub it in, 'I'll Stick Around' is the most obviously Nirvana-influenced track on the album, and made even more of a statement when it was released as the next single from the album, becoming their second UK hit and another mainstream US radio hit.

When questioned on the subject, though, Dave repeatedly denied the song had anything to do with Kurt, going so far as to tell *Rolling Stone* that the only reason he'd agreed to speak to them was in order to deny that 'I'll Stick Around' had anything to do with his lost friend, Kurt. 'It would fucking break my heart to think that people are under that impression. That was my biggest fear. Beside that, anything else is trivial and stupid. And I knew while I was recording it that it was probably the strongest song I've ever written, because it was the one song that I actually meant and felt emotionally.'

Little by little though, his guard dropped. The more successful the Foo Fighters grew in their own right, the less inclined Dave was to sugarcoat his true feelings about anything. 'By no means am I a lyricist,' he said in an early 1996 interview with *Alternative Press*. 'But a lot of times, the things you write down spur of the moment are most revealing. Now I look at [the songs on *Foo Fighters*] and some of them seem to actually have meaning.'

Asked directly by Richard Kingsmill if 'Stick Around' 'might have had something to do with Kurt's death?' Dave replied: 'Well, when you feel like you've been deprived or you've lost something you just want to move on. You just want to be here to prove that you're not gonna let whatever it is bring you down. So in a way it could be about that, but more than anything it's a song about feeling like you're lost but you're not gonna quit.' Unlike Kurt, who was never allowed to quit, despite begging to, until finally he took things into his own hands.

What Dave was about to discover though was that with control came responsibility – for everything: the good, the bad and, as the other three members of the Foo Fighters were about to find out, the ugly.

The trouble started when they came to record the second Foo Fighters album – Dave's first with the actual band. That first tour had gone on and on – and on. Nine months, a year, eventually over 16 months. Pat would keep score. Tell the others. Nate and William had never known anything like it. This was roller-coaster time for the newbies – but without the brakes or handholds. By the end of it though the band was a super-tight live act. They still hadn't found out yet, however, how they would work together once they were all in a recording studio.

Nor how the songwriting aspect was supposed to work. Out on the road they had begun to jam on some riffs at soundchecks that had already turned into fully formed Foo Fighters songs. Notably, 'My Hero', which would later become the third of four hit singles from the new album, and which nicely epitomised the everyman spirit Dave was starting to patent as part of the

Foos charm; and 'Monkey Wrench', already slated to be the lead single from the album, with its edgy juxtaposition of jaunty, grunge-lite riff and emotionally poleaxing lyrics inspired by the breakup of Dave's marriage to Jennifer. His voice breaking as he almost spits the words about remembering every single word she said, '. . . *and all the shit that somehow comes along with it . . .*'

Most of the key songs on the new album, though, would be written solely by Dave, starting with the number he had written specifically as the band's new live show opener, 'Enough Space'. Dave had picked up on how the audiences in Britain and Europe would literally begin bouncing as the band played its most exciting songs. Somewhere along the line, he had decided to write a song that helped them do exactly that; brought it into soundcheck the next day and they did it live for the first time that night, opening the show with it, making people . . . bounce.

The other two tracks that Dave wrote alone – the beautiful, ethereal 'Walking After You' and the powerful, haunting 'Everlong', both again almost certainly inspired by his painful break with Jennifer – were the stand-out moments of an album overcrowded with sonic jewels. The eerie 'Doll', which opened the album in a completely unexpected way; the quirky 'Hey, Johnny Park!', with its reverse slant on Nirvana's old quiet/loud/quiet thing; the smoky acoustic trails of 'My Poor Brain', one minute black nail-polished Velvet Underground, the next just pure Black Sabbath; others like the mid-period Beatles of 'See You', the unselfconsciously fist-pumping 'My Hero', the teasing happy ending that isn't, 'New Way Home', with its promise to 'never tell you the secrets I'm holding' . . . this is an album so clearly better arranged and produced, so obviously more thought out and less fraught, than its hurried predecessor, it still comes as a jolt to recall that it was also the album where Dave Grohl, nicest man in rock, first showed his fangs.

The album was eventually titled *The Colour and the Shape*, which seemed as good a way as any of describing in words the unsayable qualities the music evoked. But it could as easily have been called *Dave's Colour and Dave's Shape*.

The other difference between the first and second Foo Fighters albums was that this one had a real-life, true-grit producer in Gil Norton. Gil was a tough-talking British guy who had made his name making albums for the Pixies, who had eventually made their name because Kurt Cobain liked them so much he stole their sound for Nirvana. Now Dave was doing . . . what? Looking for a little of that same juice? Well, Gil was happy to oblige, but strictly on his terms. Gil played no favours and would have Dave doing take after take, push Pat into recording so many of the same parts in so many different ways he couldn't keep check on what he had and what he hadn't done. Gil would call Nate and William 'the rhythmless section,' according to William. Nate was made painfully aware that he was at best a glorified amateur. That this was his first time trying to make it in the big leagues. It was not easy for him. Years later, Nate would cheerfully admit he was 'fucking terrible'.

But it was William who was struggling most of all. He was overwhelmed with the conviction that whatever track they were working on, Dave already had the drum track he wanted 'figured out in his head'. It was true, as Dave would be the first to agree. But then he was one of the best drummers of his time: *of course he knew how the drums should go*. William was a kid who knew Dave in Nirvana was a much better drummer than he, William, in the Foo Fighters was. But what had been a hang-up on the road, now, in the studio, turned into a major trauma.

As Pat said: 'You're the drummer in a band where the singer is the greatest rock'n'roll drummer in the world, looking over his shoulder waiting for you to be as good as him. All right. That's just fucked-up pressure – and remember, William was a kid.'

It wasn't just the drums. This was Dave's baby, Dave's dream, Dave's deal. He hadn't worked this hard, come this far, to not see it through exactly the way *he* wanted it. This was the second album but the first on which the Foo Fighters would be judged as a real band. Nothing was going to be allowed to be less than it could be, in Dave's eyes. William was a good drummer. But good, for Dave, would never be enough any more. So he decided that if he wanted the job done properly he would have to do it himself. And he did. When the original sessions at Washington Farm studio in Beat Creek failed to meet Dave's soaring expectations, he took things into his own hands and – group or no group – unilaterally decided to scrap the album and start again, relocating the sessions to Grandmaster Recordings studio in West Hollywood. He simply couldn't live with William's commendable but – by Dave's standards – under-par drumming. He would be better off doing them himself, he decided

At the end of the day, Dave was the guy with the big management and record deal, with the biggest songs and ideas, with the whole map to the treasure already drawn in his head; he had every right to make such a decision. The only thing he did wrong was to not tell William. Instead, William was left to find out the hard way – by accident. The last to know, it broke his fucking heart. It broke him.

Even Nate didn't know what was going on until they got to the studio; neither did Pat. It wasn't just the drums they ended up re-recording, it was the whole album. Meanwhile, while it was happening, Dave tried to keep the whole thing under wraps, unable or unwilling to just come out and tell William. It was his first big decision as a bandleader and he only got it half right. Musically, he was on the button. Personally, he made a bad situation infinitely worse. He made William's place in the band untenable. The kid had not only lost his place on the finished album, he had been robbed of his dignity. His self-esteem, already shaky, took a fatal hit. There was, as he saw it, no way back.

Nate was freaking out, knowing how William would be when he finally found out what was going on behind his back. William, meanwhile, sensing something was up, had decided to fly down and join his buddies. But Dave caught him first, on the phone, told him not to come, that he was redoing 'a couple of the drum tracks'. Upset, bewildered, out of the loop, William phoned Nate. Told him what Dave had said on the phone. That he was redoing the drums on a couple of tracks. Then according to William, the pain still evident in his voice more than 15 years later: 'Nate goes, "He redid 'em all."'

Speaking about the incident in the 2011 Foo Fighters' *Back and Forth* documentary, Dave claimed that in the 'conversation I eventually had with William', he told him that he still very much wanted him to stay in the band and be the drummer. But that Dave would be the one playing drums on the album; maybe all the albums. In the same film, William insisted he was still unclear whether it was management, the record company, the producer, Dave, 'or all of the above' that had gone over his head and decided Dave should play the drums on the album. That in the 16 years that had passed since he walked out of the band, the decision that he would not play drums on the second Foo Fighters album 'has never been explained to me'.

He recalled straight-faced how when Dave put forward the proposition that William continue as the band's touring drummer, he baulked. 'I said, "Dude, I mean, as it is now I have to rebuild my soul. Or re-find it. If I do that [continue as just the touring drummer] it's like, see ya! Thanks but no thanks."'

William looks sad and bitter in the documentary. Dave, for his part, concedes that he knows William will never forgive him for redoing the drum parts on *The Colour and the Shape*. But it's clear that isn't the main reason William felt he couldn't go on. It was the manner in which the thing went down, the secrecy, the deception, the copping out of just letting him know what was going on, rather than fudging the issue.

But then Dave was still just a kid too.

10. Big High Heels to Fill

Finding a replacement for William Goldsmith was easy. When Will had joined the Foo Fighters it had been a gamble. Not for him, as he had nothing to lose. Sunny Day Real Estate had never really got off the grid and now they were gone anyway. Joining the drummer from Nirvana in his new venture was a no-brainer. Two years on, though, with a multi-platinum album behind them and a growing worldwide reputation, Dave virtually had his pick of brilliant drummers to take Will's place. What he was looking for though was someone who could really play, someone who, unlike Will, had already been around some, but not someone so well known – or old – Dave wouldn't feel able to 'direct'.

He found what he was looking for first time of asking in a 25-year-old blond kickass dude from Laguna Beach named Taylor Hawkins. Taylor had just come off a high-profile world tour as drummer in Alanis Morissette's live band, promoting her 33-million-selling breakthrough album, *Jagged Little Pill*. He wasn't on the album but he could be seen in the videos for two of the album's biggest singles: 'You Oughta Know' and 'You Learn'. Before that he had worked in the backing band for the Canadian actress-singer Sass Jordan, and before that as the wild-eyed skin-beater in Sylvia, an acid rock beach band from Orange County.

Born Oliver Taylor Hawkins, in Fort Worth Texas, in 1972,

Taylor – as he preferred to be known – had moved to California with his family when he was four. He'd grown up with the SoCal heat in his veins, the beach in his brains and the sand in his hair. That didn't mean he was dumb. Not all the time anyway. As well as drums, he could play guitar and piano, and he could sing – really sing. Which meant that when he joined the Foos he did for Dave what Dave had done for Kurt all those years before – added a touch of good-humoured class to the act, providing better live drums than they'd had before, and much better backing vocals. And, like Dave, he could also write – a bonus that Dave, like Kurt, would seek to augment into his own songwriting, but strictly on the singer's own well-defined terms, obviously.

Like the rest of the floating cast of session musicians living in LA, Taylor had zeroed in on news of Foo Fighters looking for a new drummer. Unlike the others, though, Taylor had an unlikely in: a cousin, Kevin Harrell, who'd already introduced him to Dave Grohl after meeting him on a camping vacation in the Ozark mountains that spring. Dave had also seen Taylor with Alanis and as a connoisseur of tight-wrapped drums played with the force and speed of a jackhammer, had taken note of his ability on the drums. When Dave phoned Taylor out of the blue, in May 1997, asking whether he could recommend a drummer for the Foos, he did so disingenuously, knowing full well that Taylor was then out of a gig. (Morissette had journeyed to India and would not begin making a new album for another year.) Dave was calling more to see if Taylor would take the bait and offer himself for the gig.

He did. Dave was overjoyed. Taylor was a dude, backing a chick was not the same as being a full-blooded member of this generation's The Who. Tall, tanned, rangy, experienced, super-confident – on the surface, at least – Taylor was, in Dave's eyes, everything that William had not been. He also had much more in common with Taylor – big band success, major world acclaim – than he did Nate or even Pat. Plus they were both drummers with big cheesy grins. They were both 'spazzes', in Taylor's words.

When Pat got the news, he was sanguine. Took it all in his stride the way Dave was used to Pat doing with almost everything. Nate, though, was a different story. Still raw from the loss of his buddy Will, Nate feared the worst: that Taylor would be another guy, like Pat and Dave, who was more LA than Seattle. More big-time; more demanding. As the bassist, Nate was the one who would be expected to work closest with Taylor onstage, too. Nate, who had all the charisma of a schoolteacher, locked into a musical partnership with a guy who was better looking than most of the chicks Nate had been with, how was that meant to work? Taylor was simply not the kind of guy Nate had ever envisaged being in a band with. 'No way.'

In the end though, Nate would do what was expected of him and find a way to help make it work. Taylor was more then the sum of his parts. He was a good kid, going out of his way to make friends with everybody. Including Nate, who initially flinched at the idea of having the kind of cars-cash-cool Californian kid Taylor represented.

The real trouble, though no one knew it yet, was Pat Smear. Three days before the next Foo Fighters tour was due to begin in May, Pat casually mentioned that he thought the band should continue as a three-piece. When everybody had stopped pretending to laugh, he filled in the blanks. He was leaving, with immediate effect.

'We said, "Pat, please stay,"' Dave later recalled. 'I went over to his apartment and cried to him for hours. I was on his floor in tears. But he just wasn't into it any more. We're always working, and it can get to you. I think Pat wanted to do other things. He wanted to do MTV's *House of Style*. He always wanted to do a record on his own. He wanted to do something else, which I totally understand.' Speaking about his decision in 2011, Pat told a similar story. 'I was just so sick of the whole thing. I didn't want to go out on another bazillion-show tour. I don't care. I just don't want to do this any more.'

Taylor wondered if it was him that made Pat jump. Maybe that had something to do with it. The band was becoming very butch and boorish, not Pat's scene. But that wasn't really it, either. Others wondered if it was to do with Courtney Love. Pat and Courtney had always been close, travelling together on Nirvana's tours on Kurt's bus while Dave and Krist shared another bus. Courtney had recently begun a very public campaign accusing Dave of everything from 'stealing' publishing money he was not entitled to from Nirvana to, as the years went by, even trying to seduce her daughter, Frances. (Something which Frances strenuously denied, forcing her mother to publically apologise.) A verbal hate campaign that would roll on for years. Insiders claimed Courtney now forced any mutual friends to choose sides. And that Pat, in leaving Dave and the Foos, had chosen which side he wished to be on.

In reality, however, Pat's disillusion was more to do with feeling compromised by Dave then divorcing his wife, Jennifer, who Pat really was still close to. This had triggered a John Lennon-style 'lost weekend'. 'I moved to Los Angeles for one year in 1997. That was post-divorce,' Dave would recall years later. Unlike Lennon, Dave didn't immerse himself in booze and drugs, he said, 'but I did all of the other things'. Banging anything that moved. Waking up in the wrong bed, on the wrong floor. 'And that's it. That was enough for me, that one year. Because how could that possibly make you feel fulfilled? That momentary reward isn't enough.'

Again, though, it's hard to believe that the androgynous Pat Smear would find Dave's sexual shenanigans so distasteful that he felt compelled to leave the band. In fact, it was all of the above and, more crucially, simply the way *The Colour and the Shape* had been recorded – then re-recorded – that put Pat's nose out of joint. He felt for Will. But not as much as he felt for himself, being asked to redo what he felt were perfectly good guitar parts over and over while Dave and Gil Norton plotted in private, after everyone else had gone home. Pat had known it was Dave's band when he agreed to join Foo Fighters. He hadn't realised though quite how much it would never be Pat's band too. He had assumed he'd at least have a say in his own musical contributions. He did not.

And there was another, never openly discussed reason why Pat was suddenly ready to bail out. Something he would never admit to Dave in a million years but which surely crossed his mind more than once in the latter months of 1997. The possibility of joining another, even bigger band than Foo Fighters. Two, in particular, both based in LA. The first, the Red Hot Chili Peppers, who had cancelled their summer US tour that year while the guitarist Dave Navarro and singer Anthony Keidis reportedly went into rehab after relapsing into drug addiction. Word behind the scenes was that Navarro, a brilliant but wayward star who had only made one album with the Chili Peppers, had played his last show with the band. Although his departure wouldn't be made public until early 1998, the feeling was that Pat was the obvious replacement. Indeed, the band had offered Pat the chance to join the band in 1993, only going to Navarro after Pat, who had already agreed to join Nirvana, turned them down.

The second band there was much speculation behind the scenes that Pat might be about to join was Guns N' Roses. In a typically tangled LA-only scenario, when the original GN'R rhythm guitarist, Izzy Stradlin, had left the band in 1991, the singer, Axl Rose, had sounded out Dave Navarro – then of Jane's Addiction – to replace him. But Navarro never turned up for any of the rehearsals set up for him with Slash and the offer was eventually withdrawn. In the meantime, however, the Guns N' Roses line-up had become so volatile that by 1997 no one was really sure who was in the band, other than Rose. Slash had quit in October 1996, Izzy's replacement, Gilby Clarke, had gone long before that. Now Axl was looking for new guitarists. Did Pat fancy his chances filling one of those slots? He certainly had the cred, and Axl at that point was all about the cred. (He eventually hired Nine Inch Nails' former guitarist Robin Fink.)

Certainly, the suggestion that Pat was about to give up a career as a rock star to appear on an MTV fashion show he had already left behind once before, seems disingenuous, at best. In the event, Dave was able to persuade Pat to stay on for another six weeks, while he frantically searched for a replacement. But this would not be easy. It was one thing to bring in a drummer to a band where few had heard of the guy leaving, quite another to bring in a replacement for Pat Smear, the other ex-Nirvana guy in the Foo Fighters and the only other compelling onstage presence in the band. (Nate, with his crablike gait onstage and head-down lost-in-his-own-world demeanour, was hardly Mr Charisma.) In the end, it would be six months before Dave felt at ease enough to announce Pat's replacement – his old friend and 'mentor' from Scream, Franz Stahl!

On paper it looked like an inspired idea. Franz had known Dave back before he was Dave. They'd grown up in the same places. Dreamed the same dreams. Having Franz come in for

Pat would be instant karma, man. Bros back together. The fact that Pete Stahl was already back in the fold working as the Foos' tour manager just made it even more perfect. Full circle, dude. Right on.

Franz was on tour in Osaka playing with a Japanese superstar named J, originally the bassist in his band Lunacy, aka Luna Sea, who were *huge* in Japan. His friend Scott Garrett, drummer in the DC punk band Dag Nasty, later of The Cult, had brought Franz into the fold just months before. Franz thought he had landed on his feet. Then he got the phone call from Dave and everything changed again – instantly. Within 24 hours he was standing on the roof of Radio City Music Hall in New York, at the MTV Music Video Awards – the Vammys – being unveiled as the new guitarist in the Foo Fighters. What a trip, man! Like it was always somehow meant to be, man. Pat played first, the band pumping through 'Monkey Wrench'. Then Franz played second, grooving through 'Everlong'. Phew, what a scoop! What a great PR stunt. What a way to begin something that was born to die even as it was being born.

Franz barely knew where he was, he was still so jetlagged from the flight. Everything was suddenly moving so fast. Pat actually did the introductions. 'That last song we played was my last with the band. I'd like to introduce you to Franz Stahl, who will be taking over. Thank you. Rock on, guys. Foo Fighters!'

It was 4 September 1997. Franz played 62 shows with the Foos in 101 days virtually back to back from then until the final show of the year at the Shepherd's Bush Empire in London on 13 December. Then a further 77 shows from January 1998 to early August, with just a couple of weeks off at the end of May. The shows were getting bigger and bigger. *The Colour and the Shape* went to No. 10 in the US, and again reached No. 3 in the UK, making the charts in seven other major countries.

'Everlong' became the band's next hit single, after 'This is a Call', the video on heavy rotation on MTV, this still in the days when MTV mattered, when it still bossed the singles and videos charts. Dave: 'It was happening to us. That thing that happens to new bands as they start to get popular.'

Franz wasn't in any of the videos, of course, wasn't part of the promotion, all of that had been done before he joined. But he did get to mime to 'Everlong' on *Top of the Pops* in London, and he did get to play 'Everlong' live on *Letterman* in the US, giving what was perhaps his most electric performance with the Foos. Franz had never been happier. After a lifetime of shitty punk rock gigs with a band no one outside of Seattle (or wherever) had really heard of, here he was, finally high in the charts. He'd have taken the gig even if he'd only half liked the songs, but he actually dug the music, thought both Foos albums were very cool. Couldn't wait to be part of their third album. What could possibly go wrong?

Taylor and Franz buddied up on the road. But when Dave and the band began rehearsing and writing, coming up with ideas for the third album, things . . . changed. Dave felt he and Taylor and Nate were 'on the same page' – but that Franz wasn't. In Scream, when it came to writing new music, Franz was in control, the leader. Now he wasn't. Not even close. It made Franz nervous about pushing himself too far forward. He just couldn't figure out when to come on strong and when to back off. In the end he just pulled away and waited to be told what to do.

Not cool. The result was the four of them couldn't fly. It was one thing onstage, powering away at well-established songs. Coming up with that vibe from scratch in the cold light of night, it just . . . would . . . not . . . work.

Nate says Dave was the last to acknowledge the situation. In a different but weirdly samey sort of way to the deal with

William, the fact that Dave was a friend of the guitarist's made it more difficult for him to try and fix what was happening. Dave had known Franz since he was 18. Firing him was 'tough, man'. According to Nate, 'there was a lot of sadness and drama' surrounding the decision to look for a new guitarist. 'It was ugly.'

But what about Franz? What did he have to say on the subject? Apart from a few brief, tight-lipped quotes here and there, Franz would simply refuse to comment, to open up and say what really went down. For years he just buried his feelings, kept the hurt hidden. Understandably. Until now . . .

It took several months of emails to persuade Franz Stahl to talk openly about his experience in the Foo Fighters. I'd just about given up when he finally agreed. We spoke over Skype, and he was warm, friendly, intelligent – and still hurt by his experience of being fired from the band. 'There's never been any sort of closure on any of it,' he said. 'And we're going on twenty years now.'

He began by reminiscing about joining the band. The thrill of getting the phone call from Dave. 'He was like, "Do you wanna join the band?" I was like, "Twist my arm, you know? You fucking kidding?"' After that, it was 'fly straight to LA, gather some shit. This was all over one weekend. Then fly straight to New York, meet these guys, go to a rehearsal place. Run over one song – then the next day I'm introduced as the new member of Foo Fighters.'

Introduced to the rock press, 'My famous quote for replacing Pat was, "I got some big high heels to fill."' Everybody, including Dave, laughed. It looked like Franz was going to fit right in. Two weeks of intense rehearsals later he was back in LA, performing with the band at the 16,000-capacity Irvine Meadows amphitheatre and the sheer scale of the job he had so glibly taken on began to sink in – and how much things had changed for Dave since their days together in Scream.

'There are so many different variables and aspects to the whole thing. I mean, obviously, him going from the original Dave Grohl from Washington, DC, and then turning into the Nirvana Dave Grohl, we're talking leaps and bounds in terms of how it changes somebody and how your whole life changes. His whole life, it was just a completely different thing . . . I also came into the band when it was really starting to kick off. The shows were getting bigger. There wasn't much time to be [friends] . . . Once I joined the band I was on a plane or on a bus. And my whole time in the band was basically working *The Colour and the Shape*, so it seemed like for a year we were just on tour.'

But while Franz was struggling to cope with his newfound status ('In my mind I was more concerned about trying to remember songs than fucking giving people a show') Dave's performance had reached a whole new level, partly through trying to compensate for the loss of Pat's louche onstage presence, partly just through his own soaring confidence as a frontman. If the first Foo Fighters world tour had been about establishing the band as a legitimate musical vehicle in its own right, the second Foos tour was all about projecting Dave Grohl Superstar.

In a nod to his illustrious past, the new show would begin each night with Dave on his own drum kit, bashing the hell out of it, as Taylor tried to keep up, before jumping down from the rostrum, grabbing his guitar and going hell for leather into 'This is a Call'. These were high-energy freak-outs. Standing next to him, in the spot where Pat used to command his own aura, on the early months of the tour Franz seemed subdued by comparison, out of his depth, lost. Though not on certain TV shows. Clearly, though, this is very much the Dave Grohl show now.

Dave still did his best to talk the whole thing up though

whenever he was questioned about the new guy. 'The thing with Franz is, it's so easy,' he gushed to the *NME*. 'I've known him since I was seventeen. So it's like having your brother or sister come out on tour.' Adding, 'The time I was in Scream was the time when I was learning to play guitar and write songs. Franz was my teacher, in a weird way. So songs like 'Monkey Wrench' or 'Enough Space' or 'Hey Johnny Park' sound like Franz wrote them anyway, because our guitar-playing is so similar.'

Things would improve for Franz – especially on smaller stages, particularly those of the various TV studios the band would find themselves on throughout 1998, where he would occasionally persuade Nate to swap sides with him, as if trying to gain as much physical as well as mental distance from his predecessor as possible – but he admits now he never really felt entirely at home. 'It was great. It was an amazing experience. [But] as far as my whole stage thing, I was a nervous wreck and for the most part I felt like I was always trying to get the gig. Even though I was on tour, every show was me trying to get the gig. At the same time I don't wanna fuck up because I don't wanna get the stare-down from Dave or any of the other guys. The whole Foo Fighters thing was just a whirlwind for me. On tour constantly, no time for this, no time for that. And that's the way it went. One minute I'm in the band travelling around the world, playing every night, and then the next minute I'm not.'

Nothing he'd ever done before had prepared him for this. At least with Will and Nate, who also shared the feeling of being out of their comfort zone for much of that first tour, they had begun small. Tiny clubs, support slots, modest college halls and theatres. For Franz, who had only ever really known the back of the van with Scream, it was straight into an arena-headlining US tour, followed by the same in Europe, then a week in Japan, two weeks in Australia, more high-profile dates in New Zealand, then back to America, and more summer festivals, plus radio, TV, press, photographs, always smiling, always up. It was everything he'd ever dreamed of and yet he'd never felt so alone.

'I think everybody has that, especially on that level,' he says. 'You're travelling around constantly and you're in *hotel rooms* – individual hotel rooms. The whole twenty years of being in Scream, I'm in a van. We're sleeping at squats. I'm sleeping right next to you. I'm hanging out with you. In the whole Foo Fighters bubble you're never really hanging out unless it's these *arranged* moments like, oh, we're in Australia, we're gonna go to the dolphin farm and swim with dolphins.'

His only real buddy on the tour was Taylor. 'On many an evening Taylor and I would go out and party and drink and hang out. I hung out with Taylor more than anybody else in the band. Not by anybody's else's fault, especially Dave. It always seemed like Dave was busy doing an interview or this and that, because he's constantly being hounded about the whole Nirvana thing. He doesn't get a fucking moment's rest. And I sympathise. I was like, "I'm glad I'm not him." He probably could enjoy himself the least out of all of us.

'There's just so much going on. It's such a different level. But I don't know I was so much lonely as I was . . . isolated. You know, in order to groove with somebody you've got to *be* with somebody, got to hang with somebody and it just happens. And if you don't, it never happens.'

As long as it all came together when the band met onstage each night, everything was doable, allowable, complete. The real trouble came after the band returned home at the end of the tour and went into rehearsal to write together for the first time.

'We got together and did a little jamming in DC,' recalls Franz, 'But it was just very . . . for me, I don't know how everybody else felt, I was just completely wiped from touring. It's a strange thing for me, because I wrote the majority of the Scream stuff and now here I'm in this band where Dave is my boss and just ... you know, I'm leery of pressing my ideas, because it's Dave's show, it's his stuff, it's his name, it's his band, it's his music ... there was a lot of trepidation for me. I really wasn't sure of how to push it – there was never anything organic because, you know, we all lived in different cities, you're not hanging out and grooving. It's: "Okay, we're going to get together and rehearse on this weekend." You fly in and it all has to happen on this weekend because you're flying out again. And it's just ...'

Horrible. Adding to the pressure was that Dave was also facing a crisis of sorts. Now living in LA and, in his own words, 'just being a drunk, getting fucked up every night and doing horrible shit', he wasn't in the frame of mind to over-concern himself with anyone else's problems. 'Living in Hollywood always seemed transitional to me. Truth be told, I fucking hated Hollywood, hated the whole life, hated most of the people we met.' To complicate matters further, Gary Gersh had also just been ousted as president of Capitol after months of behind-the-scenes friction between the 43-year-old executive and his new boss, EMI's US Deputy President, Roy Lott, unhappy with Capitol's sluggish domestic market share under Gersh, which was then hovering at a meagre 3 per cent.

The good news was Gersh was now heading for a new career in management – in partnership with the Foos' manager, John Silva. On paper, this would potentially have great benefits for Dave. Together, Gersh and Silva were talking about negotiating a new, much bigger package deal for the Foos and their Roswell label, which eventually entailed leaving Capitol in favour of RCA. It also represented a new gamble. Gersh was the key man in Dave's recording career, both with Nirvana and Foo Fighters, and if Dave had kept the Foos with Capitol, the risk was that with Gersh gone no one there would care as much and the band's still relatively new recording career might wither on the vine. Going with Gary to RCA also came with its own risks though. The only way to ensure the Foo Fighters would be taken as seriously at RCA as Dave Grohl wanted them to be was to make damn sure their next album was a slam-dunk hit. Suddenly it wasn't about making a statement of intent, as the first Foos album had been, nor a way of confirming the Foos were more than a one-hit wonder, as the second album had been. This next album would have to stand or fall by its own merits. The novelty of seeing the Nirvana drummer fronting his own band had long since worn off. The fallout over first Will then Pat was also no longer an issue. The only question that mattered now was: how much did Dave really want it? Megastar status? Oh, he would still drop names like Bad Brains into interviews, still drone on about punk rock and yadda-yadda. But what he was really aiming for was rock immortality, and that would mean aiming straightforwardly for the mainstream, dead centre. And that would mean no more second chances. Suddenly everything was up for grabs.

Dave had also begun a new phase in his personal life, leaving LA behind to buy the house in Alexandria, Virginia, where he'd gone to school all those years before, which would become his new permanent home, and along with it a new long-term relationship with Melissa Auf Der Maur, then bassist for Courtney Love's Hole, who'd released their first US Top 10 album the year before with *Celebrity Skin*. Given the increasingly tense relationship between Dave and Courtney, the couple tried to keep their affair quiet for as long as possible. But when the story finally filtered out it proved too much – and Melissa left Hole in 1999, just as Dave was finishing *There is Nothing Left to Lose*.

Not a great time then for the Foos' newest member, Franz

Stahl, to be feeling insecure about his place in the scheme of things, especially not when it came to coming up with new, commercially viable material. 'It was a very strange moment for me,' admits Franz. But equally, as he points out, 'It was a very strange moment for them. Not too long ago they'd gotten a new drummer in Taylor. Then they lost the guitar player. So it wasn't an easy time for them as well.' Hardly surprising then that the initial ideas they worked on were, in the view of both Dave and Franz, 'complete shite.' Unlike Dave, though, Franz didn't know how to respond. It wasn't his call any more.

'Like I say, I was real leery of what buttons to push and just kind of let Dave come up with stuff. And on top of that just being kind of burnt [from touring] and just not knowing my place in the band. And me just wanting [Dave] to do the right things so they don't think they've made a wrong decision. I want to keep my job as well so I'm just like a yes man. Maybe I should have been a little more . . . whatever. But the headspace just wasn't right at the time. But Dave scrapped all that shit and wrote that next record after that.'

Not cool. 'I was in an impossible situation, and maybe their unhappiness with *me* was actually the fact that they were so unhappy with the music they'd just written. Cos I didn't like it either. I mean, I never said it. But that's the way it was. Dave changed a bunch of shit, which is fine, it happens. Then we left town. We were gonna all go home and sit on it and come back and try it again.'

In a virtual repeat of what had happened with Will, the first indication Franz got that something was up was when Dave simply stopped returning his calls. 'For weeks I was trying to get Dave to send me the tapes of the new rearrangements of everything. I never got 'em – and I started to wonder why.'

When, weeks later, they reconvened in the new basement

studio – named 606, 'because it sounded like a cool number' – Dave was putting together in the house he'd bought back in Alexandria, Franz was appalled to learn he was the only one who hadn't been sent the new tapes. 'We came back after that down time and I wasn't familiar with this stuff they'd made all these changes to. So I looked like a complete fucking idiot! I said, "Dude, I kept telling you, send me this shit. Why didn't you send me this stuff?"'

Franz was back home with his wife in LA when he got the phone call that broke his heart. Unlike the phone call he got when Dave asked him to join the band it wasn't just Dave on the line this time. 'I got a fucking conference call, dude. It was the band! And . . . you know, when it's not in person like that, it's kind of suspect to me. If you can't come to me and talk to me in person there really is no validity here in your issues or whatever. They can't face me face-to-face so obviously they're not . . . their convictions are not that strong. Something else is pushing this whole situation.'

He breaks off, still lost. Did Dave do most of the talking or was it the other two? 'I don't even fucking remember. You can imagine how I felt. I really couldn't believe what was going on. I was like, "All right, all right, I'll talk to you guys later." I said, "I'm gonna come up." They didn't believe me. They thought that I would just walk away and be done with it. I remember getting off the phone and just going in my bedroom with my wife and telling her, "You wouldn't believe what just happened." I was stunned. I couldn't comprehend it. I couldn't even comment on it. I didn't know what to do. I was shocked.'

Finally, 'I was like, "Fuck this. I'm going up there. I wanna know why." Everybody just couldn't believe it happened. Like, what the fuck? It wasn't my personality. I had no problem with drugs. I was a complete, you know . . . the perfect employee.'

He chuckles self-consciously. 'I flew up there and they're fuck-ing sitting in there jamming just like nothing had happened. And I fucking bang on the door and they open the door and they couldn't even believe that I flew up there. They were stunned! It goes back to . . . guys in bands are a bunch of fucking kids, children, that really never learned to communicate with people. Or are the worst at communicating, I should say.

'So I basically go in there and just kind of break down in tears. And Nate says some stupid shit that I just couldn't believe. Just like, what the fuck are you guys talking about? But anyway . . . it was a very strange moment and I don't entirely hold them responsible for it. I mean, I do and I don't. They're a product of the whole situation as well.'

Pause. 'Taylor, who I really connected with . . . I could see the bullshit because I could see it in him. That he really wanted to fucking say something on my behalf but he couldn't because he was the new guy as well. Not only is he the new guy but he's the drummer underneath this insanely amazing drummer who's his boss! So he's not gonna say anything. It's his job too. And that always bugged me cos I could see it.

'What really fucked me about the whole thing is, if you're having issues, whether perceived or not, let's go hang out, let's talk about it and you either suss it out or you don't and that's it. That never even happened! Which I attributed to this whole machine that Dave's behind, you know. It's just cut the head off the snake and move on. Where it's a much deeper emotional attachment for me, because we're brothers, we're from the same town. It's about communicating with each other. That never fucking happened.'

Another long pause while he collects his thoughts. 'So any-way, I was like, enough of this shit, I'm out of here. You know, there's a good buddy of mine in DC, Joey Picuri, a great soundman, did Fugazi, now works for Frank Junior [Sinatra], old friend . . . he was one of the first guys to call me and he said, "Dude, the bottom line is if they don't have your back then why do you want to be a part of it anyway?" I was like, "You're right."'

Years later, Dave would describe this turbulent period in the story of the Foo Fighters as 'growing pains, played out in the public eye', adding that all bands went through the same shit. Which is true to one extent, but in another, greater sense, the fact is the Foos were always in the spotlight. And Dave, whose reputation for always handling any situation well, actually handled things badly, when it came to both Will and Franz.

But, as Paul Brannigan points out, 'You've got to have a certain amount of steel at your core in order to do what Dave's done – when it comes to it he can be quite ruthless when making decisions in the interests of his band, or indeed his own interests. The Stahl thing was probably even more of an example of where something wasn't working, Dave took action to rectify it. This was someone he'd grown up with. But when push came to shove . . .'

As Brannigan says, the Foo Fighters had always been 'very much Dave's band. There's a certain amount of collaboration in that band but Dave says constantly that this is my band, and that what I say goes, really. I think it's also just part of growing up. After *The Colour and the Shape*, Dave's a successful rock star in his own right. There's no question about that now. He's on the front covers of magazines, he's living in California. He's living the dream, as it were. So by the time it came to making [the third Foos album] he'd been divorced, he was living in Los Angeles, his whole life was changing. I guess maybe at that point in his life there wasn't an awful lot to be unhappy about.'

Not such a nice guy after all, then. Certainly that seems to have been the conclusion Nate now came to when he became the next Foo Fighter to bail out. Dave was laying up at his mother's house in Springfield, in January 1999, when he got the phone call from Nate telling him he was leaving too. Dave was bummed, pissed off, past caring almost. Livid. He told Nate he could tell Taylor himself, that he was going out to get drunk. Dave and his pal Jimmy took Dave's rental car to the nearest bar and got hellaciously fucked up. Then they 'rallied' the car over neighbourhood lawns, threw bricks threw the windows and smashed it to smithereens.

As soon as Nate got off the phone with Dave he knew he'd just made the biggest mistake of his life. The next morning Nate called Dave again and begged for his spot back. It was 6 a.m. and Dave was still drunk. Nate was beside himself, almost in tears. Dave said yeah, okay, then went to throw up. According to some, Dave has never really forgiven Nate for that. Yet in a strange way it also freed Dave to make the decisions he needed to make in future alone and without any trace of guilt attached any more. What was the point worrying about people who were just as likely to walk out on you at a moment's notice, expecting you to pick up the pieces? Fuck that shit. Dave would never make that mistake again. All three of the original 'band' had bailed for one reason or another. Sooner or later two would come crawling back – but this time *entirely* on Dave's terms.

In a strangely paradoxical sense, given its tortured origins, the third Foo Fighters album, *There is Nothing Left to Lose*, remains one of the most mellow, upbeat, certainly calmest-sounding recordings they have made. It was also – with a couple of notable exceptions – their most dull. 'Moderate rock' is how Paul Brannigan politely describes it. A fair summation of an album where only two of its 12 tracks approach the ferocity, aplomb and good humour of their more punchy predecessors.

The raunchy, attitudinal 'Stacked Actors', which opened the album, was good enough to have been on the first album, but only if Dave hadn't written a better song about the same stuff in 'I'll Stick Around'. This time though he didn't try very hard to hide the fact the song was about Courtney Love. 'I wrote 'Stacked Actors' about everything that is fake and everything that is plastic and glamorous and unreal, so if that pertains to anyone that comes to mind then there you go,' he said at the time. Courtney Love herself weighed in a few weeks after the album was released in November 1999, telling Howard Stern that she knew for sure the song was about her.

The album's only major highlight though was 'Learn to Fly', a consummate pop-rock song built on twangy guitars, strawberry-smoothy vocal harmonies and pin-sharp lyrics that wouldn't have sounded out of place on a squillion-selling Tom Petty or R.E.M. album. Full of reflections on the past 12 months, from its clear reference to dealing with Franz and the ever-fluctuating Foos line-up (*'Think I need a devil to help me / Get things right'*) to his decision to return home to Virginia (*'Make my way back home / When I learn to fly'*), this was next-level writing from Dave Grohl, a universe on from the days of meaningless lyrics and slow-fast-slow Nirvana-lite rockers. A true rock classic, 'Learn to Fly' would give the Foo Fighters their first major US hit single, reaching No. 19 on the *Billboard* Hot 100, and their biggest-selling hit worldwide.

The rest of the album, though, is merely pleasant. 'Breakout' is a formulaic Foos rocker easily forgotten the moment it ends. 'Headwires' and 'Fraternity' sound like mediocre mid-period tracks by The Police – the trio Nate, a major Sting fan, hoped the Foos would become after Franz was fired, rather than get another new guitarist in. While the breathy ballad 'Ain't It the Life' is about forsaking the LA neon for the sunlight through the trees, the sluts and empty bottles of Sunset Strip nights for the early-morning couplings of lovers in their bed, it also commits the cardinal sin of actually sounding like a Beatles-era Ringo track, only twice as long. The rest is equally shoulder-shrugging. As a result, *There is Nothing Left to Lose* was a bitter disappointment commercially, only just breaking the UK Top 10, barely equalling the sales of *The Colour and the Shape* in the US and other countries where the Foos were now famous. Had it not been for the huge mainstream success of 'Learn to Fly' – and the consequent Grammy-award-winning video, directed by former Lemonheads bassist Jesse Peretz; an incongruously literal interpretation set on a plane, only enlivened by cameo appearances from Tenacious D stars Jack Black and Kyle Glass, and Dave in multiple roles as moustachioed pilot, gay air steward, overweight female passenger, bug-eyed female Foos fan and finally himself – the album would have been a commercial disaster.

In retrospect, the title of the album said it all. It was, said Dave, 'about when you experience these emotions after you've been through a long, difficult period and you finally give in to this feeling that, quite simply, there is nothing left to lose. It can seem . . . positive, desperate and reckless.' To emphasise this newfound direction, personal and professional, Dave got the band's FF logo tattooed on the back of his neck and a black-and-white photo of it for the front cover of the album. He also resolved to ensure that whomever he hired to replace Franz on tour would come with none of the baggage both his previous guitarists had. Dave didn't need a 'friend' standing to his right onstage any more. He was sick of being sick with worry about how the other guy was getting along. He needed a guy who could play, could sing – and would do what he was told without any blowback whatsoever.

For the first time, Dave agreed to hold open auditions to find the new guy he needed for his band. More than 35 potential guitarists were auditioned at Nate's rehearsal studio in LA over a two-week period. In the band's 2011 *Before and After* documentary, Dave recalls 'the one guy who came in and hugged everybody'. The other guy who came in looking for their autographs. Then there were the shredders, the guys that thought they were in Metallica and the guys who couldn't actually play or didn't even know any Foo Fighters songs. The guys who could really play, knew every note of every song, yet just didn't really 'fit in'.

Finally, Dave found what he was looking for in the 28-year-old Chris Shiflett, whose previous claim to fame had been as the guitarist in No Use for a Name, a punk band out of San Francisco. New in town, Chris had actually been asked if he'd be up for auditioning for Guns N' Roses – who were looking, yet again, for a new guitarist. But Chris was young and smart enough to flinch from the prospect of joining a band that thanks to the madness of King Axl hadn't toured or released a new album for nearly seven years. Instead, he glibly mentioned how he'd rather audition for a real working band like the Foo Fighters. Two weeks later, he did – and got the gig.

As Chris would recall in one of his first interviews just months after he joined: 'I'd read ages ago that Franz had left and I was talking to an old friend who knew someone who works with them so he gave them a call to see what's up. Turns out they were just about to schedule auditions. I auditioned and then went home. I was camped out by the phone for the next week. Finally they did call and we played together a second time. After, I went back to their hotel, got drunk and Dave was like, "I've got to go to bed, I'll call you tomorrow." I sat by my friends' phone all fucking day and finally, at about five o'clock, they called to say it was on. That night I went out and got completely smashed on beer and sushi!

'I'd been playing in a band called No Use for a Name for four and a half years and we'd always say we wanted to open up for the Foo Fighters . . . which never happened. It took a while for the initial, 'OhmygodIamintheFooFighters' to wear off. It's not actually worn off yet, but they do make it very easy to be part of the team. It's cool.'

It turned out Dave had met Chris at a punk show in Santa Barbara when they were both teenagers. Chris was born there. Dave was in Scream and Chris was playing bass in a garage band called Rat Pack. They opened for Scream. This fact alone almost won him the gig in the Foos. A badge of honour that Dave felt meant something. Dave thought: 'He's gonna get it. He's gonna understand. He won't take this shit for granted.'

Dave made his phone call to Chris at around 6 p.m. It was Dave and Taylor on speaker telling Chris he'd got the gig. They told him: 'We start rehearsing tomorrow. Say goodbye to your friends. You're not gonna see anybody for the next year.' They weren't kidding. Eighteen months and over 200 shows later Chris Shiflett was still in the Foo Fighters and getting ready to make his first album with them.

That is, if the band stayed together long enough for that to happen. Something neither Chris – nor the other Foos – were now sure of.

11. The Honourable Thing

Then suddenly, out of the pleasant yellow sunlight came the suffocating darkness, black as a raven's wing.

The tour to promote *There is Nothing Left to Lose* began as a slyly low-key affair, some of the modest club dates like the ones in September at the tiny Troubadour in LA (capacity 350) and the equally 'fun-sized' Horseshoe Tavern in Toronto explained away as deliberately low-profile shows to introduce Chris Shiflett into the band gently. The truth, though, was that with the new album not out until November and 'Learn to Fly' not available until the end of the month, the Foo Fighters would have struggled to fill the same enormodomes that had become their staple two years before.

Instead, they pitched themselves at big TV shows and radio productions to help spread the word, beginning with two live TV appearances in Sydney and Melbourne in October, followed by two songs at the MTV Sports and Music Festival at the Hard Rock Cafe in Las Vegas; Dave's first appearance on Howard Stern's new, much-hyped radio show on Sirius, where Dave played three songs alone with an acoustic guitar; and five days later another *Saturday Night Live* performance doing 'Learn to Fly' and the track slated as the follow-up single, 'Stacked Actors'. Three days after that they were in London playing live on the Jools Holland BBC2 TV show, *Later*. Then the high-profile arts show *Nulle Part Ailleurs* (trans.: *Nowhere Else*) on Canal Plus in Paris. By the end of November they were back in New York for two shows on the 29th and 30th: MTV's *Total Request Live* and the following night *Late Show with Letterman*. After that there were various American radio shows, special events then, in January 2000 – the daddy of American talk show delirium – a two-song appearance on the *Tonight Show with Jay Leno* and, a month later, on Friday 18 February, yet another appearance on the *Letterman* show. The latter, though, would turn out to be a truly historic appearance, the band having been invited by Letterman personally to appear on what was his comeback show after a quintuple-bypass heart operation. Introducing them on the night as 'my favourite band, playing my favourite song' – 'Everlong' – he went on to explain how, listening to the song during his weeks of recovery in hospital, he'd asked specifically for them to be the band that appeared on his first show back – and that to oblige him they had cancelled some scheduled dates in South America to be there.

It was true they had been forced to reschedule three shows in Brazil. But as far as Dave Grohl was concerned it was a no-brainer. Letterman's sudden illness had been front-page news for weeks in America. Huge celebrity guests had lined up to guest-present while he was in hospital, including stellar names such as: Drew Barrymore, Robin Williams, Bill Murray, Julia Roberts, Bruce Willis, Steve Martin, Danny DeVito, and Jerry Seinfeld, to name just a few. Dave couldn't believe his luck when he got the call about the *Letterman* comeback show. With the main Foos tour starting in March, this was the kind of publicity you couldn't buy.

'We dropped everything to do it,' Dave said. 'It was an honour to be asked.' Like every other American of his generation, Dave had grown up as a teenager digging Letterman's cool, irreverent brand of humour on TV. 'I would stay up every night to see him and his band. I was an aspiring rock musician, and the *Late Night* band in the Eighties was the best rock'n'roll band on television. Their drummer, Steve Jordan, was a huge influence on me. I love Letterman – his wit, and sarcasm. I related to him. So we were obligated to play that show, not just because he's been a huge part in the career of our band, but our teenage years.'

It was, in fact, the beginning of a long and happy relationship, which would continue right up to the final ever *Letterman* show in May 2015, when they would play him out with 'Everlong'. 'I think we mean a lot to each other,' Dave told *Entertainment Weekly* at that time. 'We've traded cigars; I've given him guitars and snare drums. We gave him a guitar once as a thank you, and he got really emotional with us. It clearly meant a lot to him. He's just genuinely a warm, sweet person.'

Back on the road in America that summer the Foos got an even bigger, more sustained promotional push when they agreed to open for the Red Hot Chili Peppers on their arena-shredding tour in support of what would prove to be the biggest-selling album of their career, *Californication*. The hottest ticket of the American summer, Dave and Taylor, in particular, really loved the highs of it all. Chris couldn't believe how hard Taylor drove the whole machine along. They became pals, instantly. Even Nate liked Chris, certainly more than he ever had Pat or Franz. Like Nate, Chris was more 'ordinary'. And he was younger than Nate, and didn't have the same pedigree and pre-existing relationship with Dave as both Pat and Franz had had. For Chris, being in the Foos was 'genuinely everything that I ever wanted. This was the dream coming true.'

As it was also for Dave, the dream not being remotely punk at all, of course, but all about being in a hugely popular, worldwide-name band, playing the biggest, most lucrative shows, and being as rich and famous a rock star as it is possible to be. Never mind the cred, where's the bread? Even Nate grasped that this was now about putting on a show. Nothing fake, just something bigger, louder, *more*. These were giant rooms, you couldn't just stand there sucking your own dick, dude. Dave modelled their new live production after Queen's *Live Killers* album cover, all red, white and black stripes. They even carried a wardrobe case now, with clothes mainly red, white and black, themed tour clothes. Like, wow, man. Chris would be in a black shirt, white tie, black pants; Nate would have on a red shirt, black tie and red pants combo. Taylor would play stripped to the waist, all the young girls crying for him. Some nights Dave even came on in a tie, a proper tie with a shirt and a jacket. Was he being ironic? Was irony even still alive by then?

For Paul Brannigan, this was the tipping point in terms of the Foo Fighters becoming part of the mainstream pop culture. 'Songs like "Learn to Fly" – a lot of hardcore Foo Fighters fans are not big fans of that song but it's one of those FM-radio-type songs that really crosses over into the *real* world, beyond rock and metal and indie. It's one of those songs that people *liked*. Like one of those waltz songs, or honeymoon songs, that people get sentimental about.'

This, says Brannigan, was the beginning of 'the Foo Fighters' popularity growing away from just what was reported in the music press, to just the regular people: the £50-man who buys five albums a year; the lady putting in money on the jukebox on hen nights. These were songs that connected to the everyman character. These weren't the people that got on the phone at nine a.m. to get tickets for some gig at the Apollo, but suddenly when the opportunity presented itself to go to one of the bigger shows, suddenly all those people were interested – even if they hadn't got the first album, even if they didn't like [Nirvana] or whatever.'

The Foo Fighters stayed with it right up until August, when they jetted off for a string of major festival appearances in Britain and Europe, before heading back to the US in the autumn for their own headline tour, albeit in much smaller venues than the ones they'd been sharing with the Chili Peppers just a few months earlier. By the time they got to the Grammy awards show in January 2001, where *There is Nothing Left to Lose* won Best Rock Album (despite having come out in 1999), Dave felt entirely vindicated for whatever decisions he'd made over the past five years. Especially so, in his eyes, as he'd done it against the odds, defying whatever fate threw his way, whether it be recalcitrant band members or the vicissitudes of a record business about to endure another sea change with the advent of the new file-sharing service Napster.

'When we won for best rock album, which we made in my basement, I was so proud,' he said, 'because we made it in my basement in a crappy makeshift studio that we put together ourselves. I stood there looking out at everybody in tuxedos and diamonds and fur coats, and I thought we were probably the only band that won a Grammy for an album made for free in a basement that year.'

In the end, though, road fever got them all. At the start of the tour, they would do a shot before the show, which they called 'band prayer'. Chris: 'That turned into, "Let's do ten shots before we play."' Booze, pot, coke . . . 'We all started getting hammered before we went on stage. We got really shitty by the end,' Taylor recalled in the *Back and Forth* documentary. Fun just wasn't fun any more. They needed a break. They would get it but not in the way any of them had foreseen, most especially not Dave and Taylor.

Taylor had been going for it big time. Smack, downers, crack, anything he could get his hands on. Dave had spoken to him but the drummer was out of control. Revisited by visions of the last days of Nirvana, when it was such a huge fucking drag just being around Kurt and all his junkie 'friends', Dave told Taylor again and again how worried he was about him. But Taylor was tripped out on his own dreams, still young and famous enough to feel untouchable, he knew what he was doing, he told Dave. No problemo, dude!

Until one night it turned into a very big fucking problem indeed when the recalcitrant drummer overdosed on heroin and nearly died.

'I was a rocker. I took it to the edge,' Taylor would later claim. But that was not how Dave and the rest of the band saw it. The Foos had just headlined the V Festival in England, and the band was back at their London hotel, the Royal Garden in Kensington, the next day chilling. That evening they had all gone out together to a bar opposite, getting drunk and hanging out. Dave went back to his room early. Then got a phone call the following morning telling him the news: Taylor was in a drug-induced coma and was on his way to the hospital. 'I think it was heroin that he did,' admitted Chris, who recalled their tour manager telling him that Taylor had fucked up and was 'gonna die'.

Smack and booze, the most clichéd and lethal combo in rock, the very same formula that had done for so many, Janis Joplin and Jim Morrison to Bon Scott, Phil Lynott and so many others. For Dave it was a mind fuck. First Kurt, now this. He felt angry, frustrated, helpless, wronged, frightened. He hurriedly dressed and sped to the hospital, the Wellington North, an expensive private facility in nearby St John's Wood. For Dave, after Kurt, to go through that again, he must have just been thinking, what the fuck's happening?' says Anton Brookes. 'Yet Dave was there for him all the time [Taylor] was in London in hospital. Who was by his bed? Dave.'

Furious as he was, Dave stayed by Taylor's bedside for the two weeks he remained in a coma. The remainder of the Foos tour dates were cancelled; 2001 was effectively over. 'A part of me resented music for doing this to my friends,' Dave would comment a decade later, after the dust had settled and all the bad dreams had been left behind. But at the time he was devastated, wondering how the band could even carry on, or even whether it should. 'I just felt like, "I don't want to play any more if it's gonna make my friend die."'

It was touch and go for most of those two weeks. Doctors warned that if Taylor did come out of it he might do so mentally impaired, or so physically altered he would never be able to play drums again. When, miraculously, Taylor finally opened his eyes, Dave looked at him and said, 'Dude, it's gonna be okay.' According to Dave, Taylor's reply was 'Fuck off.' Dave: 'And I thought, oh good, he's gonna be okay.'

Once the overriding feeling of relief had subsided, though, once he knew his drummer would soon be back to 'normal', deeper, more conflicted feelings began to emerge. Why, every step of the way, were things so fucking difficult to maintain in the Foo Fighters? After the disaster of Nirvana, he had been determined to make sure his own band would never have to suffer the same shitty slings and asshole arrows. Yet every time a tour finished there was a new problem to deal with.

His personal life was also a wreck again. He and Melissa Auf Der Maur had split. Dave was forlorn. Even though it had been 'a big secret we were desperate to keep for some reason', according to Melissa, their relationship had meant something to him.

More troubling was the heavy legal dispute now reaching a sickening conclusion between Courtney Love and Dave and Krist, over the rights to old Nirvana material – specifically, 'You

Know You're Right', the last track they'd ever recorded with Kurt, when demoing new material in Seattle in January 1994. With a new single-CD 'history of Nirvana' compilation planned for the Christmas 2002 market, Dave and Krist were keen to include the track amongst the rarities. Courtney, however, was determined to stop them, insisting it would make a better addition to some future Nirvana retrospective along the lines of the Beatles' *1 Anthology* of the mid-Nineties.

In order to try and get her own way, Courtney then sued both Dave and Krist on the basis, her legal documents claimed, that 'You Know You're Right' was a 'potential "hit" of extraordinary artistic and commercial value'. It took a year for Dave and Krist's lawyers to fight it out with Courtney's legal team, before getting the outcome they felt they deserved when, in September 2002, it was announced by the Nirvana camp that the lawsuit had been settled, and that 'You Know You're Right' would after all be released on the compilation Dave and Krist were behind, simply titled *Nirvana*.

But while Dave and Krist had maintained a dignified silence on the subject, Courtney had taken her grievances public, claiming that Kurt 'hated' Dave by the end of his life. And, most ludicrously of all, that Dave was effectively taking food from her child's mouth.

'I also think she's a little bit jealous of Kurt and Dave's relationship, as proper musicians,' adds Anton Brookes. 'You know, Courtney's a good singer and songwriter, she's a good guitarist. But she's . . . she's a poor man's Kurt Cobain. And I think, to an extent, there is an inverted jealousy towards Dave. And it just seems to have festered and festered. Maybe there's financial issues that we don't know about, where she thinks she should be getting more than Dave or Krist are getting. I don't know. But I think Dave has just dealt with it admirably. He's just got on with it. Every so often he gets pissed off and frustrated and he fights fire with fire. But one thing I think Courtney's always tried to do with Dave, but he's never, ever engaged in it, is just mudslinging. Especially in this day and age with Twitter and the internet. And Courtney is so astute. Courtney should have been a scientist or something. She's ultra-intelligent. And Dave's never given her the time of day.'

Asked by Howard Stern if such plainly bizarre complaints actually hurt him, Dave confessed that they did. 'Honestly,' he said on Stern's show, 'the way I look at it is I have my version of what happened [in Nirvana]. And I have my memories. Pat [Smear] and I talk about that stuff all the time. And we laugh about the good times and we talk about the bad times sometimes. But you can't really let those things get to you … You also have to understand that circumstances were so extraordinary that everybody's got their version of what happened, you know? It's such a public event that whole thing. It's not like, my buddy Jimmy passed away …'

Hardly any wonder then that when the band got together to write material for another Foos album – Chris Shiflett's first with the band – things were once again teetering out of control. Work had begun just two months after flying back from London with Taylor. But things did not go well. Nobody seemed quite into it, least of all Dave. Nate developed what he described later as a 'shitty attitude' because Dave never seemed satisfied, while as far as the bassist was concerned things were going well. With Taylor now entirely clean and sober but still in the doghouse over his OD, he was content for the time being to merely go along with whatever his boss wanted. While Chris, who had been so looking forward to making his first album with the Foos was utterly dumbfounded, finding himself suddenly in a no man's land. He recalled how he would show up every day at the studio but never seemed to be called on to do anything. He'd hang out, drink coffee, have a late lunch, drink more coffee . . . Then go home. 'It fucking sucked.' According to Dave there was a snippy atmosphere all round. 'Infighting, whispers, blah blah blah . . .'

They carried on recording though, showing a work ethic if little else. Eventually though it became clear to Dave that he wasn't nearly as excited by the results as he should have been. In the past he'd been in a hurry to play new stuff for people. Now he wasn't sure he wanted anybody to hear what they'd been doing. It wasn't any one thing that could be easily fixed this time, either, like the drums, or the studio, or whatever. It was just . . . the whole thing. Bad vibes, man. Bummer. When they played what they had to John Silva and he shook his head that clinched it. The album would have to be scrapped, Dave decided. Nobody else except Nate disagreed.

'We had kind of a general blowout on that record,' he recalled in 2013, 'because the album sucked and we had to redo it. But it was during that process of discussing the album sucking that everybody really had a chance to air their grievances. Dave was like, "Hey man, why's it such a drag for you to come in and re-record these songs?" And I said, "Well, because I thought that the part I did was good."' But he soon came around to Dave's way of thinking. 'Having that conversation made me realise that I needed to approach what I was doing in the band differently. The good thing about that was that I think I'm a better player for the band now. I'd always relied on my instincts and said, "OK, whatever I think is going to be interesting here is going to be right for the song" and that's not necessarily the case. It changed my perspective and I would listen to the drummer more and think about what was happening with the vocal melody and think about what the general purpose of the song

On the tour bus. L-R: Chris Shiflett, Taylor Hawkins, Nate Mendel, Dave Grohl.
(Getty Images)

I'll stick around. Dave with one-time love, former Hole bassist Melissa Auf der Maur. (Getty Images)

A Fender guitar signed by Foo Fighters, 2005. It was featured in the 'Music, Mud and Mayhem' exhibition of memorabilia from the Reading Festival. (Geoffrey Swaine/ REX Shutterstock)

This is a call. Dave with newly-pregnant second wife Jordyn Blum, at a Grammy party in early 2006. (Getty Images)

(Left, above) Foo Fighters play to crowds of over 60,000 people at Hyde Park, London, 2006. (Getty Images)

The first time Foo Fighters headlined London's Wembley Stadium in 2008, 'I didn't sleep for six months leading up to it,' says Dave. (PA Images [above and left, below])

Legendary Nirvana and Foo Fighters producer Butch Vig. Working with Butch again, says Dave, was 'not unlike going back and fucking a girlfriend you had twenty years ago – perfectly natural and totally comfortable'. (Getty Images)

Dave Grohl reminisces about Nirvana on stage, headlining Reading festival in 2012. (Tom Watkins/ REX Shutterstock)

Dave Grohl's birthday bash in 2015. Smells like… success! Dave and Foos contemplate their ballooning fortunes. (Getty Images)

Dave Grohl performs on a throne-like set-up with his broken leg. On tour in 2015, after the accident that forced the Foos to cancel Glastonbury. Back on the sonic highway. (Getty Images)

was. My playing became simpler, but also more effective and direct and tighter, too.'

What nearly finished all of them off though was what Dave did next: deciding he would rather become a member of Queens of the Stone Age. Holy shit . . .

, For Chris, this was terrible news, worse than the limbo he'd endured in the studio. He'd joined the band, seen his 'dream come true' – now it looked like it was over. He could not get his head around it at all. But then neither could any of the others. Taylor, in particular, took it very badly, personally, like a slap in the kisser, payback time, maybe, he thought, for being such a fuck-up on the road. For once, Dave didn't even pretend to care. He didn't have to be there, struggling to keep the Foos on the right track. He could just go and do something more interesting, right then. So he did.

Formed in 1997 by the ex-Kyuss singer-guitarist Josh Homme, QOTSA were then one of the coolest bands on the planet rock. Neither their eponymous debut, released independently in 1998, nor their major-label debut, *Rated R*, in 2000, was a big chart success, but the band's critical reputation preceded them. If Kyuss, from Palm Desert in the Coachella valley, had been one of the forerunners of 'stoner rock', mixing wild peyote-wisdom with deep desert-sand blues, then Homme's vision for QOTSA went several steps further, advancing the prickly-cactus rhythms of Kyuss to exaggerated heights of technical expertise and dreamlike trance-music that both rocked and ruled, majestic in its decadent splendour.

In short, though they lacked any of the Foo Fighters' commercial success, QOTSA were, right then, a far more exciting proposition, musically, than any Dave had been involved with since the brilliantly real, frighteningly nightmarish *In Utero*. Always far more of a musical collective than a stand-alone

group, with each album always featuring several guest performers, from Rob Halford to Mark Lanegan, Dave joining the
Queens in the studio to record their third album, *Songs for the
Deaf*, was a surprisingly easy move for him to make. Excited by
the idea of simply becoming a drummer again on someone else's
album, he took to his new role with such enthusiasm he virtually
became a full-time member of the band, playing on the whole
album and appearing in the video for the album's lead single,
'No One Knows'.

For someone like Anton Brookes, who had known Dave since
he was the newbie in Nirvana, there was less surprise in this
latest development in the Foo Fighters' story. 'When the Foo
Fighters supposedly split up or when the Foo Fighters ditch an
album and go back in the studio, Dave's always gone with his
instincts, and his instincts, 9.9 times out of ten, have always
proved right,' says Anton. 'From sacking musicians, to bringing
musicians in, when he went off with QOTSA, everybody was
like, "Oh my god, what's happening here?" But that was part
of his development. I still think that was probably part of the
throwback from Nirvana. Like, what am I doing with my life?
He was still a relatively young man when he drummed on [*Songs
for the Deaf*]. I remember going to see them play at the Astoria
2, in London, and I'd not seen Dave drum since Nirvana. I might
have seen him drum on the odd song for the Foos or something,
and I saw him on TV drumming for Tom Petty. But to watch
him drum live again . . . To this day, I still think that's the best
QOTSA album, and I think that's partly down to Grohl. What
he contributed to that record, it cannot be taken lightly.

'And when you go and see him onstage . . . the Queens, they're
proper musicians, a proper band. And they're a cool, cult phenomenon. There's nothing throwaway about QOTSA, and to
play with them, to do something with them, you've got to be on

top of your game. When Dave went behind the stool onstage, or when you see him in the video for 'No One Knows', and he's drumming. The look on his face, the tempo of the song and he's breathing hard, you know, you can tell he's had to *train* to get there as a drummer, he's had to go back and put some time in to get there. But I think as a musician, when he recorded with them, he just went in and did it, one or two takes.'

With the rest of the Foos left in limbo for the duration, news of an appearance together onstage at the 2002 Coachella festival in California, in April, was seen as a sign of light at the end of the tunnel until it was explained to them that Queens of the Stone Age would also be appearing – with Dave on drums. Suddenly, Coachella was seen as a make-or-break date by all of them. 'We nearly broke up,' Taylor recalled in 2005. 'We didn't know what we were going to do. I wasn't surprised when we binned the demo: I was thinking, "Should we even be making records?" It was such a disorganised, unfocused time. I don't think Dave was sure of what he wanted to do and, you know, he is the leader. I think he was still in love with the Queens of the Stone Age stuff; he really wanted to go and play with them.'

The closer the date of the two-day festival approached, the more the tension grew among the freaked-out Foos. With Dave rehearsing some of the time with QOTSA, the rest of the time with his own band, the atmosphere in the Foos became unbearable. Nobody was talking any more, they just gritted their teeth and braced themselves to get through the show. When, at one rehearsal, Chris joked about how you could cut the air with a knife, a huge fight broke out between the warring members. Mainly Taylor and Dave. They finally had it out. All of it. For ever. Finally. Fuck it. Done.

Taylor hated it that Dave had gone off to play drums with QOTSA. Dave couldn't have insulted him more if he'd fucked his old lady. But Dave was now playing the long game. Foo Fighters was his band. His band; his rules. His moves. Taylor and the others would just have to suck it up. But when Taylor made a point of not going to see Dave play with QOTSA at Coachella, Dave predictably got upset, though what he expected Taylor to do, nobody knew. Taylor: 'I was supposed to be happy that Dave was having such a good time.' But he wasn't fucking happy at all. Why should he be? This was a piss-take, right? Right, Dave, man?

Says Paul Brannigan: 'The Foos were in a pretty bad shape.' Dave working with QOTSA was 'a bit of a fuck-you to his band mates. Like, if you're not bothered then I'm gonna go and do what I wanna do, you know? And it spiralled into something it wasn't supposed to be. Obviously then that sparked confrontation within the band. It led to Dave laying down the law and basically saying, this is my band and we do it this way, or we don't do it at all. Or rather, *you* don't do it at all.'

There was another quarrel between Dave and Taylor the following day, just hours before the Foos were due on stage, over the set list, during which Dave told Taylor if he didn't like it he could fucking leave. To which Taylor replied that he would be doing exactly that – right after the show.

Then came the show. Queens had gone down exceptionally well the day before, but they had been twelfth on the bill, coming on mid-afternoon. The Foos, third on the bill, and onstage early evening, went down an absolute storm, all the tension and friction causing them to virtually explode into the set. Their first show since the desultory V Festival in England eight months before, and they played brilliantly. Dave was on fire. Taylor was out of his skin. Chris and Nate just had to keep up for it to be one of their best shows ever.

When it was over, Dave asked Taylor to take a walk with him

backstage, where for the first time since the drummer's OD they talked as friends again, brothers reunited. Dudes. The following morning it was agreed they band would meet up again at Dave's studio in Virginia, and see what happened when they revisited some of the material from the aborted album.

'Theoretically, that should have been the end of the Foo Fighters – their staring-at-the-abyss moment. Once they managed to negotiate that then suddenly everything was a bit easier. Everybody knew their place. Everybody knew how things operated. But that fight was their defining moment. Once they got that out of their system then everyone understood how things operated and whatever Dave chose to do, they always had the faith in him that he was coming back. These are the things that Dave wants to do and we'll just chill here until he comes back,' says Paul Brannigan.

Their first day back at 606, Dave walked in with a brand-new song. It was called 'Times Like These' and it seemed to say it all, with its heightened message of 'a brand new sky to hang the stars upon tonight'. A song that Dave admitted had been about the choice he'd been wrestling with all year: 'Do I stay or run away?'

For Dave it was a musical rebirth. They re-recorded the whole album in a week, out at 606, as before with the third album. Only this didn't sound anything like that. This sounded darker, heavier, less sure, yet more powerful, more passionate than ever before. They called it *One by One*, as if in homage to their new stated belief in taking things one day at a time. One second at a time. One breath in and one breath out. This was the way it would be from now on, Dave was sure. The others, most of all Taylor, could only agree. What else could they do? What else would they *want* to do? It was get onboard the bus time or get off – for good.

In the end all the fussing and fighting meant the album would cost over a million dollars to complete. For Dave, it was an easy decision to make. The most monumental track on the album was 'All My Life', one of the few survivors from the original aborted sessions. First time around it had cost hundreds of thousands of dollars and taken weeks to try and get right. The newer, post-Coachella version took half an hour and was done and dusted in the 606 basement, and, according to Dave, 'became the biggest fucking song the band ever had'.

Stupendously anthemic, like something The Who might have done in their 'Won't Get Fooled Again' prime, 'All My Life' became the calling card of the new album, one of the corner-stones of the Foo Fighters' live set that remains so to this day. It also became their biggest single in the UK since 'This is a Call' when it reached No. 5 in September, before repeating its success around the rest of the world, including the US, where it became another mainstream Top 40 success and went to No. 1 on the Alternative Rock chart. As a result, *One by One* became the Foo Fighters' biggest-selling album yet: their first No. 1 in the UK, Ireland and Australia; and by far their biggest chart success in the US – No. 3 – so far.

Released just two months after *Songs for the Deaf* had become the Queens of the Stone Age's big commercial breakthrough, the knock-on effect for both bands was extraordinary. While Dave's added profile had brought QOTSA greater mainstream visibility – not least with the brilliantly executed 'No One Knows' video – there's no mistaking either the obvious influence working with the Queens had had on Dave's own approach. Unlike its lack-lustre predecessor, *One by One* positively bristled with nailed-on power, achingly tight rhythms and unashamedly me-first drive.

There were some more self-consciously balladic moments – the juddering 'Disenchanted Lullaby', the turgid 'Tired of You', the discursive 'Lonely as You' – but the main thrust of the album's 11 tracks was determinedly 'up', decidedly shiny and new and almost unnervingly bold. In the final analysis, *One by One* sounds like what it is: two halves of two quite different albums bolted and sheened into one, the best moments all to be found on the singles, with 'Times Like These' justly following 'All My Life' high into the world's singles charts.

If Chris Shiflett's influence is anywhere to be found it was not immediately obvious, although he shared band writing credits with Taylor and Nate. The main message was: we are back, bigger and better than before. Well, they were certainly bigger. Over the course of the next two years the band would tour like there was no tomorrow, making hay it seemed while the sun still shone, headlining a brace of sold-out shows at London's Wembley Arena; then the 16,000-capacity Colour Line arena in Hamburg; the 17,000-capacity Arena in Berlin; the 25,000-capacity Showground Arena in Sydney; and, back in the States, giant rock landmarks like the 17,000-capacity Cobo Center arena in Detroit. At the same time, they now became everybody's favourite rock band – especially for the people that didn't feel they especially liked rock.

When, finally, the dice stopped rolling and they came off the road long enough for Dave to decide what their next move would be, it was the start of 2005, halfway through a decade they had so far spent almost entirely on the road. Time for something . . . new. Something . . . different. But what exactly? Privately, Dave considered taking up the offer of writing his first film score. 'Walking After You' had been used in the movie version of *The X Files*; and Dave had written 'A3120' especially for the soundtrack album of the 1998 movie *Godzilla*, and more recently the track 'The One' for the soundtrack to the Jack Black movie *Orange County*. Other, bigger offers had come in since then. But after such a long period of time away on the road Dave wasn't sure what he wanted to do, except that it had to offer some much-needed contrast to the life he'd been living.

In the end, he simply sat down, alone, just him and his acoustic guitar, and began writing. No big ideas, no real agenda, just stuff that took him away of its own accord. Pretty soon he had ten new songs, all acoustic, reflective, pure, and no idea what to do with them. He thought about a solo album. Perhaps the time was right for something like that? But Dave Grohl hadn't worked his nuts off these past ten years building the Foo Fighters up into an unstoppable machine to allow it to diffuse into solo albums and side projects right now. Especially right now, on the back of his biggest sales success since the height of Nirvana. Besides, what would a Dave Grohl solo album really mean? How would that be different from making another Foo Fighters album, where he had the final say anyway?

So, somewhat reluctantly to begin with, not entirely sure what he was proposing, he played the songs to the others in the band. 'Who's to say what we should sound like?' he told them. Nate agreed. The fact that the songs weren't what one would have expected from a Foos record was precisely 'why [they] should go on the record'. When Dave ran the idea past the grown-ups at Gold Mountain though, they frowned. An all-acoustic Foo Fighters album? Really, seriously?

So Dave came up with a better idea that allowed him to have his cake and swallow it whole. A double album, one all-electric and razzed up; the other all-acoustic and spaced out. 'I have to have loud rock music in my life somewhere,' he explained in Classic Rock, in 2005, likening the whole to 'the bottle and the hangover'. The hard rock side of the bargain being 'my Jack-and-Coke record' and the acoustic side 'my Sapphire-and-Martini-with-Kylie record.'

Shrewd as ever, Dave was deflecting from the fact that what he'd really set out to do was make the grandest possible musical statement yet. Something akin to the great double concept albums of the Seventies that he still adored, like Led Zeppelin's monolithic *Physical Graffiti* or, going further back, the Beatles' groundbreaking *White Album*. 'I wanted to do something special,' he shrugged. As a result there would be a panoramic feel to the finished album, which Dave had now decided to call *In Your Honor*, that also summoned up such self-aggrandising double-album works as The Who's much-maligned-at-the-time *Quadrophenia*, or the Rolling Stones' equally misunderstood-first-time-around *Exile on Main Street* double – something heavily underlined by the all-electric album, with its filmic title track.

The album was recorded at another new studio Dave had purpose-built, this time in Northridge, California, which he named Studio 606 West and that took nearly four months to finish constructing. Meanwhile, the band rehearsed in North Hollywood's Mates Rehearsal Studios, where 'we ended up with three or four different versions of about thirty songs', according to the album's co-producer, Nick Raskulinecz, who added that 'it got to the point where I didn't want them to play the rock songs any more. I was afraid they were going to get stale.'

After the crooked lightning of *One by One*, the two-CD release of the grandiose *In Your Honor* in June 2005 was greeted with suitably gasping amounts of awe by Foo Fighters fans – enough to make it their best-selling album since their first two, going to No. 2 in both Britain and America. 'I look at this album as kind of the end of one chapter and the beginning of something new,' Dave proudly told the US music industry bible *Billboard*. 'With the rock record, we finally got the aggressive, anthemic thing down. With the acoustic album, it offers some kind of look into the future of things we're capable of doing and the direction we could move if we wanted to.'

Reviewing the album for the *New York Times*, the estimable Jon Pareles seemed to agree, describing *In Your Honor* as 'an unexpected magnum opus', though he felt strongly that 'the rock CD overpowers the acoustic one', but that 'among the quieter songs, there are enough supple melodies and hypnotic guitar patterns to suggest fine prospects for a follow-through album'. A more accurate appraisal followed in *Rolling Stone*, where Barry Walters hailed the acoustic album over the electric, pointing out not unreasonably that *In Your Honor* 'could have been easily pruned down to one disc', complaining not unjustly that several of the electric rocker tracks 'strain so hard that the melody gets lost', lurching along in a 'cartoonish headbanging fashion' that 'accentuates the band's self-inflicted one-dimensionality'.

But Dave Grohl, nicest man in rock, people's champion and world's greatest everyman capable of doing just about anything, no longer cared deeply about what the reviewers had to say, pro or con. His career had now moved past that. He was now dealing directly with his people. The advent of social media had seen to that, through MySpace, then Facebook and of course the spanking new Foo Fighters website. As did his plan to embark on a one-off acoustic tour of theatres. In the new age of 'event media' in the music business, Dave, sharp as ever, had grasped the nettle and come up trumps again, announcing a detour from the band's already planned arena tour to do seven smaller acoustic shows in July and August 2006, beginning at the Seattle Paramount Theater, on 11 July, the setting for so many classic pre-fame Nirvana shows, and highlighting at New York's Beacon Theater, on 21 August.

Aware of the limits of all-acoustic shows, stretching back to his experience with Nirvana's *Unplugged* show more than a decade before, Dave also announced that the band would be augmented on stage by a violinist, Petra Haden (recently of Beck and Green Day), and a keyboardist, Rami Jaffee (formerly of The Wallflowers and Everclear), both of whom also appeared on *In Your Honor,* plus the ace percussionist Drew Hester, who had recently produced Taylor's side project, *Taylor Hawkins & the Coattail Riders.*

And that was not all, the best being kept for last – cue drum roll: the return of Pat Smear! Pat, who had most recently been playing reunion shows – minus Darby, of course – with The Germs would be coming along not as a fully fledged member, Dave stressed, but as a 'touring guitarist'. The idea was to perform live for the first time most of the songs from *In Your Honor*'s second, more mellow side, along with whittled-down versions of all the biggest Foos hits. Pat's return came as a huge surprise to Foos fans generally, but most especially to Chris Shiflett, who had no idea what was going on until Dave let him know just weeks before. But then Dave no longer felt the need to consult with anybody on anything when it came to decisions about what he was going to do with his band. Chris, though, admitted he was aghast. 'To me that was just a guy that wanted my job,' he said of Pat. 'I was just like, "You've got to be fucking kidding me."' Pat, with his hotwired sense of entitlement, claimed not to feel weird about it at all, only in the sense that he hoped it didn't freak Chris out too much. And if it did, then, well . . .

In fact, Pat had been angling for a return to the Foo Fighters almost from the moment he'd left nearly ten years before. Watching from the sidelines as the band got bigger and bigger without him, he realised that, boy, had he made a fucking big mistake. When he heard that Franz had been booted out, he began calling Dave, 'just to say hi', making noises about wanting to come back. According to Chris, he'd only been in the band a couple of months when 'Pat almost came back'. Dave didn't know that Chris had got wind of the fact that he and Pat had been speaking and scheming together again. But Chris, shrewdly, said nothing, just waited to see which way the wind was gonna blow. Dave, more wary than ever of making another bad public move, after the loss of first Will, then Pat and now Franz, knew he had to tread carefully, though. The announcement about Chris joining the band had already gone out. Now he was gonna announce that, actually, that was a mistake, and Pat was back? Uh huh. Also, could Pat really be relied on not to let him down again? Dave had cried and begged Pat not to leave. He promised himself he would never allow himself to be put in that position again.

According to Pat, it was all his decision: 'There was at least a couple of times where I called Dave and said, "I want back." Then when it looked like it might actually happen that was when I got scared,' he declared in the *Back and Forth* documentary. But Dave knew he had to play his cards close to his chest. Simply couldn't afford to make any more rash moves. So he fobbed Pat off with some time's-not-right guff and told him: maybe next time, buddy. Then tucked the idea away in his back pocket like a get-out-of-jail card while he waited to see how things turned out with the latest version of the band.

Chris, meanwhile, not knowing what to believe, never stopped looking over his shoulder, his feeling during those years: 'It probably will end, sooner than I want it to.' Dave's idea to finally bring Pat back as a 'touring guitarist', strictly for the acoustic shows, was a wonderfully subtle way of testing the water. Pat didn't get a free pass back into the Foos and Chris maintained the illusion that he had not been usurped in the band. When, as things turned out, Chris and Pat instantly hit it off, from their very first rehearsal, it opened the door wide for Pat's full return.

Not yet but very, very soon. Dave had already decided. It was just a case of getting round to actually letting the guys know. Hell, yes, it was awkward to begin with. Dave of course just pretended not to notice. He'd learned by now that that was the best way for him to operate in such circumstances. He'd made his decision, let the others figure out their own ways of dealing with it.

Meanwhile, Pat's return, albeit in a minor role to begin with, was greeted with joy by longer-standing Foos fans, and deep fascination by the younger generation. Chris was a very good guitarist and a perfectly serviceable foil for Dave's livewire on-stage persona. But having Pat back in the band brought back a much greater sense of character and destiny to the Foo Fighters; a much greater sense of fun. As Charles R. Cross points out, 'The early Foo Fighters had a sense of humour that was sarcastic. It was really Pat Smear's sense of humour. Early on I think Pat had a much bigger role in keeping everybody grounded. Pat is just the kind of guy that is no nonsense. He frankly has the sense of humour far closer to the sense of humour that Kurt Cobain had than anybody else I've ever met in rock.' And no one was more aware of that than Dave Grohl.

When the acoustic dates sold out, three more shows were added, over three consecutive nights at the Pantages Theatre in LA, which would be filmed and later released as the live CD and in-concert DVD *Skin and Bones*. When Clive Davis, then the president and *grand fromage* at RCA, came to one of the acoustic dates he helped clear Dave's thoughts on where to go next. Dave had been thinking it would be great to have an acoustic experience, and a rock experience, for separate audiences. Hence: the jumble of acoustic and electric dates that year. It was Clive who told him: why not do both together?

It seemed so obvious yet it took someone of Clive's stature

– someone who had signed Bruce Springsteen, Billy Joel, Aerosmith, Pink Floyd and dozens of other superstars – to say it before the light bulb went on in Dave's head. Dude, if Clive thought it was a good idea then what are we waiting for?

From here on in, the Foo Fighters would become far more than its constituent parts. It was no longer a case of what happens is we lose one member or bring another back, the new live version of the Foo Fighters would be a constantly evolving travelling circus of musical super-troupers who cared more about entertaining the crowd than they did pining for credibility.

'I always remember Dave talking about when he first met Neil Young, how that made him realise the band had longevity,' Anton Brookes recalls. 'You could forge it into a career. A band didn't have to self-combust after two or three albums. Even after ten years, it could go on and on. He also saw the close-knit family which Neil Young's community is. In the kitchen there was Neil Young, his wife, band members and their family, preparing food for everybody. Something as simple as that, Dave saw that as an indication that actually you don't have to be stereotypical: that you can go your own way. That he'd earned the right.'

12. Not Like the Others

In Your Honor and the subsequent Skin and Bones tour hadn't just allowed the Foos to step off the treadmill, it had shown Dave Grohl that there were different ways of doing things. The Foo Fighters had spent the first decade of their career with their foot on the gas, rocketing down their own sonic highway, learning to fly. But now it was time to head off-map and see where they ended up.

'After that tour, I finally realised the possibilities hidden in a lot of our songs,' Dave told *Billboard*. 'We had been kind of caged by the fact we were just a four-piece rock band. With additional instrumentation, which we'd never really experimented with before the last album, we could take songs from ground level to soaring heights.'

Grohl's reputation as the nicest man in rock had been cemented years before, but ever since the demise of Nirvana, he'd been a serious contender for the title of Hardest-Working Man in Showbusiness. The instruments had barely even been packed away after the Skin and Bones dates before the seeds for the Foo Fighters' sixth album were already being sown in his head. He refused to entertain the thought of going back to the heads-down, arms-aloft arena rock with which his band had made their name, but neither could they repeat *In Your Honor*'s binary electric/acoustic split.

'We've been a band for thirteen years,' Dave explained. 'Album after album, we've tried to redesign what we do. Not reinvent, but just make it all a little prettier. We wanted to experiment and go deeper melodically. The first record to me sounds like it could have been a garage hardcore band. The idea now is to step it up and make *Odessey and Oracle*.' He was joking, but only just. He was referring to the 1968 album by British band The Zombies. A work of peculiarly English psychedelia made by men who looked like they'd never touched a psychedelic drug in their lives, *Odessey and Oracle* was destined to remain little more than a footnote in rock's history books before a turn-of-the-millennium reappraisal rubber-stamped it as a bona fide cult classic. Re-creating an album along the hazy lines of *Odessey and Oracle* might have been a big ask even for Dave, but the point remained: the Foo Fighters' horizons had opened up. Some said they had opened up a little far, perhaps, put off by the sheer overindulgent weight of the double *In Your Honor* set, but for Dave Grohl it was now anything goes.

Part of the challenge was simply to stave off boredom. What does the rock star who has seemingly achieved everything do next? He'd spent the last decade and more playing the part of the textbook rock star, 'running around a stage with a beer in my hand, singing my fucking throat out . . . You do get to the point where you think, "Man, there's got to be more than just that, so let's explore a little bit more."'

But there was another reason for his burning desire to keep moving forward. In April 2006, Dave became a father for the first time when his wife, Jordyn, gave birth to a daughter, Violet Maye. While most new dads find themselves locked in a hellish cycle of sleepless nights and nappy changing, fatherhood only seemed to amp up his already irrepressible energy levels. More importantly, it flicked a switch in his brain. Suddenly, he found that having a daughter fed into his songwriting in new and entirely unexpected ways.

'It made me feel like the big picture had opened up so wide that I wasn't afraid of anything any more, to try things I've never done and to say things I've never said before,' he gushed to *Kerrang!*. 'It changed everything about the way I write. Now when I get fucking angry or defensive or something, I just want to rip someone's fucking head off. When I feel love, I feel it in fucking every cell of my body. So it just makes me fucking more alive. So when you're writing music with that in mind or that in your heart, everything just blooms into this fucking incredibly colourful feeling.'

This newfound energy could instantly be heard in the new ultra-vivid songs he was writing. Abandoning the laboured electric-or-acoustic approach of *In Your Honor*, early demos for the prospective album featured songs that ranged from what the frontman described as 'wall of noise hard shit' to 'fucking mellow piano ballads.' Unlike its predecessors, however, there was no over-arching concept or philosophy behind the process. 'The only philosophy that Dave had for this record was anything goes,' said Taylor Hawkins. 'After playing that acoustic tour we shed some of the fear of incorporating mellower stuff with the heavy stuff.'

The process of actually writing the album was no different to the way the band had worked before. Dave always kept an acoustic guitar to hand whether he was in his studio or his lounge watching TV on the couch. Ideas would be sketched out; if they worked, he would bring them to the band's practice space to turn into 'big loud rock songs' – or, in some cases, quite the opposite. After the turf wars and near implosion of the early 2000s, these days the rest of the band were just happy for their fully acknowledged leader to shoulder the songwriting burden.

But if it was now crystal clear who was in charge, they weren't unaware of the scale of his responsibilities.

'We have a lot of people that work for us,' the newly sober Taylor said. 'Every time Dave puts a pen to paper or picks up the guitar, it's a big deal. I don't think he thinks about it like that, but every time we're due for a new Foo Fighters record it's like, "Okay, Dave, what do you got?"'

That said, Dave's determinedly unconventional approach to the new album needed an equally unconventional producer. Various names were bandied around, but there was one the frontman kept returning to: Gil Norton. Of course, the Foos had history with Norton – both good and bad, in Dave's eyes. He hadn't forgotten what a hard taskmaster the producer had been on *The Colour and the Shape*, with the scorchingly honest approach of a drill sergeant. Yet for many that remained still one of the best Foo Fighters albums and Dave was equally mindful of how effectively Norton had elevated the songs to another level, giving the Foos' sound the extra punch it needed while sharpening its sleek pop appeal.

The one consistent criticism of every Foo Fighters album since then had been that they had never really reached outside their comfort zone. Gil Norton, Dave decided, would be the perfect man to help push them up a gear. Norton, who had been involved in numerous critically acclaimed projects with artists like Patti Smith and Feeder, had nevertheless not enjoyed a huge international hit since he'd last worked with the Foos a decade before. He was more than happy to work with them again. The first step was to spend two weeks sitting at a table, alone with Dave, deconstructing everything he had written so far, focusing on the minutiae of what made a song work: arrangements, structure, melody, dynamics, harmony ... As they progressed, they whittled the songs down from 40 to 20 to, finally, just 12, stripping things back and then painstakingly rebuilding them, piecing things together, said Dave, 'like a little Lego fire truck'.

This ultra-methodical approach chimed with the singer's own determined streak – an aspect of his character that he no longer tried to conceal from the public. It seemed the more of his working methods he revealed the more his fans liked it. Liked it that it was Dave in charge. Liked it that it was Dave's band, Dave's direction; Dave's full attention they were getting every time they played one of his songs or bought one of his tickets.

'We went and sat in a rehearsal space for about four weeks,' Grohl recalled. 'We got deep. We'd play a song a day, and I mean *a song a day*, from noon to midnight. By the time we got to tracking, we were like the fucking Bad Brains – the tightest band in the world.' Of course, Dave had absolutely no intention whatsoever of turning the Foo Fighters into Bad Brains. His gaze was now firmly on claiming the same territory huge international mainstream rock acts like U2 and Coldplay occupied. He just liked to throw names like Bad Brains into the conversation to somehow make him feel more real. Like he was still one of us. When in fact he had not been that for too long now.

For the volatile Taylor Hawkins, who had yet to join the band when they recorded *The Colour and the Shape* with Norton, it was an eye-opener – albeit one he actually came to enjoy. 'We basically played each of these songs a hundred different times, trying every little thing every different way,' he recalled with a smile. 'With him we took each song down to the studs and remodelled it completely. Gil's whole philosophy is to stretch things out as far and wide as possible to see where these songs could go.'

Having decided which tracks made the grade, the band entered Studio 606 West – 'our fortress', as Dave now called it – in March 2007 to start recording. It wasn't all work and no play, though. Dave and Taylor embarked on a competition to see who could go longest without shaving. The result, after nearly four months' recording, was a pair of luxuriant beards. 'I was looking like [late Beach Boys drummer] Dennis Wilson in his homeless period, hitching on the Pacific Coast Highway with a bottle of orange juice and vodka in his hand,' Taylor boasted, while Dave compared himself to heroically hirsute ZZ Top frontman Billy Gibbons.

Mid-recording, the band descended en masse on the LA Forum to see Black Sabbath spin-off band Heaven or Hell, featuring Dave's friend and sometime collaborator, Tony Iommi. The trip was one part team-bonding experience, one part frat boys' night out. A tour bus was duly hired, and someone thought to supply beer bongs – a typically American device to aid consumption of vast quantities of booze at a rapid rate. Unsurprisingly, Dave's recollections of the gig were hazy, though he woke up the next morning with a painful reminder of the evening's hijinks: a cracked rib.

But the most surreal moment occurred during the Superbowl on 4 February. The pinnacle of the American football season, this battle royale between the Chicago Bears and the Indianapolis Colts was watched by an estimated 90 million people in the US alone, plus millions more worldwide. By 2007, the half-time show had become an integral part of the glitzy, garish spectacle – every A-list superstar from Michael Jackson to U2 had played this 15-minute musical interlude in front of a huge TV audience. In 2007, it was Prince's turn. Coming off the back of a decade-long cold streak, the Purple One's career was on the up again and he was determined to put on a half-time show to remember. And, despite torrential rain, that's what he did, serving up his Eighties hits 'Let's Go Crazy' and 'Baby I'm A Star', before launching into electrifying covers of 'All Along the

Watchtower', Creedence Clearwater Revival's 'Proud Mary' . . . and the Foo Fighters' 'Best of You'.

Taylor was watching the Superbowl on TV with the Foos' former producer Nick Raskulinecz and members of Rush, who were working with Raskulinecz on their latest album, and couldn't believe what he was seeing. 'I'm outside smoking a cigarette with [Rush drummer] Neil Peart and someone sticks their head outside and goes, "Uh, dude, Prince is doing your song,"' he told MTV.

There was no small degree of irony in Prince's cover. Just five years earlier, Prince had blocked the Foos from releasing their version of his gloriously sleazy 1984 funk rock classic 'Darling Nikki' in the US, pompously proclaiming that bands should 'write their own song'. Whether his own take on 'Best of You' was a heartfelt tribute or belated dig wasn't immediately clear. 'Dude, I have no idea why he did it, but I'd love to find out,' Taylor told MTV. 'The thought went through my head that maybe he was doing it as a sort of "Fuck you" to us, or maybe he really likes the song. Either way, it was pretty amazing to have a guy like Prince covering one of our songs – and actually doing it better than we did.'

As the beard-growing competitions, drunken hijinks and unexpected superstar tributes indicated, there was an optimism and energy to the sessions that had been absent just a few years before. The studio buzzed with the confidence of a band truly hitting their stride. The end result of this hot streak was both the most focused yet musically diverse record the Foos had made in years. While it had its share of ready-made arena rock anthems in the shape of 'The Pretender' – its compelling 'What if I say I'm not like the others' refrain the mission statement of the whole album – and the assuredly breezy 'Long Road to Ruin', elsewhere Dave boldly attempted to mix things up. He cited

Metallica as an influence on the gnarly 'Erase/Replace' ('I still listen to *Kill 'Em All* at least once a week,' he claimed), while 'Cheer Up, Boys (Your Make Up is Running)' was effortless thrash-pop that Grohl only half-jokingly compared to R.E.M. and their 1989 mainstream breakthrough album, *Green*. At the other end of the spectrum was the stripped-back 'Stranger Things Have Happened', a song whose hushed tension wouldn't have been out of place on Nirvana's *Unplugged* album, and acoustic instrumental 'The Ballad of the Beaconsfield Miners', a song featuring virtuoso acoustic guitarist Kaki King and a tribute to the 17 men who narrowly escaped death during the collapse of Tasmania's Beaconsfield mine in April 2006.

There were some unexpected left turns as well. The piano-led 'Statues' was Dave unashamedly tapping into his inner Paul McCartney; the result wouldn't have sounded out of place on a 1970s Wings album. 'I was quite nervous about putting it on the record because it's a big departure,' he confessed. 'Then I thought, "What the fuck? That's exactly why we should put it on the record."'

The new album also found Dave finally accepting his role as a serious lyricist in a way that he'd never allowed himself to before. Long gone was the guy who rubbished his own lyrics, getting in his excuses early, claiming he only wrote them quickly, almost as an afterthought. It had never been true, only now he no longer felt the need to apologise for voicing his increasingly mature emotions. A large part of this was down to the changes in his domestic circumstances. 'I used to be scared,' he told *Clash* magazine. 'I used to be afraid to say certain things, but after becoming a father, the big picture really does open up a lot and you realise that life's too short to hold back those things that you've always wanted to do or always wanted to say.'

No Foo Fighters album would be complete, of course, without speculation that at least one song was about Kurt Cobain. In this case, it was 'Let It Die'. In fairness to the critics, the lines 'A simple man and his blushing bride / Intravenous, intertwined' seemed to point in only one obvious direction. The fact that it echoed the same quiet/loud dynamics as Grohl's old band only amplified the probable connection. This time, though, he didn't bother to deny it. '[It's] a song that's written about feeling helpless to someone else's demise,' he told the *Mail on Sunday*. 'I've seen people lose it all to drugs and heartbreak and death. It's happened more than once in my life, but the one that's most noted is Kurt. And there are a lot of people that I've been angry with in my life, but the one that's most noted is Courtney. So it's pretty obvious to me that those correlations are gonna pop up every now and again.'

The song that was emblematic of what the Foo Fighters were doing with the album though was the closing track, 'Home'. A stark, startling pared-down piano ballad, it was as far from 'This is a Call' or even 'Learn to Fly' as it was possible to get. This is Dave Grohl, 38-year-old husband and father, baring his soul.

'I sat and wrote the lyrics in about ten minutes, sang it once, listened to it, and just felt overwhelmed by how revealing it was,' he said, simply. 'It made me feel quite vulnerable, so much so that it's hard to listen to. I get really choked up thinking about all the time I spend away from the things that are important to me. It's tough being away on tour; it's even tough just to be talking about how much I wish I was with my family.'

'Home' also gave the album its name. Whereas in the past Dave had agonised over album titles, favouring the direct and to the point, here he wanted something that summed up the album's breadth and diversity; something that gave it the weight it deserved. There was a line in 'Home' that fitted perfectly:

'Echoes, silence, patience and grace, all of these moments I'll never replace.' *Echoes, Silence, Patience & Grace* . . . The sixth Foo Fighters album had its name.

'I thought it was nice because it's open to interpretation and it's a beautiful title,' Grohl told *Clash*. 'I think the album is beautiful in its diversity and its melody and its musicality.' Not all of his band mates were on quite the same page, though. Taylor, as usual, for one, led the charge, declaring the album far too polished for his taste. 'It's pristine,' he complained to *Drummer* magazine, 'a Steely Dan version of the Foo Fighters.'

But Dave had learned to take such utterances with a pinch of salt. If Taylor wanted to play boss in an interview with a *drumming* magazine that was fine by Dave, who now had bigger fish to fry. 'At the end of the day, I wanna jump up onstage in front of 80,000 people and make 'em kick up dirt for a few hours,' he informed *Q* magazine in yet another cover feature. 'But the quality and craft of what we've done is far above anything we've ever done before.'

That desire to 'jump up in front of 80,000 people' was now closer to being fulfilled than he knew. The Foo Fighters finished work on *Echoes, Silence, Patience & Grace* in June 2007, and the album was set for release three months later, in September. But before that there was the matter of the biggest performance of the Foo Fighters' career so far: Live Earth.

On 21 January 2007, the unlikely team of former US Vice President-turned-environmental-crusader Al Gore and A-list hip hop producer and singer Pharrell Williams had announced a series of seven simultaneous benefit concerts taking place on 7 July under the banner of Live Earth. These shows would be held on each of the seven continents, and were collectively designed as a consciousness-raising exercise for global warming and climate change issues – a hot-button topic ever since the release of Gore's Oscar-winning documentary, *An Inconvenient Truth*, the previous year.

Live Earth stuck closely to the template laid out by the landmark Live Aid concert more than 20 years earlier: every A-list band and superstar under one roof – or, in this case, seven roofs – where the eyes of the world could focus on them. The European Live Earth show, where Dave and the Foos would be high on the bill, was the biggest of all. Held at London's enormous, 86,000-capacity Wembley Stadium, the bill brought together the biggest names in pop (Madonna, The Black Eyed Peas, Pussycat Dolls), alternative rock (Red Hot Chili Peppers, Snow Patrol, Razorlight) and hip hop and R&B (Beastie Boys, John Legend, Corinne Bailey Rae). There were high-profile reunions (Genesis, Duran Duran and, to the delight of Dave and the rest of the Foos, spoof Eighties rockers Spinal Tap), housewives' favourites (James Blunt, Paolo Nutini) and even a lone representative from the world of heavy metal (Metallica, dude!).

It was into this billion-dollar line-up that the Foo Fighters found themselves parachuted. For Dave Grohl, it was an opportunity to engage with politics for the first time since his days on the Washington, DC, hardcore punk scene – though, this time, it would be in front of an audience that ran into the billions. 'I grew up in Virginia, where we had beautiful seasons, summer, winter, spring and fall,' he said ahead of the show. 'In LA you don't get that, you get heat, and in the last six years I've lived here every summer has gotten hotter than the one before. My priority is to look out for my daughter's future, not to mention the wellbeing of the human race.'

On the day of the show, London was bathed in sunshine – ironic, given the cause behind the show. For Taylor, it really was a baptism of fire. The day's entertainment kicked off with the SOS Allstars, an all-drumming supergroup featuring Hawkins alongside his hero, Queen sticksman Roger Taylor, and Chad Smith of the Red Hot Chili Peppers, plus more than 40 back-up drummers from backgrounds as diverse as the British Army and East London bhangra institute The Dhol Foundation. Watching from the side of the stage, Dave was suddenly made ecstatically aware of the sheer scale of the day. 'You see Wembley Stadium with all of those people and it's like jumping into a cold lake, like "Holy fucking shit this is HUGE!" Not to mention two billion people watching it on television!'

The Foo Fighters found themselves in the slightly surreal position of being the night's penultimate act. Even more sur-really, they were sandwiched between burlesque-themed girl band Pussycat Dolls and the Queen of Pop herself, Madonna. 'I thought it was kind of funny,' Dave told the *NME*. 'I just thought, "All right, let's do this!"'

At precisely 9.17 p.m., following an introduction by comedian-lately-turned-political commentator Russell Brand, the Foo Fighters took to the Live Earth stage and launched straight into a ferocious 'All My Life'. The MO for their 20-minute set was exactly the same as Taylor's latest heroes Queen's had famously been at their now-legendary Live Aid show: get on, play the hits, knock 'em dead. As well as 'All My Life', their five-song set featured 'My Hero', 'Times Like These', 'Best of You' and a startling, stripped-down 'Everlong'. The response from the crowd was uninhibited euphoria. 'Once we got to the middle of "My Hero",' said Dave afterwards, 'I was like, "Ah, I think I've got these fuckers in the palm of my hand!"'

Dave was charm itself, his Every Dude persona utterly in keeping with the serious-but-celebratory tone of the day. The Foos themselves looked like a band that had finally come to terms with the idea of being an arena rock act – or, in this case, a fully fledged stadium rock act. The show might have been called

Live Earth, but this was the Foo Fighters' own Live Aid moment. Speaking to *Kerrang!*, Dave said as much. 'I realised that we could jump into a stadium like that, somewhere that size, and feel like we owned the place for the time that we were onstage.'

'They were a big band in *Kerrang!*'s world, a big band in *NME*'s world,' says Paul Brannigan, editor of *Kerrang!*. 'But they were still a level below that of Metallica and U2, the Stones and Springsteen. They weren't anywhere *near* that kind of plateau. The big turning point seemed to be Live Earth. That was the first time you thought, "Oh, hang on, wait a minute . . ."'

The only question now was: when would Foo Fighters play Wembley on their own? Dave neatly sidestepped the question by joking about returning for a five-night stand, only to politely shoot down the idea. 'I don't think that's feasible. For that moment it felt like that massive stadium had shrunk into a tiny room, and when that happens it's the greatest feeling in the world! If we could do that again it would be good,' he added almost as an afterthought, albeit a prescient one given that little over a year later the Foos would return to Wembley, 'that massive stadium', this time strictly on their own terms.

For now, though, there was a more pressing matter: the release of *Echoes, Silence, Patience & Grace*. The Live Earth show and a subsequent 'secret' appearance on the second stage at the popular British V Festival had only served to ratchet up anticipation for the new album. Things were taken up several notches further with the release of the barrelling first single, 'The Pretender', which became their biggest hit in America and Britain since 'Best of You' two years before. The album hadn't even been released yet, but Foo Fighters had become one of the most talked-about bands on the planet again.

When *Echoes, Silence, Patience & Grace* arrived in September, however, it did so to mixed sales reactions. Unlike *In Your*

Honor, it entered the UK album chart at No. 1. In America, though, it only got as high as No. 3 and would become the first Foos album not to achieve platinum status for over a million sales. Partly, this was due to the rapidly collapsing state of the record industry as downloads took over from hard-copy CD sales. Mostly, this was simply due to the fact that the Foo Fighters' career had now plateaued in America. They were about to become one of an increasing number of high-profile rock acts whose albums would still enjoy full-spectrum publicity campaigns by an adoring media, but whose actual sales initially took them high into the charts, only for them to descend just as rapidly soon after.

Most of the reviews were lukewarm. In America, *Rolling Stone* made nice noises but only gave it three and a half stars. *Spin* yawned pleasantly and gave it 6/10, insisting that 'two-thirds of these tracks sound a lot like songs Grohl has done before'. In Britain, the *Observer* damned it with more faint praise, describing it as 'undemanding arena rock that's just leftfield enough not to jar alongside Grohl's previous incarnation'. This was not the reaction Dave had been hoping for. By this stage in their career, the Foo Fighters may have been virtually critic-proof – but Dave wasn't. It was now he decided he would simply bypass the critics and take his message straight to the fans.

On 5 September, nearly three weeks before the album's release, the Foo Fighters played a short, six-song set at Studio 606 West, four of which were brand-new songs: 'The Pretender', 'Cheer Up, Boys (Your Make Up is Running)', 'Long Road to Ruin' and, as an all-too-earnest finale, 'Home'. It would be the first step on a touring treadmill that would run through to the end of 2008 and see them play more than 110 shows in venues ranging from tiny clubs to huge stadiums. This was no longer about building his empire; for Dave, this was now a pilgrimage to the faithful. The road to rock'n'roll Damascus.

In early November, just five weeks after the album's release, the band opened the MTV Europe Awards show at the Olympiahalle in Munich, playing a medley of 'The Pretender' and an arena-rocked-up version of the Sex Pistols' 'God Save The Queen' (whether the latter was in 'honour' of the British monarchy's German roots is unclear). Although the Foos eventually went home empty-handed, losing out on the Video Star and Headliner awards to French dance duo Justice and Brit-rock titans Muse respectively, Dave happily accepted the job of hosting the so-called VIP 'Glamour Pit', interviewing assorted winners and celebrities. It was a mark of his own increasing celebrity, as well as his studied nice-guy reputation, that he'd been tasked with the job in the first place. The band were also given their own 'Fantasy Suite', where they played a separate set featuring guest stars ranging from Josh Homme to rapper CeeLo Green.

Less than two months later, the MTV Awards would be overshadowed by the biggest music event of the year – one which Grohl was only involved in as a spectator. On 10 December 2007, the three surviving members of Led Zeppelin – guitarist Jimmy Page, singer Robert Plant and bassist John Paul Jones – reunited onstage at the 12,000-capacity O2 arena in London to play their first full show since the legendary band split up following the death of drummer John Bonham in 1980.

The clamour for a Zeppelin reunion had grown exponentially louder as the years passed, though the band themselves had consistently turned down increasingly ridiculous sums of money to get back together. But this was different. It was a tribute to the late founder of Atlantic Records, Ahmet Ertegün, the man who had signed and mentored Led Zeppelin way back in 1968. This was no cash-grab – the O2 show was a true one-off, and a comparatively intimate one at that.

Given the size of the band and the uniqueness of the occasion, it was the must-attend show of not just the year, but of the entire decade. The VIP guest list read like a celebrity *Who's Who*: rock legends such as Mick Jagger, Paul McCartney and Jeff Beck rubbed shoulders with the supermodels Kate Moss and Naomi Campbell. While the newer generation of music stars were represented by the likes of Noel Gallagher, Marilyn Manson and, of course, Dave Grohl.

The Foo Fighters' frontman had never made a secret of his love of Led Zeppelin, even when he was a 16-year-old punk rock brat. John Bonham was his idol. Less well known at the time was that Dave was now a prime candidate to replace the late Bonham at the O2 show. His own drumming style was directly inspired by Bonham's hard-hitting but percussive approach. 'I am at their beck and call,' he had told the *NME* after the Zeppelin show was announced in July 2007. 'But Jason [Bonham, son of John] should be the one . . . everyone knows that. He's a fucking phenomenal drummer. But if I got that call, what the fuck do you think I'd be saying? "Hey, Chris and Taylor, let's take a little break for a few days. I'll see ya later!" But I don't expect that to happen.'

In the event, it was Jason Bonham who rightly took his father's place on the Zeppelin drum stool. The O2 show was a simple triumph, with Grohl declaring it one of the best nights of his life. It was in the rosy afterglow of the Zeppelin reunion that he looked back over 2007 and proclaimed it the band's best yet. 'I can't imagine how this year could have been any better. But, at the same time, I can't believe that this will be the best year of my life because they just keep on getting better.'

The end of the year, though, brought a new reality check to the situation Dave and the Foos now found themselves in. 'I remember at one point thinking, "God, I wish our band was as big in America as it is in Britain,"' he confided to *Kerrang!*. '[In the UK] we're treated like this world-class rock band. Then we go home and we're playing in theatres, much smaller places.' He was being disingenuous, but only slightly. While his band were festival headliners in the UK and across Europe, they were still capable of pulling large crowds in the US.

On 14 January 2008, the Foo Fighters launched the US leg of the *Echoes, Silence, Patience & Grace* tour with a show for LA's KROQ radio station at a Hollywood sweatbox, The Troubadour. Coincidentally, it was also Dave's thirty-ninth birthday, and the band were joined onstage by their old friend Lemmy, bearing a cake for the birthday boy. The tour proper kicked off two days later at the decidedly less-fabled Frank Sinatra Theater at Bank Atlantic Center in Sunrise, Florida, and continued through such venues as the Fed-Ex Forum in Memphis and the Jobing.com Arena in Glendale, Arizona.

As the corporate nomenclature of the venues they were playing suggested, this was the Foo Fighters' biggest and most extensive US trek yet, with a touring infrastructure to match. To get this particular show on the road involved eight musicians (including touring musicians Rami Jaffee, Drew Hester, Jessy Greene and their old friend Pat Smear), 35 crew members, six tour buses and nine trucks. More importantly, it also represented the point where Grohl had to reconcile his view of arena rock as a teenage punk with the realities of the position the Foo Fighters now found themselves in – namely, their status as an arena rock band. 'I was a cynical pothead,' he told *Q* in early 2008. 'Like, "This is stupid, this place is so big." It made no sense. But now, I guess it does.'

It wasn't just the size of the venues that had changed. It was Dave himself. The snotty punk rock kid would have barely recognised the grinning, audience-conducting ringmaster he had become. The middle-aged man Dave now was knew that the people who made up a typical Foo Fighters crowd didn't come for political reasons or to find answers to The Big Questions. They came for a good night out. Playing arenas wasn't a case of them selling out. It was just a case of Dave being honest about what people loved about his band, and their place in the scheme of things. 'I think people should be entertained. The last thing in the world I want to do is challenge someone with our concert. I want people to feel included in what's going on. I don't want them to think I'm anything that I'm not, so I try my best to feel completely at ease. I would like for the audience to look at the band and feel like they're looking back at themselves.'

If Dave had any niggling doubts about his band's status in America, they were at least partly banished by the 50th Grammy Awards, held this year at the Staples Center in Los Angeles. The Foos were nominated for five awards, two of which they went home with: Best Hard Rock Performance for 'The Pretender' (which they performed on the night in front of a roomful of sedate, suited-and-booted invitees) and Best Rock Album for *Echoes, Silence, Patience & Grace*, beating such heavyweights as Bruce Springsteen and John Fogerty in the latter category.

There was very little time for celebration, however. The day after the Grammys, the Foo Fighters' tour machine was already rolling on to the next date. As the effective CEO of the whole operation, the success of the tour, and of the band, fell on Dave's shoulders. While he was never onc to complain about the heavy workload, he had become aware that, as a father, there was more to life than just being in a rock'n'roll band. For the first time in his life, Dave mused on the idea of taking time away from the band for domestic reasons.

'The key to longevity is balance,' he explained to *Spin*. 'And I love the band like a family. But I've realised that the most important thing is my life outside the band. Without this, everything else would fall apart.' Family was now all to Daddy Dave. Speaking again to Q, he talked of how being a husband and a father had 'centred' him. 'Personally and honestly, it's something that I'd always imagined happening,' he said. 'I grew up with a tight family. I'm probably one of the few rock musicians that didn't have a fucked-up life. I mean, my parents divorced when I was seven years old and we grew up with no money. But we got by with very little and we were still the happiest people in the world.'

But then, as Anton Brookes points out, Dave Grohl was always more grounded than your average rock star – and more private. Fatherhood may have altered his perspective on the rock'n'roll industry in particular and the world in general, but his family weren't there to be paraded as tabloid bait.

'Dave is very closeted actually when it comes to his private life and his family,' says Anton. 'You never see him in the tabloids. You never read about him doing something silly or involved in something. You occasionally see snaps of him with his wife and kids where they've gone out somewhere. But it's very few and far between.'

He may have been out of reach for the tabloids, but Dave always seemed to have time for pretty much everyone else, not least his fans. 'Sometimes I've been with Dave and we've gone out just to grab a sandwich or something in between interviews, or just get out of the hotel or the record company,' says Anton. 'But as soon as he walks into somewhere, it's all, "Ah, Dave Grohl!" Dave just plays along with it, and he gives the people what they want. He knows what to do. He's a seasoned pro. He's very intelligent. He knows how to play the game. For that twenty seconds people are in his face trying to connect with him, he'll give them what they want. Then they'll walk away feeling like a million dollars. Which then allows Dave just to get on with his life.'

Of course, part of the reason for this is that Dave was – and is – still a fan boy at heart. This was put beyond doubt in May 2008, when he wrote an open letter to Metallica via the pages of *Metal Hammer* magazine. The heavy metal band were working on their latest album with the producer Rick Rubin, and as a long-time fan, said Dave, he wanted to show them some love. The letter opened with the gushings of a star-struck fan.

'Hey, it's Dave!' he began. 'Remember me? Yeah, I'm the guy that's been listening to your band faithfully since 1983.' He talked about buying the first Metallica album, *Kill 'Em All*, from a mail order catalogue, and how that record 'changed my life'. Then he offered some characteristically enthusiastic support: 'I can't wait to hear the new shit, and no matter what you guys do I'll always be the first one at the shop waiting to hear it. I'm sure you'll come out and blow everybody's fucking minds, because you're fucking Metallica! Good luck. And don't release it until it's kickass. PS Have you finished recording the drums yet?'

It was a letter that reaffirmed his nice-guy credentials, though there was an interesting subtext. Dave may have been a true-life Metallica fan, but it was also written by someone who was now their equal. For, in 2008, Dave Grohl had every reason to be brimming with confidence. Just four weeks after the open letter was printed, the Foo Fighters returned to the scene of their greatest triumph yet: Wembley Stadium. And this time they were the main attraction. The Foos' two Wembley shows, on Friday, 6 June, and Saturday the 7th, had been announced a few months earlier. For Grohl's biographer Paul Brannigan, who had followed the band since their inception, the step up to a stadium took a lot of people by surprise.

'Things have always grown for the Foo Fighters,' he says now.

'But there's a massive leap between two nights at Brixton Academy and two nights at Wembley Stadium, yet that was done within the space of fifteen years. If you're watching from outside and hadn't been paying too much attention, you'd see the Foo Fighters doing Wembley and think: "How the fuck did that happen?" It wasn't like they were notching up a string of Top 10 singles. It would have been quite easy not to have noticed the curve they were on.'

No one, however, was more surprised than Dave. The frontman admitted he wasn't convinced the band were big enough to fill the stadium. To his amazement, both shows sold out instantly. 'Someone said it's 85,000 tickets and we're like, "We'll never sell that out, are you crazy?" And then two nights at Wembley sell out in a fucking day or whatever? Honestly, can you imagine that happening?'

His apprehension was understandable. Headlining two nights at Wembley wasn't just the biggest achievement of his career so far, it was by far the most prestigious. If they pulled it off, the Foo Fighters would be elevated to rock's A-list. If they fell flat, then . . . well, that didn't bear thinking about.

It was with this in mind that the Foo Fighters pulled out all the stops on those two balmy nights in June. The capacity crowd gazed down on the vast stage in the centre of the Wembley pitch. It wasn't so much 'in the round' as 'in the square'. The revolving main stage was covered by an illuminated pavilion, while a lengthy runway led down to a smaller stage where the band would perform a semi-acoustic set. This same attention to detail was extended to the backstage area, where a replica of Dave's favourite London rock dive, the Crobar in Soho, replete with skulls, burning black candles and a permanent soundtrack of sheer heaviosity, had been created to entertain the VIP guests.

The first night's show was as gloriously memorable as

anything they'd yet done. The 20-track set list covered all bases, from the latest album right back to Dave's Nirvana-era B-side, 'Marigold', recalled only by those whose memories were now longer than their hair. After traversing the length of the runway for an extended 'This is a Call', the singer offered up a lovingly irreverent tribute to the audience: 'Hey! Hey! Hey! Wembley fucking Stadium, ladies and gentlemen, I love each and every one of you fucking assholes tonight!'

If the first show was a triumph, it was the second night that truly elevated the Foo Fighters to the next level. 'We knew from the beginning this wasn't just going to be an ordinary show,' a clearly jubilant and emotional Dave announced near the end of gig. 'We knew that this country, you guys, you made us the band that we are today. So we'd like to invite a couple of very special guests: Mr Jimmy Page and Mr John Paul Jones from Led Zeppelin.'

The roar that greeted the appearance of the two musicians could probably be heard across the Atlantic. Just six months after the already-legendary Led Zeppelin comeback show, Dave had managed to pull off what would turn out to be the closest anyone would get to another Zep reunion. At the end of 2007, he had sat in the audience at the O2. Now two of the three surviving members were onstage with him.

Page and Jones played two Zeppelin songs with the Foo Fighters. For the first, the old Zep warhorse, 'Rock and Roll', Taylor stepped up to the microphone, allowing Dave to get to finally live out his John Bonham fantasies behind the drum kit. Then the latter stepped back to the front of the stage for a triumphant 'Ramble On'. 'Welcome to the greatest day of my whole entire life,' an emotional Grohl told the crowd as Page and Jones took their bows. This was stadium rock as it should be done: on the grandest of scales. If their Live Earth show was a party in someone else's house, this was bigger and far more significant. For those two nights in June, Wembley Stadium was The House That Dave Grohl Built.

The significance of the show wasn't lost on anyone. Fourteen years into their journey, the Foo Fighters had done what no one up to and including Dave Grohl had expected them to do: they had secured a seat at rock's top table. The two Wembley shows were the moment when the Foo Fighters were admitted to the pantheon of the greats, bigger even perhaps than Nirvana, certainly in terms of mass widespread recognition. The moment when Dave Grohl was anointed as the heir to the Seventies rock gods he had once worshipped. Not that the man himself would ever admit it.

'Did I enjoy it? Yes and no,' Dave told *Kerrang!* in the days after the gig. 'I mean, I was pretty nervous beforehand, but it was an amazing night. The crowd were great, and come on, having Jimmy Page and John Paul Jones onstage? How could I *not* be excited about that? The question now, though, is where do we go from here?'

The answer, as would soon become evident, would be right back to the start.

13. Wasted

On Wednesday, 14 January 2009, Dave Grohl turned 40. If this landmark birthday gave him cause to look back, then he would have been both proud and bewildered at what he saw. In the 19 years since he'd joined Nirvana, his life had been a rollercoaster ride, punctuated by triumph, tragedy, chaos, struggle and, ultimately, vindication. The Foo Fighters' two huge Wembley Stadium shows the previous summer had been their crowning glory, and on the back of them Dave had called that whole year the finest of his life. Little did he know going into 2009, and his fifth decade, that he would have to recalibrate what he meant by 'finest'. For the fan boy inside Dave, what was on the horizon was arguably more exciting than anything he'd done before.

The tour for *Echoes, Silence, Patience & Grace* had officially come to an end in September 2008, and the band temporarily went their separate ways. Nate Mendel reconnected with his old band, Sunny Day Real Estate, who had reunited for a tour (the line-up included Mendel's former Foos colleague, the drummer William Goldsmith), Taylor Hawkins was asked to complete an unfinished song by the late Beach Boys singer and drummer Dennis Wilson which appeared on a reissue of the latter's classic 1977 album *Pacific Ocean Blue*, and Chris Shiflett diverted his attention to his side project, Jackson United, who had recorded a new album at Dave's Studio 606 West (and which featured guest spots from both Dave and Taylor).

Dave's own constitutional inability to take a holiday ensured he was not out of the spotlight for long. In November 2008, he presented an award to the surviving members of Led Zeppelin at a ceremony held by GQ magazine in London. A month later, he appeared at the annual Kennedy Center Honors in New York, paying tribute to that year's inductees, The Who, and leading a rollicking version of their 1978 hit 'Who are You' as Pete Townshend and Roger Daltrey looked on from the balcony.

In the year of the US presidential election, there was also a run-in with the Republican candidate John McCain. Despite his father's former job as a political speechwriter, Dave had spent his life publicly avoiding politics. But when McCain used the Foos' 1997 song 'My Hero' as a campaign track, Dave decided enough was enough.

'The saddest thing about this is that "My Hero" was written as a celebration of the common man and his extraordinary potential,' said the band in a statement. 'To have it appropriated without our knowledge and used in a manner that perverts the original sentiment of the lyrics just tarnishes the song.'

According to the Washington Post, the McCain campaign duly noted that the song was used properly under blanket licensing (which does not require the artist's permission), and all proper royalties were paid.

But Dave had something far bigger on his plate than living out his Roger Daltrey fantasies or tackling errant US politicians. He had long harboured plans to work on 'a sweet little side project' with his old friend, Queens of the Stone Age's leader, Josh Homme. Except the scale of the Foo Fighters' success meant there was no such thing as 'a sweet little side project' any more. Certainly not given the line-up Dave was considering.

'The next project that I'm trying to initiate involves me on drums, Josh Homme on guitar, and John Paul Jones playing bass,' he had told *Mojo* magazine back in 2005. 'That wouldn't suck bratwurst.' Three years on, his fantasy supergroup was about to become a reality. The first step had been when Dave presented Zeppelin with their *GQ* award. 'I think by then my nerves had gone away, and I realised I could consider Jones a friend,' Dave recalled. 'I rang Josh from the airport and said, "Hey man, I'm going to ask John Paul Jones if he'll jam with us."'

In the vast round hole that was Led Zeppelin, Jones was the closest thing they had to a square peg. The bassist was the original 'quiet one' – a crack musician and arranger who had no truck with the rock'n'roll clichés that swirled around Zeppelin. After his former band split up in 1980, he went on to work with a dizzyingly diverse array of collaborators, among them the British goth band The Mission, US alt rock giants R.E.M. and Greek-American avant-garde diva Diamanda Galás. Like Dave, he was a man constantly in search of new experiences and new collaborators.

By the start of 2009, a year after Zeppelin's triumphal comeback gig at the O2 in London, Jones found himself in a strange position. With Robert Plant unwilling to commit to a full-blown reunion, as originally planned, the band were in limbo. Jones and Jimmy Page had tested the water with various replacement singers, including Aerosmith's Steven Tyler and Myles Kennedy of a rising US rock band, Alter Bridge, but it had all come to nothing. When Dave invited Jonesy to his birthday in LA, he had an ulterior motive.

'I had my fortieth birthday party at a Medieval Times restaurant, watching men from Long Beach, California, pretend they're English knights,' Dave told *Q*. 'I invited two hundred of my friends and we reserved the whole bar. We were drinking chalices of Coors Light and eating with our hands. They make the birthday announcements in the middle of the show: "We'd like to wish a happy birthday to Bryan! He's seven today! And Lucas, who's sixteen! And Dave! He's turning . . . *forty*?!" That was quite a night.'

Dave cunningly seated Jonesy next to Josh on what he called 'a blind date'. If the two didn't get on, there would be no band. Fortunately, they hit it off straight away. 'Dave never mentioned John to me until December, and I didn't even believe him until January,' added Homme. 'What was good about Medieval Times was that there was no risk of pretension. It broke the ice. With a lance.'

For Dave, the prospect of forming a dream supergroup with two musicians he knew and hugely admired was more than just wishful thinking. Just as joining Queens of the Stone Age earlier in the decade had provided him with a vital release valve, so this new band would help relieve the pressure of being the boss of Foo Fighters, Inc. Two days after their chalice-quaffing night out at Medieval Times, the three men met clandestinely at Homme's Pink Duck studio, located on the aptly named Stoner Avenue in Burbank. 'It was white knuckles,' Dave recalled. 'It was like cramming for a test. To be honest, I was fucking nervous. It was just a blur. But the second jam it was like, this is on. It had a real forward motion to it, and I think we all understood we had to grab hold of it.'

A few days later, Jones had to fly back to the UK. It gave everyone time to mull over what they'd done and work out if it had a future. Dave and Josh turned to each other and asked: 'OK, should we be a band?' The answer, unequivocally, was 'yes' – something, to their relief and delight, Jones agreed with when they spoke to him.

The trio didn't waste any time getting started, entering Pink Duck in February 2009. The set-up couldn't have been simpler: Josh Homme on guitar and vocals, John Paul Jones on bass and all manner of keyboards, Dave Grohl back behind the drum kit, where he was most comfortable in this setting. Originally calling themselves Caligula until they discovered, as Dave put it, 'about seven other fucking bands called the same thing', they eventually settled on Them Crooked Vultures as 'a name of no significance' for their new group.

For Dave and Josh, it was a welcome opportunity to break from the readily identifiable sound of their day jobs. Them Crooked Vultures were driven by a lack of boundaries. Here, anything went, from sludge-metal noise to James Brown-influenced funk grooves. 'The only reason you have for doing it is the pure love, joy and thrill of collaborating with the other people in the room,' Dave explained. 'Because of that I wanted to do some crazy stuff that I'd never done before.'

But there was an elephant in the room. John Paul Jones had been one half of the greatest rhythm section in the history of rock, alongside John Bonham. While Dave could hardly contain his excitement at playing alongside one of his heroes, he knew that it would be foolish to try and fill Bonham's shoes. 'I relieved myself of the pressure of playing with John by thinking, "Okay, obviously I am not going to be the best drummer he has ever played with; I'm not even going to try to be!!" So it was easy that way and honestly, while we were recording or jamming, I just wanted to entertain the other guys and do something that might make them laugh, might make their jaws drop, or might take them by surprise.'

The fact that a trio of high profile musicians had joined forces wasn't a surprise. All three of them thrived on collaborations and keeping things fresh. What was a shock was the fact that they did it all in secret. They may have been in three of the most successful rock bands of their respective generations, but the world at large didn't have a clue that it was happening at all.

Dave, for one, didn't want anything to distract from what they were doing. 'We had this wonderful opportunity and we didn't want to see it tarnished by anything from the outside.'

Not that Dave was in any danger of becoming a Howard Hughes-style recluse. In March 2009, he appeared on 'Run with the Wolves', a pummelling track from the latest album by British dance-punk overlords The Prodigy. The collaboration came about over a year earlier, after Dave told Prodigy's mainman, Liam Howlett, that he wanted to get back behind the drum kit. Howlett called his presence on the album 'inspiring'. The same month, Dave popped up on the US comedian Greg Proops's TV chat show, where, poker-faced, he recited the lyrics to the famously OTT metal band Manowar's song 'Gloves of Metal' and 'All Men Play on Ten' as if they were the greatest works of poetry ever written. Keeping a commendably straight face he recited such immortal lines as: *'While I'm burning up my gear, there's a fire in your ear / That won't stop until the day you die . . .'*

Them Crooked Vultures were the main focus of his attention now, though. On 9 August, six months after they had first rehearsed at Josh's Pink Duck, the three musicians broke their self-imposed vow of silence with their first public appearance, a low-key show at Chicago's Metro Club. Despite little advance fanfare, word inevitably leaked out and the midnight show was thronged as the new band ploughed through an 80-minute set comprised of nothing but Them Crooked Vulture originals.

'The reason people came is because I'm in the Foo Fighters, Josh is from Queens and John was in Led Zeppelin,' Dave observed in *Drummer*. 'But nobody had heard any of the music, not a note. Everyone had these huge expectations because of our reputations, but they didn't know what to expect; we had managed to protect the project and we gave people a unique experience. For that hour and a half those people just sat, watched and listened.' It was at that gig that Dave realised that Them Crooked Vultures was more than just a group of A-list rock stars jamming together – that it was a band. 'After that first gig, I just wanted to do it again,' he said.

He soon got his wish. Less than two weeks after their live debut, an untrumpeted slot opening for the British indie rock upstarts the Arctic Monkeys in London introduced them to European audiences. In October 2009, they kicked off a world tour; their self-titled debut album followed on 16 November.

Dave told the *NME* that the album was 'the most exciting thing I've done in my entire life'. Jones took things even further: 'It's a dream. It's like the old Zeppelin days.' Ironically, given all their talk about dispensing with boundaries, it sounded suspiciously like Queens of the Stone Age with a turbo-charged rhythm section, though that was hardly a hindrance: the album entered the Top 15 on both sides of the Atlantic. Dave's great adventure with Them Crooked Vultures would take him all the way through to the end of October 2010. During that time, all three members said they were keen to record a follow-up album, though it has yet to materialise.

Typically, TCV wasn't the only thing Dave had on his plate. In April 2009, Dave's wife, Jordyn, had given birth to the couple's second daughter, Harper Willow. And then there was the day job. Where his stint with Queens of the Stone Age in 2002 had been a result of his unhappiness with the Foo Fighters' internal machinations, Them Crooked Vultures were fuelled by the excitement of three musicians at the top of their respective games sparking off each other. 'The Foo Fighters have always been my priority,' he told *Classic Rock* magazine. 'The bond that we have as people is even stronger than the bond we have as a band. The Vultures was like going off and fucking some beautiful chick for a while, but there's no way that I would feel the love that I have for my wife or my family with some hot fucking girl.'

Indeed, Dave hadn't forgotten about the Foo Fighters. The band had started working on new songs during soundchecks on the *Echoes, Silence, Patience & Grace* tour. When that trek ended, they went straight into Hollywood's Grand Master Studios to record the 13 new numbers they had come up with. 'Rather than just forget about them or letting them sit around until we were ready to make another album we thought, "Let's go in and put them to tape now,"' he explained.

At first he had toyed with the idea of simply releasing the new songs without fanfare, promotion or even an accompanying tour – the sort of thing David Bowie would do to great effect four years later. But Dave felt that something wasn't quite right. The songs weren't ready, for starters. Plus the idea of the Foo Fighters putting out a record and not doing anything on the back of it was unthinkable. 'We wouldn't be able to just sit around at home if we had a new album out, and ultimately we just want to go out and play, so rather than jump back into another cycle of things, it felt like a good idea to stop,' said Dave. 'So we recorded that shit and stopped.'

But Dave couldn't leave the Foos alone entirely during his time in the studio with Them Crooked Vultures. At one point, he was shuttling between material for both bands. But the sheer workload he'd taken on caused another problem. Midway through recording Them Crooked Vultures' album, Dave had a health scare. Between working simultaneously on the Vultures and the Foos, as well as being kept awake most nights by his newborn baby, Dave reckoned he was only getting about three hours' sleep a night. Something had to give – and he ended up being rushed to the local ER when his wife feared some heavy chest pains might be the start of a heart attack. 'They ran all these tests on me,' he later recalled, 'did X-rays, and then finally turned round and told me that I needed to stop drinking so much coffee!'

But the songs the Foo Fighters had recorded at the end of 2008 weren't entirely wasted. The same month as Them Crooked Vultures released their debut album, the Foo Fighters issued their first greatest hits record. It was a decision their leader wasn't entirely comfortable with. The band's record company had been pressuring him for a compilation Foos album ever since *One by One*, but Dave had resisted the idea, calling them 'the kiss of death'. But now the label was *demanding* one, and Dave was contractually obliged to deliver. That was what he told the media anyway. 'It seems premature, because we're still a functioning band,' he told Radio 1. 'These things can look like an obituary. I think there are better songs than some of those [on the album].' What he was reluctant to explain was that, as the head of his own label, he wasn't 'contractually obliged' to do any such thing. But there would be a four-year gap between *Echoes* and the next Foo Fighters album, and Dave knew he needed to plug the gap somehow. For all their bold words about how brilliant the Vultures album was, it hadn't sold even half what a normal Foo Fighters album would be expected to. With the Foos' *Greatest Hits* released the same month as Them Crooked Vultures, Dave had shrewdly ensured he would once again be having his cake and eating every last mouthful of it too. When the Vultures album failed to sell anywhere near as many copies as *Greatest Hits*, plans to record a follow-up were quietly shelved while Dave turned his attention to resurrecting his career with his own 'real' band.

Partly to ease his conscience and ensure that long-time fans weren't getting completely ripped off, Dave decided to add two brand-new tracks that had been written on the last Foos tour:

the billowing, Tom Petty-esque 'Wheels' and the snarling pop-thrash of 'Word Forward'. The former song was released as a single a few weeks before the album's release, but it had received its world premiere when the Foo Fighters broke their hiatus to play an Independence Day concert honouring military veterans on the White House lawn – the first of many appearances that Dave and the band would make at the most famous residence in America.

Significantly, both 'Wheels' and 'Word Forward' had been re-recorded for the *Greatest Hits* album with Butch Vig, the man who had produced Nirvana's *Nevermind* nearly 20 years earlier. Dave had bumped into Vig at a party earlier in the year and asked if he was interested in the pair working together again. 'We had so much fun doing it,' Vig told *Rolling Stone* of the sessions. 'We realised we hadn't worked together on an album since *Nevermind* – and he goes, "Dude, man, do you want to make the next Foo Fighters record?"'

Dave would prove to be a man of his word, but that was a few months away. Before that, there was the small matter of bidding farewell to 12 months in which he'd formed a band with two of his closest friends and musical inspirations and welcoming in the New Year. This he did dressed as Olivia Newton-John at a fancy dress party themed around the Seventies musical *Grease* thrown at Studio 606 West. For once, Dave was able to let his hair down – even if that hair was in the form of a fetching blond wig. But beyond the usual Christmas break, there was no chance of a holiday – nor did Dave want one. 'My life is a fucking holiday,' he declared. 'I don't need a vacation from the adoration.'

Luckily for him, the first half of 2010 was as busy as the last few years had been. Them Crooked Vultures' world tour would take them through to the end of July, when they played their last major gig at the huge Mount Fuji Festival in Japan. The tour was punctuated by the sort of disparate and occasionally bizarre events that only a man like Dave Grohl would encounter. On 2 June, he made his second visit to the White House in less than a year when Paul McCartney received the prestigious Gershwin Award for Popular Song from the Library of Congress. In front of President Barack Obama, the ex-Beatle sitting next to him was honoured with an all-star ceremony which featured Dave covering the classic Wings song 'Band on the Run' and culminated in an all-star finale of 'Hey Jude' which saw McCartney, Dave, Stevie Wonder, Jack White and the night's other big stars joined by the President and his wife, Michelle. 'We went upstairs to meet him before the gig,' Dave recalled. 'His wife is gorgeous, man. She has the air of a president whereas Obama has the vibe of a laid-back surfer. He really puts you in a good mood.'

Even weirder was an offer Dave got to play on an unfinished song by Michael Jackson, the erstwhile King of Pop who had died the previous year. Dave met funk rock star Lenny Kravitz at a film awards ceremony in early 2010. Kravitz informed him that he had an incomplete song he'd worked on with Jackson in 1992 called '(I Can't Make It) Another Day'. Did Dave fancy playing drums on it? Of course he did.

Dave and Butch Vig worked on a massive-sounding drum track. 'I sent it to Lenny and he's, like, "Dude, this is going to be awesome,"' said Dave. And then . . . nothing. Dave never heard back from Kravitz again. Then he stumbled across the track in question online. 'You know what they used?' he said, dumbfounded. 'One snare hit. That's it. I don't know who's playing drums on it, but it ain't me. It says: "Featuring Dave Grohl". And it's like: "It does? I can't hear me in that!"'

There was a much happier outcome a few months later, when Dave was invited to perform at Dimebash, the annual tribute concert to 'Dimebag' Darrell Abbott, the former Pantera guitarist who was shot and killed onstage during a gig in Columbus, Ohio, in December 2004. Dave and Dimebag had crossed paths countless times during the early Nineties, sharing bills as readily as bottles of Crown Royal whiskey, and the late guitarist was just as garrulous a host as the Foo Fighters frontman. Since his death, Dave had become close to Darrel's long-time partner, Rita Haney.

The charity gig took place at a Sunset Strip hangout, The Key Club, and featured a line-up that included members of Slayer, Dio, Puddle of Mudd and Marilyn Manson's band. It was organised by Rita, who persuaded Dave to join the fun. 'He was all down for it,' she says today. 'He said, "Yeah, I'm gonna be in town, so we'll come out and do some songs." But a few days prior to the gig, I went to touch base with him because I hadn't heard from him. I was thinking, "Don't pull out on me now!" He finally got back to me the day before and said, "Look, I've got a problem . . ." He sent me a picture of him on a mountain bike. He had wrecked and scraped his whole chest and fractured a couple of ribs.'

While Dave's injuries were hardly life threatening, they did preclude him from playing drums at Dimebash as originally planned. Instead, he wound up jamming with Lemmy and Motörhead's guitarist Phil Campbell on 'Ace of Spades'. 'That was one of Lemmy's least favourite songs to do when it's a jam but it was really cool,' says Rita. 'I remember Lemmy saying, "I don't normally do that song, but I will." So they did that tune and then Dave came out and played bongos with [Slayer's drummer] Dave Lombardo on [Black Sabbath's] 'Planet Caravan'. It was so awesome! It turned out to be way more memorable than what we had planned.'

For Rita, Dave's appearance sums up his attitude to the people in his orbit. Many other stars of his magnitude wouldn't even consider turning up to a club gig for free, let alone with fractured ribs. 'Dave was like Darrell,' she says. 'He can take over a room very quickly and make you feel at home, like you've known each other for ever, within just seconds. To have that thing inside you that you can pull out and draw everyone in is amazing. Dave has that trait and it's genuine, and that's why you feel so comfortable – because you know it's genuine. A lot of musicians or actors inhabit this persona of what they think people will expect. When they create this persona, sometimes they don't realise that they're trapping themselves and they can't be who they want to be offstage. I mean, you know you're not going to see him or someone from Slayer out picking flowers!'

Dave's appearance at Dimebash was doubly impressive given that work was already well underway on the Foo Fighters' seventh album. Them Crooked Vultures had barely walked off-stage after the final gig of their tour in July 2010 when Dave reconvened the rest of the Foos in Los Angeles. Except this time there would be some significant changes – luckily, all of them positive. For one, Pat Smear was officially back in the band as a full-time member. Dave dropped some sizable hints when he tweeted photos of his on/off band mate in the studio. No less significant was the return of Butch Vig. Dave had followed up his offer of getting the *Nevermind* producer to work on the new Foos album.

But the most radical departure of all wasn't who was recording the album, but where they were recording it. Rather than hire out an expensive studio facility, or even record in the Foos' own Studio 606 West complex, Dave opted for the most unlikely location of all: his garage. 'He calls me and says he's got some stuff he wants to play for me,' Vig recalled in *Nylon Guys* magazine. 'I get to his house and the first thing he says is, "I really wanna do this in my garage." Then he said he wanted to record on tape with no computers. They'd just played some shows at Wembley Stadium, and he told me, "We've gotten so huge, what's left to do? We could go back to 606 and make a big, slick, super-tight record just like the last one. Or we could try to capture the essence of the first couple of Foo Fighters records."'

For Dave, the driving motivation behind the new album would be to take the band back to basics. Aware that among diehard Foos fans the orthodoxy now was that the first two FF albums were still their best, his aim was to try and re-create the speed and spontaneity with which that material was created. Then get it down on tape – literally – in as old school a way as possible. Enter Butch: 'I truly believe that the environment and the atmosphere in which you make a record should dictate and define what the album sounds like,' said Dave. 'If you're being real, then the way you feel comes out.'

But there was another bonus to recording it in Dave's back-yard. It ensured that he could spend valuable time with his growing family. He may have wanted the next Foos album to crackle with the same energy it did when playing live, but the days of pretending the wishes of the others really had anything to do with the big decisions were over – and both sides were now happily reconciled to that. Dave's eldest daughter, Violet May, frequently wandered into the studio while her father was working. 'I'd come up [to the studio], clean up all the fucking beer bottles and vacuum this room, mop the fucking floor,' he pretended to complain in *Classic Rock*. 'And I'd work until six o'clock, go down and have dinner with the family, read them stories and give them baths and put them to bed. And come back up here, work until ten p.m. and then go to sleep. That was it.' Well, not quite. He still had his wife, nanny, pool guy, housekeeper and extended family to help out occasionally too. Plus his own band and producer to do his bidding as well.

Dave had been working on songs for the new Foo Fighters album when he was on the road with Them Crooked Vultures, honing the demos the band had recorded on their last tour in various hotel rooms around the world then hooking up with Hawkins whenever he returned to Los Angeles. If there was a mission statement for the new album, then it would be, according to Dave, 'fucking heavy'.

'I love mellow music,' he told *Hot Press*. 'I can write sleepy, beautiful fucking ballads all day long. But then I thought: "Fuck that!" I'm forty-two now, I don't know if I'm going to be able to make this record when I'm forty-six or forty-eight or forty-nine. So I thought: "All right, well, it's my last chance. So I'm going to go for it."'

Despite Dave's ongoing desire to keep things moving forward, there was an unavoidable edge of nostalgia to the sessions in his garage. Working with Vig again was, as Dave put it, 'not unlike going back and fucking a girlfriend you had twenty years ago'. Though it was, he added, 'perfectly natural and totally comfortable – he's the same person he was twenty years ago'. Again, though, this was a fairly rose-tinted view of the 46-year-old producer. In the intervening years Vig had enjoyed his own roller-coaster ride to success with his post-Nirvana band Garbage, selling over seven million albums worldwide. He'd also continued as a producer, recording multi-platinum albums for Smashing Pumpkins, Soul Asylum and Green Day, among others. This would be a meeting of minds between the two; a joint statement on how far they had come and how deeply they both felt the need to prove themselves once again.

The producer wasn't the only blast from the past. For one of the songs they were working on, 'I Should Have Known', Dave tapped up his old Nirvana band mate Krist Novoselic. The pair had stayed in touch in the years after Kurt Cobain's death, and Novoselic had even added backing vocals to a Foo Fighters song, 'Walking a Line', recorded during the *One by One* sessions. But this was the first time the pair had actually played together in the studio since Nirvana. Factor in the presence of Butch Vig and Pat Smear, and this was the closest anyone would get to a Nirvana reunion – albeit, with one glaring absentee. For Vig, seeing the pair in the same room for the first time for nearly 20 years was an intense experience. 'Krist was standing there saying: "Hey, how's it going?"' Vig told *Esquire*. 'My brain is going "Holy shit!" Dave opens up a bottle of wine, a friend had sent me a bottle of bootleg whiskey, we started sipping on that, and just sat down and told stories. We were there until about two in the morning. It was powerful, all those memories came flooding back.'

Working with Novoselic and Vig inevitably sparked memories both conscious and subconscious for Dave. He admitted to the *Daily Telegraph* that he dreamed about their late band mate. 'I've had a few dreams where Kurt shows up and I'm so blown away. "Wait, you never died?"' he said. 'For whatever reason, he'd just been hiding. And the three of us get together to be a band again. It's totally weird.'

Novoselic wasn't the only guest Dave invited to appear on the album. The dense, bristling 'Dear Rosemary' found him trading vocal and guitar lines with Bob Mould, former frontman with the influential Minneapolis hardcore punk pioneers Hüsker Dü, a band who inspired both the impressionable young Dave and the oversensitive young Kurt. For the Foo Fighters frontman, it was a chance to work with yet another hero and pay back something that was owed.

'I was a huge fan of Hüsker Dü,' Dave told *Mojo*. 'Their album *Zen Arcade* is one of the most underrated American rock'n'roll records of all time. I met him for the first time last summer and said, "You know, I'd be nowhere and nobody without your music, right?" And he very politely nodded and said: "I know." I had this song that I imagined would be a duet between us, and he obliged. What an honour to have that sort of moment with one of your heroes.' Mould was no less effusive in his praise, likening Dave to the former US President Bill Clinton. '[Dave has] amazing people skills,' Mould told *Nylon Guys* magazine. 'And he never forgets anyone's name. Dave's in this position now where he wants to share the riches of his success. He wants people to know about the artists who've made an impact on him. It's really touching.'

The informal atmosphere fed into the recording, and they worked fast. The album was finished in early December, just 11 weeks after they started. The band and Vig, plus the engineer Alan Moulder and filmmaker James Moll, celebrated by playing a secret gig at a Los Angeles karaoke bar, Paladino's, the very night they wrapped up the record. 'Honestly, we finished the last mix and an hour later we got in Alan's car and drove down to the club and I walked right up onstage,' Dave told the *NME*. 'It was like this sappy Hollywood ending with me, Butch, Alan and James walking down the driveway knowing that we weren't coming back to make the record tomorrow. It was so *Gone with the Wind* it was ridiculous.'

The seventh Foo Fighters album was released on 12 April 2011. Titled *Wasting Light*, after a line from the jagged, pointed 'Miss the Misery' ('*Don't change your mind / You're wasting light . . .*'), it was deservedly more positively received by the critics than *Echoes, Silence, Patience & Grace*. When *Spin* hailed it as 'Dave's most memorable set of songs since 1997's *The Colour and the Shape*', it was as if Dave had written the review for them. This was exactly what he wanted to hear. While even the stuffy British broadsheet the *Daily Telegraph* called it 'tough but accessible, reliably catchy, yet also as surprising as the last'.

If Dave's plan was to strip away the baggage of success and reconnect the Foo Fighters with their musical roots, then he had achieved his desire. His insistence that it was also the 'heaviest' Foos album was borne out in tracks like the serrated 'Rope' and the titanic 'White Limo'. The latter, a gnarled noisefest with barely decipherable lyrics (written as quickly and unthinkingly as anything on the first Foo Fighters album), was the first full track to be unveiled from the album. Fittingly for such a heavy monster sound, it was accompanied by an amusingly low-budget video featuring Motörhead's mainman, Lemmy, as the Foo Fighters' personal chauffeur, driving the band around LA in – yes – a white limo.

'That was another goofy idea from Dave,' Taylor Hawkins guffawed. 'He was mocking some of his favourite old-school punk rock videos. You know, the ones guys used to make on the cheap back in the early Eighties with a couple of handheld VCR cameras.' Asked what he thought of Dave, Lemmy echoed pretty much everyone else who had ever met him: 'Great guitarist, great drummer, great singer – what more do you want? Dave has shown the world it's possible to be a success and a nice guy at the same time.'

Lemmy may have become a buddy, but there was another, altogether more bizarre celebrity encounter shortly after the album's release. In April 2011, Prince booked a string of 21 dates at the LA Forum. The Foo Fighters' relationship with Prince was a strange one: the singer had blocked the band from releasing their cover of 'Darling Nikki' almost a decade before, only to cover 'Best of You' during a memorable half-time performance at the 2007 Super Bowl. Despite all that, Dave was a huge fan of the musician, and attended one of the shows (arriving on what he called a 'party bus'). At the venue, he bumped into a roadie friend, who told him: 'Prince knows you're here. He wants to jam.'

'The end of the night, I'm standing next to this black curtain,' Dave would later recall in *Rolling Stone*. 'I pull it back – there's Prince with Sheila E. I go, "Hey, man, great show." He says, "When do you want to jam? How about Friday?" "All right, cool!"' On the allotted day, Dave returned to the venue and in the backstage catering area bumped into Prince, who immediately invited him to jam on a 'bad-ass' ten-minute version of Led Zeppelin's 'Whole Lotta Love'. Dave played drums while Prince pulled out his best Jimmy Page moves. At the end of the jam, Prince told him: 'We should do that, man! What are you doing *next* Friday?' Sadly Dave didn't hear from Prince again and the promised follow-up jam never happened. In fact, some of his friends didn't believe the original one took place either. 'I *swear* it happened!' Dave insisted. 'I swear. And nobody saw it.'

In between the comedy promo videos and superstar jams, the Foos had an album to promote. In typically down-to-earth fashion, they opted to launch it with a tour of fans' garages. 'We'd recorded *Wasting Light* in Dave's garage,' explained Nate Mendel, 'so we thought, "We'll go play in other people's garages."'

For Dave, there was 'poetry' in the idea of a band that could sell out Wembley recording an album in a garage. To him, it wasn't just a neat gimmick – it was about the idea of taking rock'n'roll out of the stadiums and back to where it belonged. It was also a brilliant marketing gimmick that attracted better than usual publicity. If, musically, *Wasting Light* was a direct reaction to the success the band had attained over the past few years, then promotion-wise this was Dave at his most up to date and cutting edge, taking nothing for granted. He may have been the nicest man in rock, but he was still the cleverest too.

'Kids got too smart and crafty,' he said in Q. 'There's part of me that feels like rock musicians aren't as crafty and criminal as they used to be. My generation were stoners, dropouts and petty thieves. We played music on the weekends to forget about the shitty jobs we had to work. There was never any career option, because, what, you're playing in a little hardcore punk rock band and you're going to sell a million records? No. You just did it for kicks.'

The album's release was accompanied by a documentary, *Back and Forth*. Filmed by Oscar-winning documentary maker James Moll and named after one of the highlights of *Wasting Light*, it was a look back over the Foos' illustrious career, from the tragic end of Nirvana through to the deliberately lo-fi recording sessions for the new album. But amid the footage of the band and their kids larking around in the swimming pool *chez* Grohl, there were other elements that made for less comfortable viewing – not least the less-than-amicable departure of their original drummer, William Goldsmith, and the band's near-dissolution in the wake of Taylor Hawkins's drug overdose.

'It hasn't all been fun,' Dave admitted. 'We've had moments when we didn't want to be a band any more. The director, James, he's not a music guy. So his focus was the personal relationships and the people. He got us to say things we might not even say to each other. Which I believe is one of the reasons we've managed to stay together – we just don't tell each other everything. Some bands hire therapists to help them work shit out. That would completely destroy our band. From the beginning, we wanted to make it clear that this was not like drama club. We did not want any bullshit.'

'I could tell Dave had to digest it and figure out a way to come to terms with it,' said Nate. 'The part about William leaving the band, he felt really beat up about that. That's something that's never been resolved between us. Hopefully the film dealt with it. Everything that needed to be said was said.' If the *Back and Forth* film was a heavy-duty experience for the Foo Fighters personally, the *Wasting Light* tour that ran through spring and summer of 2011 was the exact opposite. The band worked up a list of a staggering 75 covers that they, as Dave put it, 'want to fucking goof off in front of 70,000 people'.

The work they put in paid off when the Foo Fighters played a two-night stand at the 65,000-capacity Milton Keynes Bowl – their biggest UK shows since headlining Wembley Stadium nearly three years before. On top of what was effectively a greatest hits set, they covered 'Young Man Blues' (a song written by Mose Allison but made famous by The Who on their classic *Live at Leeds* album), roped in support acts John Paul Jones and Seasick Steve for a version of the latter's 'Back in the Doghouse', and called Alice Cooper up for a rapturously received one-two of 'School's Out' and 'I'm Eighteen'. As such, the two Milton Keynes shows were the perfect snapshot of what Dave now wanted the Foo Fighters to be. 'The most important thing to me is that we do what's right, we do what's real, and that we're a fucking blazing live band,' he told *Nylon Guys*. 'When I show up at a festival and we're the headliners, and I've got grey hair in my beard, I want the kids who played the twelve slots before us to look at us and be like, "Damn, those guys are old but, fuck, they're really good."'

Dave's self-deprecation only extended so far. One of the most monumental anniversaries of his career was looming, and there would be no room for joking here: 24 September 2011 marked 20 years since the release of *Nevermind*. It was something that Grohl couldn't help but be aware of. 'For me, it's a personal landmark,' he told the *NME*. 'My life was split in two by *Nevermind*. I don't remember the making of it, nor the day that it came out. But it caused a profound change in my life.'

Amid the non-stop chaos that came with the job of being CEO of Foo Fighters, Inc., the album's anniversary provided a moment of reflection for Grohl. Not least in terms of the impact his old band had on his own life, let alone their millions of fans. 'It's funny – for years I've been navigating in and around the shadow of Nirvana,' he told the *Irish Independent*. 'When I say "shadow", it's not meant to sound negative. It's a reality. When [Foo Fighters] first started as a band, I didn't want to talk about Nirvana because Kurt had just died and it was hard for me to talk about it without getting really upset. Then as time went by, it was easier to talk about. But there was more to talk about with the Foo Fighters. And the Nirvana questions sort of went away. Of course, now they are coming back.'

To mark the anniversary, Grohl, Novoselic and Butch Vig teamed up for various interviews, and the band's old record company reissued an extended version of the album, but there was no high-profile reunion gig or mawkish tribute to Kurt Cobain. It was celebratory but respectfully muted. It was everything Kurt Cobain would have wanted.

As 2011 turned into 2012, Dave's status as the most well-connected man in rock was put far beyond doubt. If he wasn't jamming with Eighties rock'n'roll pin-up Joan Jett onstage at the US Lollapalooza festival and co-writing a song, 'Any Weather', for her next album, he was rubbing shoulders with members of boy band *NSync at an Elton John AIDS Foundation charity evening, or bonding with veteran blues rock icon Bonnie Raitt, who admitted she was a 'huge fan' of the Foo Fighters. Most improbably of all, Dave even appeared in the big screen version of *The Muppets* – appropriately enough, making a cameo as a replacement for the windmill-armed Muppets drummer, Animal.

Uncharacteristically, he also found himself embroiled in controversy – albeit of the type that erupts online rather than in the real world. At the 2012 Grammy Awards in Los Angeles, the Foo Fighters cleared up, picking up five of the six awards they were nominated for including Best Rock Song (for 'Walk') and Best Rock Album (for *Wasting Light*). It was during his acceptance speech for the latter that Dave – sporting a Slayer T-shirt – celebrated *Wasting Light*'s proudly lo-fi conception and launched a broadside against plastic pop music: 'To me, this award means a lot, because it shows that the human element of music is what's important. Singing into a microphone and learning to play an instrument and learning to do your craft, that's the most important thing for people to do . . . It's not about what goes on in a computer.'

Shortly afterwards, he was forced to backpedal. 'Never has a thirty-three-second rant evoked such caps-lock post-board rage as my lil' ode to analogue recording has,' he said in a statement, going on to explain that as a fan of everything from 'Dead Kennedys to deadmau5', he loved all music with a 'human element'. Adding: 'Look, I am not Yngwie Malmsteen. I am not John Bonham. Hell, I'm not even Josh Groban, for that matter. But I do the best that I possibly can within my limitations, and accept that it sounds like me. Because that's what I think is most important. It should be real, right?'

Minor bumps in the road aside, 2012 was the year that the Foo Fighters established their place amid rock's A-list, and Dave became a peer of the rock stars he'd idolised as a kid. That summer alone, he played 'Miss You' onstage with the Rolling Stones (and jammed with both Mick Jagger and the actress Kristen Wiig at the after-show party), became the most frequent musical guest on *Saturday Night Live* with his eleventh appearance (one more than Paul Simon) and teamed-up with

Neil Young and The Black Keys at the Global Citizen Festival in New York's Central Park.

It was at the latter show that Dave announced the Foo Fighters were taking a break. 'Without making a big deal out of it, we don't have any shows after this,' he said from the stage. 'This is it. Honestly, I don't know when we're gonna do it again.'

The rumour mill immediately cranked into action and speculation sprung up that the Foos had finally reached the end of the line. For the second time in a few months, Dave had to issue a statement clarifying what he'd said. 'I was serious,' he wrote. 'I'm not sure when the Foo Fighters are going to play again. It feels strange to say that, but it's a good thing for all of us to go away for a while. It's one of the reasons we're still here.'

Proving there was a world of difference between what Dave Grohl considered a hiatus and what the rest of the world thought of as a proper break, he then announced his most ambitious idea yet: a big-screen documentary on the fabled LA studio Sound City.

'A year in the making, it could be the biggest, most important project I've ever worked on,' Dave concluded with that big goofy smile. 'Get ready . . . it's coming.'

14. For Everlong

On 12 December 2012, the biggest concert of the decade so far took place at New York's fabled Madison Square Garden. More than 18,000 people had crammed into this cavernous venue to witness an all-star benefit gig dubbed 12-12-12: The Concert for Sandy Relief, designed to raise money for the victims of Hurricane Sandy, which had ripped through the northeastern states of America, leaving $65 million worth of damage in its wake. Like Live Aid and Live Earth before it, the bill featured a line-up of A-list stars, among them the Rolling Stones, Bruce Springsteen, Eric Clapton, The Who and Kanye West. Closing the show was Sir Paul McCartney, who, as an ex-member of the Beatles, was the biggest star of them all.

Five songs into his eight-song set, McCartney introduced three guest musicians to the stage: Krist Novoselic, Pat Smear and, of course, Dave Grohl. With Grohl behind the drum kit and McCartney on a cigar box guitar, this ad hoc supergroup launched into a song McCartney announced they'd recently written together.

The song itself, titled 'Cut Me Some Slack', was a heavied-up garage rock jam that channelled the Beatles' proto-heavy metal anthem 'Helter Skelter' and the kind of raucous noise with which Grohl and Novoselic made their name. While the song might have been unfamiliar, no one watching could fail to note the significance of the occasion: it wasn't the first time Dave and

Krist had shared a stage, but it was the first time they had done it while Dave sat behind a drum kit since the crazy daze of you know when. For the 18,000 people in Madison Square Garden, and the millions watching the live broadcast on TV at home, this was the closest they'd come to a Nirvana reunion – and a Nirvana reunion with a Beatle standing in for Kurt Cobain at that.

Charles Cross, who witnessed a later performance from the same line-up in Seattle, has a typically unique perspective on the occasion. 'When Dave and Krist played with Paul McCartney, everybody thought that was the greatest. More people cite that as the greatest show that ever happened in Seattle than they cite any of the Nirvana concerts. The idea of suddenly you have a linkage between the Beatles and these other two guys . . . it was the *rawest* Paul McCartney ever has been. It's by far and away the greatest show Paul McCartney ever gave, short of any show he ever gave next to John Lennon. You could literally witness Paul as just kind of like, "Where the hell are we going next?" It kind of brought Paul back to the club in Hamburg. And it brought Nirvana back to these early kinds of things where nothing was planned. They had rehearsed it but it seemed as though it was being created in that moment. And that was one of the keys to great Nirvana.

'If I were going to say something negative about the Foo Fighters, I guess it would be, sometimes in concert, that aspect of it was there early on but I'm not sure if it's always there now. In the early Foo Fighters shows, when you saw them, you felt like what you were witnessing was being created at that moment. Who they were, where it was gonna go, whether it was gonna be chaotic or fun or focused, you could see that all happening.

'One of the problems when you become a superstar band playing festivals to 100,000 people – how do you manage to do that? How do you manage to keep that alive? That's quite a challenge. But Dave had that onstage with Paul McCartney and Krist Novoselic. There is a special connection between Novoselic and Dave. When those two guys are together it truly is better than any other rhythm section that Dave has been in. And it's not because Krist is the world's greatest bass player. It's because they have a musical intuitiveness that is there. And that gets lost when people talk about Nirvana or even when they talk about the Foo Fighters.'

But Dave, as usual, had another surprise up his sleeve. Taking to Twitter after the New York performance, he revealed that 'Cut Me Some Slack' would be the first song from the soundtrack album to an upcoming documentary he was directing, *Sound City*. Not content with the Foo Fighters becoming one of the biggest rock groups on the planet, the man at the centre of that empire was now moving into film. Why not? He'd been everywhere else.

It had been only a matter of time before Dave made the transition from musician to filmmaker. His career had been marked by a combination of fierce ambition and restless drive. The Foo Fighters always had fun with their promo videos, but it was *Back and Forth* – the career-spanning documentary that accompanied the Foo Fighters' seventh album, *Wasting Light* – that truly sparked his interest in making his own films, one that would plug into his love of music and its history.

In May 2012, six months before his historical onstage collaboration with McCartney and his old Nirvana colleagues, Dave had announced that he was producing and directing a film about what he described as 'America's greatest unsung recording studio'. The film would take its name from the studio in question: Sound City, a legendary facility in Van Nuys, California, where such illustrious artists as Neil Young, Fleetwood Mac, the Red Hot Chili Peppers, and dozens more had made their breakthrough records.

For Dave, there was a personal connection to the ramshackle Sound City. It was there, in the summer of 1991, that Nirvana had recorded *Nevermind* with the producer Butch Vig. Dave had long been impressed by the studio's analogue mixing console, a vintage Neve 8028. The Neve was utterly out of step with twenty-first-century digital recording techniques, but Dave just loved its warm sound and the fact that it provided a link with both the studio's past and the history of American music from the late Sixties right up to the present day. When it came to recording *Wasting Light* in his studio, Dave contacted Sound City to see if they could buy the Neve board.

'They were like, "I'd sell my grandmother before I'd sell that board,"' he recalled. 'I was like, "Okay, just saying." [But] it was only a matter of time before they closed, and they asked me if I was serious about buying [the console]. It didn't cost as much as you think."

The Neve board became the seed of the story for Grohl's subsequent film. It provided a springboard for him to look at the studio and many of the bands that recorded there. But it was also an opportunity for Grohl to celebrate what he called 'that feeling you get when you put five guys in a room, hit "record" and the hair on the back of your neck stands up'.

'When Sound City closed [in 2011], it was a very sad day,' he told *Rolling Stone*. 'That place was like a church. The list of people that recorded there reads like a virtual Rock and Roll Hall of Fame: Neil Young, Fleetwood Mac, Tom Petty, Cheap Trick, Slayer, Rage Against the Machine, Weezer, Metallica – and Nirvana . . . That funky old place had the best drum room in the world. The drum sound at the beginning of 'Smells Like Teen Spirit' – that's Sound City.'

For Grohl, the film was a labour of love. Initially conceived as a YouTube clip, it grew into a year-long project that involved him taking responsibility for interviewing many of the bands and artists who had recorded there, from Fleetwood Mac's Mick Fleetwood and Metallica's Lars Ulrich to easy listening kingpin Barry Manilow. As a first-time producer and director, it was a baptism of fire. 'When I did the first Foo Fighters record, I did it in six days and played all the instruments,' Dave reminisced. 'I didn't know what I was doing. I like that record because it's so naïve and it is what it is. It's not the greatest record in the world, but to me, it's, like, cool. Same thing goes for the movie. I don't know how to make movies, but I could tell you the story of Sound City like that' – he snapped his fingers. 'So why would I need anyone's help? We rounded up the coolest people we knew and it was fucking great.'

Dave's hands-on involvement gave the film an extra dimension that separated it from every other music documentary. As part of the film, Dave would also write songs with various collaborators, which would then appear both in the finished movie and on a subsequent soundtrack album. Among the people he worked with were the Eighties AOR pin-up Rick Springfield, Slipknot's frontman Corey Taylor, and Fleetwood Mac's singer Stevie Nicks, the latter of whom sang on 'You Fix Me'.

'I'm still a nerdy rock fan and these were huge experiences to me,' Dave told *Kerrang!*. 'But logistically, the project was nuts! That's when I needed help! The Stevie Nicks song was something I wrote for *In Your Honor*, but we didn't use it because the music sounded too much like Fleetwood Mac. The song was just sitting there, so I sent it to her and asked what she thought. She said, "I love it!"'

But the biggest coup of course was the involvement of Paul McCartney. The Foo Fighters had played onstage with McCartney during the celebrations for Liverpool's year as the European Capital of Culture, while Dave had also joined the legendary Beatles star at the 2009 Grammys. Nearly 20 years earlier, Dave had also been part of the band who re-created the Beatles' music for the biopic *Backbeat*. But McCartney's involvement in the *Sound City* documentary would be the first time the two parties had ever been in the studio together.

It was Grohl who invited McCartney to jam at Sound City Studios when he was next in Los Angeles. In the mind of the Foos frontman, they would blast through some classic rock'n'roll staples like 'Long Tall Sally'. 'He was the one that said, "No, no, no, no – let's write a song. Let's write and record a new song in the three hours we have there,"' Dave recalled. He had also invited Krist Novoselic and Pat Smear along to the clandestine session. Inspired move, lucky break, opportunistic wheeler-dealing, looking back on it a few months later, Dave still couldn't believe it had actually happened.

'I love Paul so much,' he told *The Times*. 'Not only because he is a great person, but because he is a fearless musician. He walked in here with the bass and the Les Paul: two of the most iconic instruments in music history. And he decides to play a cigar-box guitar in front of everyone, to record a song. Not a lot of people would do that. To sit down and start from scratch and three and a half hours later have this raucous fucking jam come together – it was huge. It really was a huge, full-circle moment.'

The result of this superstar jam session was 'Cut Me Some Slack', which echoed both the Beatles and Nirvana. Yet it wasn't until halfway through the session that McCartney realised the history of the people in the studio with him. 'It was magic for me, playing with these guys,' said McCartney. 'To tell you the truth, I didn't kind of know who they were . . . Then, during the session, I hear them talking: "Wow, we haven't played that since

Nirvana." So I found myself in the middle of a Nirvana reunion, and I was very happy.'

The events surrounding the 'Cut Me Some Slack' session made up the climactic final quarter of the *Sound City* documentary. The rest of it told the story of the studio through the artists who recorded there and the staff who worked there. Grohl spoke to more than 150 people in total (though not all made it into the finished movie). There were archival appearances from Johnny Cash and, naturally, Kurt Cobain. The end result was more than just the story of the vintage Neve 8028 soundboard – it was a loving tribute to the cradle of so much great American music, and also a tantalising glimpse of a creative process that normally remains hidden from the general public.

Sound City premiered at the Sundance Festival in Utah on 18 January 2013. It was during Sundance, at the Park City Live venue, that Dave unveiled the Sound City Players, a band-come-collective featuring a rotating cast of musicians who appeared in the film. Among them were Stevie Nicks, Rick Springfield, Creedence Clearwater Revival's John Fogerty, Lee Ving of punk rock band Fear, and Krist Novoselic. The Foo Fighters themselves were the core band – a task that entailed them having to learn 50 songs in just ten days.

Such was the demand for the gig that tickets changed hands for $1500 a piece. The crowd certainly got their money's worth – the band played for more than three hours, making it through 35 songs. Dave would subsequently take the Sound City Players on the road with him to New York, Los Angeles and London. Despite the all-star line-up, there was one band whose songs he was conscious to avoid: Nirvana. 'You know, that's hallowed ground,' he explained to *The Times*. 'We have to be careful. We have to tread lightly. We have talked about it before, but the opportunity hasn't really come up, or it just hasn't felt right. And we did have an idea for the London gig that maybe we would do a Nirvana song, but it didn't pan out. The person we wanted to do it with wasn't available.'

The film, the Sound City Players shows and the subsequent album of collaborations recorded for the documentary, *Sound City – Real to Reel*, were all rapturously received. This was Dave Grohl the music fan in his element, his love for his chosen subject – music, in all its forms – shining through. 'I consider this to be the most important thing I've ever done, artistically, of all the albums I've made, of all the bands I've had the pleasure of being in,' Dave told the audience at the film's premiere. 'I really feel like the *Sound City* movie, its intention is to inspire the next generation of kids to fall in love with music as much as I did.'

Despite the effort involved getting his documentary to the screen, Dave's adventures in filmmaking hadn't taken him away from his day job. On 20 February 2012 – the day that would have been Kurt's forty-sixth birthday – Dave appeared at the Brit Awards in London to present an award to The Black Keys. During an interview with the radio station XFM, he was asked when the Foo Fighters would start work on their next album. 'Well, I'll tell you, we have been in our studio writing, and in the past few weeks we've written an album,' he said. 'And we are going to make this album in a way that no one's ever done before, and we're pretty excited about it . . . It's a little ways off – it's not ready to happen right now – but I think next year is going to be a really big year for the Foo Fighters, without question.'

Dave's promise that his band would make an album 'in a way that no one's ever done before' would eventually prove to be just that. But before that, the Busiest Man in Rock had a full calendar. In April, Dave and Taylor inducted the veteran Canadian prog rock trio Rush into the Rock and Roll Hall of Fame.

The young, pre-punk Grohl had his mind blown by Rush's 1976 concept album, *2112* – not least by the drummer Neil Peart's hyper-technical approach. 'It fucking changed the direction of my life,' he told *Rolling Stone*. 'It made me want to become a drummer.' Of course, he'd said similar things in the past about John Bonham, Keith Moon, Ringo Starr and Rat Scabies, but that didn't make it any less true in Dave's starry eyes.

His and Taylor's appearance at the ceremony was character-istically funny. After officially inducting Rush with an effusive, heartfelt and hilarious speech, the pair returned to the stage dressed in white silk kimonos – and, in Dave's case, a blond wig – in honour of the band photo from the back sleeve of *2112*. They then proceeded to blast through that album's opening track, 'Overture', before being joined by the three members of Rush themselves. 'It's terrifying to play your favourite band's song in front of your favourite band,' Dave gushed afterwards. 'It's one thing to sit in the basement and woodshed *2112*, and its another to stand in front of Rush in a fucking kimono and a wig and try to use a wah-wah pedal in your platform shoes.'

Rush weren't the only band whose orbit the Foo Fighters found themselves in during the summer of 2012. In May, Dave joined the Rolling Stones onstage in Anaheim, California, to add guitar and trade vocal lines with Mick Jagger on their 1971 classic 'Bitch'. A month later, the whole band appeared as John Fogerty's backing band on a turbocharged update of his old Creedence Clearwater Revival hit 'Fortunate Son', from his album *Wrote a Song for Everyone*. 'It was palpable, the air,' Fogerty said of the sessions. 'You could tell a band was in there. It was a unique group of people.' There was also a return appointment with Paul McCartney for Grohl, Krist Novoselic and Pat Smear, this time at Safeco Field in Nirvana's hometown of Seattle. As well as playing 'Cut Me Some Slack', this time they joined McCartney on the Beatles classics 'Get Back', 'Helter Skelter' and 'The End', plus a romping version of Little Richard's old rock'n'roll staple 'Long Tall Sally'.

Amid all these high-profile hook-ups, Dave didn't stop writing. He collaborated with Joan Jett on a song for her new album, *Any Weather*, and produced an EP by a country outfit, the Zac Brown Band, appropriately titled *The Dave Grohl Sessions Vol. 1*. 'They're unbelievable,' he said. 'The band is so good . . . we didn't fuck with computers, we tracked live, four-part harmonies around one microphone. It's rocking.'

There were also tantalising hints of what the Foo Fighters' eighth album might be about. In August 2013, Butch Vig confirmed that he would be producing the new record. 'It was a very short hiatus,' Vig said of the band's break. 'We're going to start recording the new Foo Fighters record at the beginning of next year.' A few weeks later, Chris Shiflett posted an Instagram photo revealing that the band had already completed 13 new songs. In an interview with *Rolling Stone* in November, Dave ramped up anticipation about the new record even further. 'It's badass,' he said. 'We're doing something that nobody knows about, it's fucking rad. We begin recording soon, but we're doing it in a way that no one's done before and we're writing the album in a way that I don't think has been done before.'

Aside from a pair of shows of in Mexico in December (announced with a hilarious YouTube video featuring the actor Erik Estrada from the Seventies TV show *CHiPs* as a leather-clad biker, and a cameo appearance from Dave's bare buttocks), the Foos were suspiciously quiet as 2013 gave way to 2014. For Dave Grohl, his attentions were at least partly on his imminent second visit to the Rock and Roll Hall of Fame. This time, though, it wouldn't be to induct another band – in 2014, it was Nirvana's turn to be inducted.

The Rock and Roll Hall of Fame had been set up in 1983, by the Atlantic Records mogul, Ahmet Ertegün, and a team that included *Rolling Stone*'s founder, Jann Wenner. With a museum in Cleveland and an annual induction ceremony, it was the closest thing the music world got to the Oscars. The list of stars already inducted read like a *Who's Who* of music – everyone from rock'n'roll pioneers such as Elvis Presley and Little Richard to contemporary stars like the Rolling Stones, U2 and Bruce Springsteen. According to the organisation's rules, artists were only eligible for induction 25 years after the release of their first record. 2014 was the first year Nirvana were eligible – their debut album, *Bleach*, having been released in 1989 – and, unsurprisingly, they were a shoo-in.

Although Dave hadn't played on *Bleach*, he was still an integral part of the band. 'For once . . . I'm speechless,' he said in a statement. 'From the basements to the dingy clubs, to the broken-down vans to . . . the Rock and Roll Hall of Fame. I'd like to thank the committee not only for this induction, but also for recognising Nirvana for what we were: pure rock'n'roll. Most of all, thank you to all of the fans that have supported rock'n'roll throughout the years, and to Kurt and Krist, without whom I would not be here today.'

But there was one potential issue lurking in the wings: Courtney Love. The relationship between Kurt's widow and the two surviving members of the band had gone beyond fractiousness and descended into outright war. In November 2011, onstage at a festival in Brazil, Courtney had publicly accused Dave of '[taking] money off my kid's table', referring to her daughter, Frances Bean Cobain. Worse was to come. In 2012, in an increasingly venomous series of Twitter postings, Courtney accused Dave of trying to seduce Frances. Dave immediately shot down the accusations with a statement: 'Unfortunately, Courtney is on another hateful Twitter rant. These new accusations are upsetting, offensive and absolutely untrue.'

More tellingly, Frances Bean herself denied her mother's claims. 'While I'm generally silent on the affairs of my biological mother, her recent tirade has taken a gross turn,' she said in a statement. 'I have never been approached by Dave Grohl in more than a platonic way. I'm in a monogamous relationship and very happy.' Courtney later withdrew the allegation.

In the build-up to the show, which was held on 10 April 2014, at the Barclay Center in Brooklyn, onlookers began to wonder what the night might hold. Given that both Dave and Courtney wouldn't just be onstage for the induction but sharing a table as well, there was the strong possibility of some very public fireworks. Incredibly, the exact opposite happened. Nirvana's induction into the Rock and Roll Hall of Fame was moving, celebratory and, ultimately, a chance for the two warring parties to rebuild bridges. On the night, it was R.E.M.'s Michael Stipe – a longtime admirer of the band, and a friend and mentor's of Kurt's – who introduced the band, before Dave, Krist Novoselic and Kurt Cobain's mother, Wendy O'Connor, gave their own emotional speeches. Dave also paid tribute to the four drummers who preceded him in the band, and talked about the punk rock spirit that inspired them all.

And then it was Courtney's turn. Approaching the microphone to a mixture of cheers and boos, she was in uncharacteristically concise mode. 'I have a big speech,' she said. 'But I'm not going to say it. This is my family I'm looking at, all of you. Brother Michael, Brother Krist, Grandma Wendy, Mr Grohl . . . David.' She then walked over to Dave and gave him a very public and heartfelt hug. 'That's it,' she added. 'I just wish Kurt was here to see this.'

For Dave, making up with his old enemy was almost as much of a triumph as the actual induction. 'You know, the wonderful thing about that night was the personal side of it,' he told the *Hollywood Reporter* afterwards. 'It was the Hall of Fame ceremony, but it meant so much to all of us personally that sometimes you forgot about the other stuff – like the arena and the trophy – and focused on real, personal things. I saw Courtney walking past [earlier in the night], and I just tapped her on the shoulder and we looked each other in the eyes and that was it – we're just family. We've had a rocky road. We've had a bumpy past, but at the end of the day we're a big family and when we hugged each other it was a real hug.'

As was tradition, the surviving members of Nirvana – including Pat Smear – played a brief set for the crowd. Just as Kurt Cobain had rejected the macho stereotypes of rock 25 years before, so his band mates chose to do the same by recruiting a quartet of female singers to take his place at the Hall of Fame: Grohl's sometime collaborator Joan Jett came on to sing 'Smells Like Teen Spirit', Kim Gordon of Sonic Youth tackled 'Aneurysm', the indie rock singer-guitarist St Vincent covered 'Lithium', and most startling of all, the 17-year-old New Zealander Lorde – who wasn't even born when Kurt Cobain died – turned in a spine-tingling performance of 'All Apologies', with Krist on accordion.

'We thought, "Wait, it has to be all women,"' Dave told *Rolling Stone*. '"Don't even ask anyone else. If we can fill the Rock and Roll Hall of Fame performance with these incredible women singing Nirvana songs, then we'll have achieved our own revolution." It also added a whole other dimension to the show. It added substance and depth, so it didn't turn into a eulogy. It was more about the future. I haven't played those drum parts since I was twenty-five,' he continued. 'I'm forty-five now. We played for ten fucking hours each day. After the first night of rehearsals, I limped home, had two glasses of wine, three Advil, took a hot shower and slept for ten fucking hours. That's a coma for me, because I never sleep.'

There was a second, unpublicised show later that same night at the 250-capacity St Vitus club in Brooklyn. As well as Joan Jett and St Vincent, Dave and Krist also recruited Dinosaur Jr's mainman, J Mascis, and John McCauley, singer with the indie rock outfit Deertick, a band that sometimes play sets of Nirvana covers under the name Deervana. McCauley had received an email from Dave asking if he wanted to sing on 'Serve the Servants' and 'Scentless Apprentice' at the show. McCauley initially thought it was an April Fool's joke by one of his friends. It was only when Dave's manager, John Silva, followed it up that he realised the offer was serious.

'It felt like when you're a kid and you sleep over at a friend's house and you become part of your friend's family for the night,' McCauley said. 'When I got up onstage, it was a lull, because we were trying to figure out what song to do next and there was just feedback and us yelling at each other and Dave was like, "Wow, this is like a real Nirvana show!" I'm having a hard time believing it ever happened.'

Dave's high-profile presence at the Hall of Fame ceremony momentarily drew attention away from the new Foo Fighters record. His claim that this would be a revolutionary new record, one done 'in a way that no one's ever done before' was a huge promise to try and keep. But the mystery was soon resolved when it was announced that he was making a TV series for the US channel HBO that would pick up where *Sound City* left off. It would see the frontman visiting eight studios around America: Chicago's Electrical Audio, Rancho De La Luna in California and Inner Ear in Washington, as well as similarly legendary facilities in New York, Austin and New Orleans. As with *Sound City*, Grohl would speak to artists who had worked in each studio and, with the Foo Fighters, record a new song in each. There would be the series and an accompanying album, both to be called *Sonic Highways*.

The album would feature songs from each episode, each with a different guest musician. This would be 'a love letter to American music', said Dave. 'We've been recording at some different locations, but we're almost halfway done with the recording and it's going well,' said Butch Vig, who had been enlisted once again to produce the album. 'It sounds different – we've thrown a few things into the mix, in the recording process, that are going to give the record a different sound and a different feel. It's been a challenge, but it's also been exciting.'

In May alone, Grohl and the Foos appeared in two different cities as part of the ongoing recording-sessions-cum-musical-travelogue. There was a surprise Foo Fighters gig at the legendary Washington, DC venue the 9.30 Club. Ostensibly a birthday party for Big Tony Fisher, bassist with local 'go-go' heroes Trouble Funk, it found Dave teaming up with members of Bad Brains and his old band Scream – including Franz Stahl – before capping out the night with an unannounced Foo Fighters set. A few days later, the band appeared at New Orleans' prestigious Preservation Hall, where they were joined by local musicians, the Preservation Hall Jazz Band. By mid-August, both the *Sonic Highways* album and the TV series were finished. The title reflected the Foo Fighters' sense of musical wanderlust and their attempt to document the indigenous American music of the twentieth and twenty-first centuries.

Yet, as Dave revealed, it could all have been very different. 'At one point I thought, "You know what would be really funny? To re-record the first Foo Fighters record as the band we are now,"' he told the *NME*. 'Cos the first record isn't the Foo Fighters; it's just me. So what if, for the twentieth anniversary, we went in and re-recorded the first record – same songs, same arrangements, in sequence – but as the Foo Fighters 2014? Taylor was like, "Are you out of your fucking mind?! That's the worst idea ever! People would fucking hate it!" And Pat said, "That's exactly why we should do it!"'

In the event, Dave ditched the idea and instead focused on *Sonic Highways*. Picking up where *Sound City* left off, it would be the most ambitious project he'd ever put his name to – musically and personally. Pulling it together had taken 18 months – the majority of which had taken place in secret. 'After making the *Sound City* movie, I realised that the pairing of music and documentary worked so well because the stories give substance and depth to the song, which makes a stronger emotional connection to it,' he told the *Hollywood Reporter*. 'If you know the story behind the artist, or the story behind the studio, or the song, it widens your appreciation for the music. The four-minute-long video is a blessed thing but sometimes it can be just an image. And these stories and these people give so much more depth to the music.'

For Dave, the *Sonic Highways* project was both 'the history of American music broken down to the cultural roots of each place' and a look at the Foo Fighters' own place in it all, as they approached their twentieth anniversary. His original plan had been to visit studios all over the world. Logistics prevented that, so they focused instead on eight studios in the US, some of which he had a personal connection with. Inner Ear Studio in Arlington, Virginia, where Dave recorded with Scream, was the cradle of Washington, DC's hardcore punk scene, though arguably the place with the most personal connection for him was Robert Lang Studios in Seattle, where he had recorded his last tracks with Nirvana a few months before Kurt Cobain's death – and all of the first Foos album.

Other studios, such as New Orleans' Preservation Hall, Austin's Studio 6A and The Magic Shop in New York, were chosen purely on account of Dave's curiosity for his subject. 'We get to spend a week in each city, and by the time we leave each place, I feel like I know the people, I know the food, the music,' he explained. 'Seven days is enough to get a little bit of each city under your skin. And New Orleans is just so deep – there's not only a musical community but it's a community of families where generations of musicians have been playing music in the city for hundreds of years . . . It was just fuckin' magical.'

In each city, Dave spent time interviewing the key players who had helped shape its music scene – and by extension, the music of America. In the episode centred on Washington he spoke to Big Tony Fisher of Trouble Funk and Fugazi's singer and DC hardcore punk linchpin Ian MacKaye, whom Dave knew from his days on the city's punk scene. In Nashville, his interviewees spanned several generations of country icons, from Dolly Parton and Willie Nelson to latter-day stars such as Zac Brown. In New York he bridged the worlds of rock, avant-garde and hip hop with help from Kiss's Paul Stanley, Sonic Youth's Thurston Moore and LL Cool J.

One of the most insightful interviewees was Steve Albini, owner of Chicago's Electrical Audio studio and the guy who had produced *In Utero*. Speaking now, two decades after they last worked together, Albini notes that Grohl is 'still basically the same dude – way more money and obviously comfortable with his station in life, but still goofy and gregarious, still sick with talent'. Albini's work with everyone from the Pixies to Jimmy Page and Robert Plant has seen him build a reputation as the most no-nonsense producer operating today. Not for him the extravagance or egos of the modern music industry – Albini famously views major labels as an unnecessary evil, and the bands who sign for them as little more than puppets. Foo Fighters, however, he says, are one of the few exceptions.

'It's pretty clear the Foo Fighters as a project is Dave Grohl expressing himself rather than anybody else pushing him around,' says Albini. 'His music may or may not be to your tastes, but it's genuinely his, he's going to pursue it his way and he doesn't seem to care if other people get it. I don't know what more you can ask of an artist.'

For Dave, pulling together the *Sonic Highways* project involved a superhuman effort of will. This was more than just roping in a few mates to play a gig. By taking on the role of TV producer, Dave stepped far outside his own comfort zone. 'I was on the phone conferencing with agencies and corporations, trying to round up money to do this,' he told *Rolling Stone*. 'Part of me felt sick inside. But I justified it: "I'm doing something good. I'm doing something people will appreciate."'

The TV series made its debut on 17 October in the US and was an instant critical success. It certainly fulfilled Dave's promise of being 'a love letter to American music'. Effectively an eight-part musical travelogue, each episode featured multiple interviews, done by Dave himself, and culminated in the recording of a song with a musician associated with the studio – in Chicago, it was Cheap Trick's Rick Nielsen; in Austin it was the rising bluesman Gary Clark Jr; in Los Angeles it was the Eagles' guitarist Joe Walsh. Other guests included Dave's former Scream band mates on the raucous 'The Feast and the Famine' (recorded in Washington, DC), the Nashville-based country singer Zac Brown, who added vocals and 'devil-picking' to the sleek 'Congregation', and David Bowie's longtime producer Tony Visconti, who arranged the strings on the seven-minute epic, 'I am a River'.

The *Sonic Highways* album followed less than a month later. Despite the multitude of guests, it sounded undeniably like a Foo Fighters record, even if it smoothed out the rough edges of the wilfully raw *Wasting Light*. For Dave it was both the logical culmination of his lifelong obsession with music and definitive proof that even though he was the leader of one of the most successful rock bands of his generation, he was still a fan at heart – albeit one with a huge amount of pulling power and clout.

'He absolutely calls the shots now,' says Paul Brannigan. 'He can obviously do whatever he wants. He's just done an HBO series. He's not gonna be short on offers to direct other music documentaries. He's already making videos, he did one for Soundgarden [2013's 'By Crooked Steps']. He can pretty much flick through the Rolodex of popular culture at the moment and pick out anybody in the musical world and say, "Do you fancy doing something?" There are no barriers absolutely now to whatever he chooses to do. Whether that's a good thing for the Foo Fighters remains to be seen, but certainly from Dave Grohl's perspective, you've got to think you're in a pretty sweet position right now, however you choose to move on from this. It really does seem like a pretty limitless horizon at this point, whatever he should choose to do.'

Dave certainly pulled in the big names to a gig held to celebrate his forty-sixth birthday party at the Los Angeles Forum in January 2015. The band were joined by Kiss's singer, Paul Stanley, Van Halen's frontman, Dave Lee Roth, the Tenacious D duo of Jack Black and Kyle Gass, Jane's Addiction's singer, Perry Farrell, and, for a climactic cover of Chuck Berry's 'Let It Roll', the Motörhead mainman, Lemmy, ex-Guns N' Roses guitarist Slash and Ozzy Osbourne's six-stringer, Zakk Wylde.

Rita Haney, widow of the late Pantera guitarist Dimebag Darrell, suggests that Grohl relishes the role of bringing people together. 'He's like David Lee Roth,' says Haney from her home in LA. 'He's just got that grin. He hit me up to see if I could put him in touch with Zakk Wylde to see if Zakk would do that birthday thing he was doing. It was like a day or so before and we were texting and I said, "What are you up to?" and he said, "I'm bored in the studio, just messing around with the Charlie Brown theme." I was like, "I need to hear this." He immediately sent me this audio. It was really funny. He's a character – always positive. He's not one of those energy vampires. Just a positive guy.'

For Paul Brannigan, Dave Grohl remains the same person he first met in the Nineties, just less available. 'It's harder to get to him. I remember running into Dave at other gigs in London, or in America, where he wasn't playing but he would just be there, watching some other band. That still happens, but not quite so often as it would have done in the late Nineties. And he's got a family now and whatever. But when you sit in front of Dave it doesn't seem that anything has particularly changed. It doesn't seem that different from sitting in the pub getting drunk with one of your friends, talking about some obscure seven-inch records or AC/DC albums or whatever. You almost have to remind yourself that this is somebody that is going to be headlining Glastonbury, and doing two nights at Wembley.'

Dave's own journey from gawky punk rock kid through personal tragedy into bona fide rock god is one of the more unlikely success stories of the last 20 years. If nothing else, it does show that sometimes nice guys do finish first. 'Out of the fires, phoenixes rise, and that's exactly what Dave's done,' says Anton Brookes. 'And he's done it in a dignified way. He hasn't raped the carcass of Nirvana. He's not used that golden ticket to fulfil his career. He was given opportunities because he was Dave Grohl from Nirvana but he had to earn that right. People were waiting sharpening the knives in the wing, waiting for him to fall so they could launch into him.'

Anton draws a parallel between Dave's own fandom and the levels of devotion he inspires in his band's following. 'The fans love them. With every new record that came out, the fan base grew and grew. [To the point now where] it's dads and sons, mothers and daughters. They can enjoy them on almost a spiritual plateau together. Both get the same yet something different from the band.'

It's no surprise that 2015 has seen the Foo Fighters play to more people than ever before. The summer was to have seen the Foo Fighters undertaking another two-night stand at Wembley Stadium as well as an even more prestigious debut headlining slot at the iconic Glastonbury Festival, the five-day celebration of music that takes place in the southwest of Britain and regularly attracts audiences of upwards of 150,000 people. As Metallica's 2014 appearance at Glastonbury proved, headlining the festival has the power to take a band to an entirely new audience.

Unfortunately, though, when Dave Grohl broke his leg when he fell from the stage during a show in Sweden in June, it put all those plans in abeyance. A downer for Foos fans but an even bigger blow to the band. At the time of writing, Grohl has just told *Rolling Stone* that he's making progress in his recovery, saying, 'I'm starting to do a little bit of rehab exercise and the cast is off. The swelling's down. The pain's gone. It's just a matter of getting those kick-drum muscles back, man. I can't fucking lose those. That's important to me. So I'm sitting here, moving it around, doing my exercise as we speak.'

In the meantime he is using a removable boot and points out that his accident could have been much worse. 'I could have done some real damage. This is pretty gnarly, but it could have been a lot worse.' He said his physical therapist told him, 'It was

basically like my ankle got into a forty-mile-per-hour car crash.'
Ouch!

Having been forced to cancel seven dates, including those huge
UK shows, the Foos are now back on tour in the US, with Dave
singing while seated on a giant throne, his leg raised in front of
him on a chair. He joked that the 'easiest part of my whole day'
are the shows, 'the rest of the time, I'm hobbling around trying
to brush my teeth and pack my bags and walk down the street
and get a cup of coffee. The challenge is the other twenty-one
hours of the day.'

They will be back, possibly as soon as next summer when
Glastonbury will be simply the latest staging post on a career
that, 20 years ago, would have been unthinkable by everyone up
to and including Dave Grohl himself. But while he has achieved
so much in his career thus far, the future has endless possibilities. There is now talk of a follow-up album and series to *Sonic
Highways*, this time based in Britain. Meanwhile, Dave Grohl
has become the rock superstar it's now against the law not to
love.

But what of the city that first made him famous – Seattle?
I end by asking Charles Cross what the word on the street in
Seattle is these days about Dave Grohl and his Foo Fighters?
If anyone is qualified to judge, it is he. Typically, he pulls no
punches in his assessment.

'Well, it's complicated,' he says. 'You know, a lot of the members of the bands in Seattle that didn't become super-famous,
but even the guys that did, even the guys in Pearl Jam or Soundgarden you run into . . . they are pretty down to earth. Very
little ego. If you acted like you were a big deal in Seattle you're
very quickly going to become isolated from the community of
musicians, writers, club owners. If there is a secret to the Seattle

ethos, it is that everybody is equal, depending on the quality of the songs they're writing and the live performance they're putting on. It didn't matter how many records you sold. It didn't matter how famous you were or how many magazine covers you were on. There's a couple bands that didn't make it big, like Pure Joy and Love Battery, to name just a couple, that are not as big as the bands that became big, and everybody cares about them just as much in Seattle, that supports their shows. You see superstar musicians at their shows, or you did in the day when they were around.

'So the Foo Fighters were born out of that. I mean, Sunny Day Real Estate plays a *huge* role in the Foo Fighters. And though Sunny Day Real Estate is not very known far and wide, everybody when they talked about the Foo Fighters early on, nobody said it's the guy from Nirvana. Everyone said it's the guy from Nirvana and the guys from Sunny Day Real Estate. That was in the same sentence. There was no comma between those two. That's how people in Seattle approached it. And that is a key to understanding Seattle.'

20 years on, however, 'Dave's got a very carefully cultivated public image where he's able to . . . He has everything that Kurt never could have. He can both be the nicest guy in music and a simple guy who just loves music. And yet he's also the head of a major corporation and the leader of a huge band. So he has both the capacity to be a huge star and yet also walk through the public as though he is the everyman. Kurt wanted that but he never got that. Kurt was either completely unknown or overnight he was massively famous. He couldn't have it both ways and if Kurt were alive now, I have to say that's probably what he would most admire about Dave, more than the music. He would be, "Dude, how on earth did you manage to pull this off? How can you have these two personalities in the public?"'

Anton Brookes, who was there with Kurt and Krist long before they had ever heard of Dave Grohl, and who was also there when the latter made his seemingly impossible transition to global superstar on his own terms, has the final word.

'A lot of people like rock'n'roll to be straightforward,' he says. 'They put music on and it's escapism. They don't want music that is a refection of your life; you want something that is happy, jolly with a bit of meaning to get you through the day. And that's what the Foo Fighters is. Where Nirvana was the crutch for a generation. It was propping up people. Even today, the disenfranchised youth around the world, teenagers are still finding angst within that message of Kurt's angst.

'I think Dave, deliberately, from the get-go, was like: that's what Nirvana did, I'm going [the other] way. Because, can you imagine, if Dave even attempted playing a Nirvana song live? Can you *imagine* what the media would have done to him? Can you *imagine* what Courtney's reaction would be? It's been hard enough for Dave to stand up to a lot of unfair slings and arrows and accusations without that.'

Instead, Dave set his sights high. Impossibly so, it seemed at so many junctures. Nonetheless here he still is, higher up in the clouds than ever.

Anton smiles. 'You look at him from playing to small crowds to arenas and now stadiums, and he pulls out all the stops. It's really funny. When Dave goes onstage, he's always been a performer. As a drummer, he was your archetypal sarcastic joke-telling drummer who made everybody laugh. That was part of his character and part of his charm and appeal. I always thought with Dave, though, that was a bit of a smokescreen that he used to keep people away. I always thought Dave used that as a gauge to get to know people. And as you got to know him and he got to know you, then the real Dave came out. But if you didn't get to know Dave, all you got was like, "Hey," and a slap on the back. All smiles and teeth and goofiness.

'I think that's probably something he learned from being in Nirvana, which kept his sanity and kept him safe and kept a lot of the trappings that come with rock'n'roll away. Especially the parasites; the people that latch on to bands and performers. I think Dave learned the hard way from seeing what happened with Nirvana, and used to that to his own devices.

'I think also as a songwriter, as a musician, he just blossomed and got better with everything he's done. I always marvelled and laughed at Dave when he was onstage because he'd come running out . . . As soon as he beamed onstage, as soon as he came onstage and he smiled, the audience just smiled back. They loved him. And he camps it up. He's a rock'n'roll star but he's Benny Hill! He'll be running and pretend to trip or something, and laugh and point at the crowd. He smiles and he talks to them and he tells jokes and he burps and he farts and whistles. To be fair to Dave, after a couple of years he was no longer Dave from Nirvana. He became Dave Grohl of the Foo Fighters who *was* in Nirvana. Where some of the media dubbed him the Grunge Ringo, he quickly outgrew that and he blossomed into one of the greatest songwriters and musicians that the planet has had to offer for a long, long time.'

And his story is not even half over yet.

Index